Bootlegger

Bootlegger

✦

Max Hassel, The Millionaire Newsboy

Ed Taggert

Writer's Showcase
New York Lincoln Shanghai

Bootlegger
Max Hassel, The Millionaire Newsboy

Writer's Showcase
an imprint of iUniverse, Inc.

For information address:
iUniverse, Inc.
2021 Pine Lake Road, Suite 100
Lincoln, NE 68512
www.iuniverse.com

ISBN: 0-595-26013-6

Printed in the United States of America

Contents

Foreword

If I had been in a hurry to finish this book, the reader would have missed some of the best parts. After the first five years of research, I always had the feeling there was more to come. And there was. Vital information about Max Hassel's life came to light from the most unexpected people and places in the past year. It was like striking gold when sources began appearing out of nowhere to greatly enhance this story that took about nine years to complete.

The book did not turn out to be what I originally planned to write. Having written a series of articles for the *Historical Review of Berks County* about Reading's long history of racketeering, I hoped to enlarge on those pieces by writing about the City of Reading during Prohibition. I soon found out that Max Hassel was such a dominant and interesting character that I wanted to focus solely on him.

Retracing the life of a racketeer in a small city is an inexact exercise. There are not a lot of traceable facts about his formative years, nor the many secrets he shared within the bootleg fraternity. Like other racketeers who rose above the pack, Hassel left few written records. His breed was more interested in covering its tracks rather than keeping records of its achievements and failures. His frequent bouts with law enforcement are well documented, but far less was written about this man of social conscience and goodwill. The charitable causes he supported, the synagogue projects he subsidized, his annual holiday giving, and his generosity to friends and employees—just how much of that do we know? He never went to prison, but we can only speculate how he managed to dodge conviction time after time. What went on in attorneys' offices and what deals were made that vitalized political corruption?

Max never rose to the prominence of the Chicago Tommy Gun crowd, or the Lower East Side gangsters who became crime bosses and to this day are glamorized by Hollywood and television. He did not take the path of violence followed by so many of his Prohibition peers, which is why he became a footnote in the annals of organized crime. His reputation as a fair and honorable beerman was of the variety rarely found in his circle of associates.

I don't profess to be a historian and this book is not a social history. I have relied heavily on local and national newspaper archives, biographies of Prohibition racketeers, local and federal court documents, the records in several county and city governmental departments for much of the information found here.

When I arrived in Reading in 1956 to work for the *Reading Times* I was assigned to the police beat. An aging police detective, Charlie Dentith, liked to talk about the old days. I enjoyed his tales about Max Hassel, the "Millionaire Newsboy," who made and spent millions during his career as one of the country's biggest bootleggers. Almost with reverence, Charlie talked more about Hassel's many charitable endeavors than about his underworld successes. Although Charlie worked for the Police Department during the latter years of Prohibition, like many cops he made a few extra bucks at the bidding of Hassel and company. It was the majority attitude of the Reading workingman in the 1920s that whoever kept the beer flowing was to be praised, not dishonored.

I regretted later that I really didn't tap Charlie's wealth of inside information about Max. In later years, I realized what a complex, adventurous, courageous, humanitarian, tax-dodging character Hassel was. It was not easy trying to figure out his real estate deals. The Internal Revenue investigators realized that the first time they tried to pin Max down for unpaid income taxes. Just as he used dummy buyers in many of the buildings he bought, he also masked his generosity behind anonymous donors. Who can really say how much he gave to the community, or how much high-powered beer he sold, or near beer for that matter?

Dozens of seniors in their seventies, eighties, and nineties, even a couple of centenarians have shared stories with me. Asked to stretch their memories to recall how it was during Prohibition, occasionally they offered different versions of the same event. If the conflicting viewpoints seemed important, I've offered both for the reader to pick and choose.

As with any nonfiction, the research process couldn't move forward without the aid of helpful librarians and archivists. Vallie Reich consistently came up with the answers to my many questions during her volunteer stints in Reading Library's Pennsylvania Room. Lenora Adams, another volunteer in the Berks Prothonotary Archival Center, located the transcript of an immigration hearing that had eluded me. First a local judge directed me to the Philadelphia Federal Building. A clerk there said the document should be on file in the Berks County Courthouse. Until Lenora found the transcript that proved so helpful, I doubted it would ever surface. Jon Del Collo and other employees in the Recorder of Deeds office assisted me when I stumbled, and Clark Kent in the Register of Wills office often pointed me in the right direction.

George M. Meiser 1X, Berks County's foremost historian, was always helpful with his photographic memory of places, dates, and people, and several times directed me to old-timers with ties to Max Hassel and the Prohibition era. William McShane loaned me old Reading Brewery ledgers that were found in the former Reading Hardware Building when he bought it and opened his Neversink Brewery and Canal Street Pub.

Among the octogenarians, nonagenarians, and centenarians, and a few relative *youngsters* who helped me relate to the past were Ed Marks, Tom and Kitty Promos, Jake Heffner, Bernie Dobinsky, Claude Mervine, Myrtle Quier, Norman Kaplan, Charlie Reed, Chet Hagan, Wilson Austin, Jules and Alyce Bookbinder, Paul Hill, Polly Wagner, Mary DeAngelo, Shirley Shirey, Earl Wiswesser, Florence Goodhart, Bill Mason, Jon DelCollo, Jim Davis, Jim Williams, Jere Verdone,

Rabbi Joel Weintraub, Paul Kantner, Ed Engle, and Andy Kent. Several have died since sharing their memories with me.

The lone surviving relative of Max Hassel I was able to contact was Dr. Sarle Cohen, a nephew. He was born four years before Max died. Through his and other family members' efforts, the Hassel Foundation, created by Max's late brothers and sisters more than forty years ago, is perpetuating the Hassel legacy of benevolence.

Latecomers in the research process were cousins Bill and Fritz Moeller whose forebearers played important roles in the beer empire Hassel created.

I was able to bring the book to a strong conclusion when Joe Stassi, a 95-year-old Prohibition gangster, appeared out of the blue to reveal a story about his close friend, Max Hassel, that was his secret for almost seventy years. Kudoes to Fred Tamarri for his tip about the *Gentlemen's Quarterly* article written by Richard Stratton in which old Joe bares his soul. Bob Garfield had the contacts to direct me to Stratton.

Mary, my wife, likes to point out my mistakes. Therefore, whenever she slackened off as chief editor of this book, I reminded her to get back to work and prove me wrong. For the fifth and final edit, my former colleague and current *Reading Eagle* columnist, Joe Farrell, did a thorough touch-up job that was greatly appreciated. Neighbors and friends, Connie and Dave Levering, gave it one last helpful read.

Son Brian, serving as go-between with Iuniverse.com, the publisher, solved computer problems that were beyond my limited skills.

And thanks to all the others I might have forgotten who assisted in one way or another.

Ed Taggert

1

Budding Entrepreneur

A big majority of notorious bootleggers during Prohibition were established gangsters by the time the "Great Experiment" was launched. The teenage gangs of the Lower East Side slums of New York City spawned hardened criminals who eventually grew into the capos of organized crime. For them, Prohibition opened a window of opportunity that they exploited. They quickly filled the vacuum the 18th Amendment created when it banned the production, distribution, and sale of alcoholic beverages throughout the United States.

Bootlegging became a profitable industry that attracted young men who were experienced thieves, extortionists, robbers, and practitioners of violent crimes. Among the very few who didn't fit the profile of the Prohibition racketeering heirarchy was Max Hassel. He was not a product of the Lower East Side.

Max grew up on the streets of Reading, Pennsylvania. This was an industrial town, a union town where railroaders, steelworkers, machinists, and knitting mill workers earned high marks for their work ethic. When Prohibition arrived in 1920 the heavy flow of immigrants that began before the turn of the century was still swelling the city's population. Max Hassel, soon after he arrived from Latvia in 1911, was eager to join the bustling multi-ethnic work force of this thriving town. He had already established a remarkable business resume by the time the 18th Amendment to the U.S. Constitution changed the course of social history in this nation.

Max still occupies a special niche in the memory of oldtimers. As Reading's foremost bootlegger of the Roarin' Twenties, he left a legacy of nonviolence and benevolence. It is not unreasonable to believe that Prohibition changed the life of this promising young man. Friends and associates have insisted he was more businessman than racketeer. But the business he chose was illegal at the time, and he ignored the law to achieve wealth and notoriety—and finally, legendary stature in death.

Max was born Mendel Gassel on April 24, 1900, in Latvia. He became Max Hassel as a youngster, and his father, Elias, eventually referred to himself as Ellis Hassel. Although Max attempted to have his name legally changed, his problems with the law always gave the courts reason to forestall the process.

The migration pattern of families who arrived in Reading early in the 20th Century had the husband making the long uncertain voyage first. He sacrificed personal comfort for several years, saving his earnings to pay passage for his wife and children. With the family reunited, the potential for success in the land of opportunity depended as much on ambition and fortitude as it did on training and education.

Latvia was ruled by Russia at the time Elias Hassel made the drastic decision to move his family to America. Under Tsar Nicholas II, widespread anti-Semitism throughout the Russian empire became official policy with the passage of laws restricting Jews even further. The Gassel family lived in the city of Dvinsk on the Daugava River. Elias and Sarah Gassel had five children: Mendel in the middle, preceded by Fannie and Calvin, and followed by Morris and Lena. The siblings were educated in a *chedar,* a religious school where the rabbi taught them the Hebrew alphabet and prayers. Children were encouraged to read and study as many books as were available. Material ambition was not encouraged. The brightest were counseled to follow the calling of the rabbi. Would Max Hassel have taken the religious path had he remained in Latvia?

Many Jewish families migrated to the United States to flee harassment and persecution, others to escape poverty. What Elias's reason for leaving is not known, but accompanied by 14-year-old Fannie, he joined the exodus first. They arrived at Ellis Island, then journeyed to

Reading in 1908. The father opened a small tailoring business, assisted by his daughter, already a skilled dressmaker.

It is possible that Max Abramson came to America about the same time. He, too, traveled from Russia, settled in Reading, was a tailor and eventually married Fannie in 1913.

In the fall of 1911, Sarah and the other four children left Dvinsk by train for the 225-mile trip to the Baltic seaport of Liban (now Liepaja). They boarded the S.S. Kursk, one of the Russian Asiatic Steamship Company's newest transports, for the eleven-day trip to Ellis Island, landing on September 22, 1911. The family then took a train to Reading.

Meyer Lansky, one day to become a major force in organized crime, also came to America on the S.S. Kursk, arriving only six months before Max Hassel. Their lives would become entwined in a dramatic episode a couple of decades later.

When Max reminisced in later years, he liked to tell friends it was a Friday evening when the Gassel family exchanged hugs and kisses at Reading's Franklin Street Station of the Philadelphia and Reading Railway. Within days, the children were enrolled at Park Public School, Perkiomen Avenue and Franklin Street. Knowing he would be following his father to the United States, it is possible Max learned some English if such instruction was available at his synagogue. When he and his siblings arrived in Reading, they also attended the Thomas Severn School at 512-514 South Sixth Street, which provided crash courses in English to all immigrant children. It was better known as the Americanization School.

Florence Mason turned 100 in 2001, but she remembered when the Gassels moved into their first home at 231 South Eleventh Street. A year younger than Max, she lived in the same block and attended Park School. Florence acknowledged with a telling grin that she did not associate with any of the Gassel children because in those days, "it wasn't the thing to do. American-born residents didn't go out of their way to welcome Jewish newcomers." Florence recalled that the Gassel children were always well-groomed and polite in class. Although the family had not completely escaped antiSemitism, Elias could assure his children that the police did not indiscriminately intimidate or arrest law-abiding people regardless of race or religion. The family had escaped the life-threatening prejudices of their Russian oppressors.

Kesher Israel Synagogue was chartered in 1913, occupying a building on the southeast corner of North Eighth and Court streets. The Gassels went there to worship. Rabbi Yood, probably an itinerant religious leader, held classes for teenagers, teaching them to read the Torah in English. Max was one of the rabbi's best students. Acquaintances remember that Max worked at losing his Yiddish accent at an early age, something that didn't concern many immigrants. In line with his early sense of business, Max must have realized the benefit of gentrifying his English.

It is not documented exactly when Mendel Gassel unofficially changed his name. At a naturalization hearing in 1933 he said he began calling himself Max Hassel as soon as he arrived in this country. This says something about his individuality: an 11-year-old with the moxie to chance such a dramatic switch. Some immigrants were determined to blend in; others held tight to their heritage. Within a few years, his father was using Hassel as the family name.

There is no record of delinquency in Max's formative years. He was a well-mannered, attentive pupil at Park School, and later at the Ninth and Windsor streets grammar school. But earning power was more important than a formal education to this ambitious youngster. He was a quick study, always soaking up whatever was needed to earn a buck. In the school of hard knocks he majored in tact and common sense, seasoned by a strong work ethic and a dash of daring. These qualities carried into adulthood. He developed a strong sense of social justice, but his search for knowledge was focused on the business at hand.

After a year or so at the South Eleventh Street house, the Hassels moved to 528 North Eighth Street. While in this neighborhood, it is quite possible Max became acquainted with Abe Minker whose family ran a grocery store a few blocks south on Eighth street. Their paths definitely crossed during the early years of Prohibition, but Max was never a member of Abe's wild North Eighth Street gang. While Max, barely out of his teens, leaped to the forefront of bootleggers, Abe didn't reach his peak as a racketeer until the 1950s.

With his parents' permission, Max quit school at 14, restless to make his mark. It was not uncommon for youths to leave school after seventh or eighth grade. Ellis and Sarah were only too happy to have another wage earner in the family. And Max was eager to accept responsibility. This was in keeping with the Jewish tradition of helping and honoring thy parents.

Youths under 16 were required to obtain working papers to get regular employment. Max was hired as a cash boy at Pomeroy's, Reading's largest department store at Sixth and Penn streets. This job kept him hustling as counter clerks constantly summoned runners to fetch change from the vacuum tube system popular in that era. Also working as a Pomeroy cash boy was Ralph Kreitz, Reading's future slot machine kingpin. In 1951 Kreitz testified at a U.S. Senate Organized Crime Committee hearing that his only contact with Max Hassel was as a teenager when they worked together in the department store.

But it wasn't all work. Like most kids his age, Max enjoyed sports. He played shortstop on a sandlot baseball team. As an adult he was something of an exercise freak and a golfer with a substantial handicap.

It didn't take long for Max to make his first important impression. George Pomeroy, co-founder and president of the Pomeroy retail chain, soon recognized Max as a cut above the usual stock boy or money runner. Pomeroy's son, George Jr., who succeeded his father as president of the company, had this to say when he appeared in later years as a character witness for Max:

"My father selected him (Max) from among the cash boys to serve as his own personal messenger. And Mr. Hassel was his messenger for probably a year. Then after talking it over with Mr. Pomeroy, he left to take up some newspaper business, as I recall it. He didn't make as much money as he had hoped to in that business, so he came back after maybe six months and my father rehired him. He was then with the store for more than a year, eventually becoming a clerk in the men's furnishing department. He left to go into the cigar business. But I know my father thought very well of him and spoke about him on many occasions."

That was a typical description of Max by people who knew him as a teenager. When he left Pomeroy's the first time he became a *Reading Telegram* newsboy. Newspaper customers remembered him as polite and quick to make the proper change. Personal appearance was a priority throughout his life.

After his second tour of work at the department store, he took his first major gamble at 16 by giving up a steady job to start a cigarmaking business. He also resumed hawking the *Telegram*, becoming a familiar figure at Sixth and Penn streets. Competition was fierce among several daily newspapers, most selling for two cents a copy during the World War I era. The Reading Times Company printed the *Telegram* and other publications in its North Sixth and Walnut plant. The Reading Eagle Company building was on the southwest corner of Sixth and Penn, directly across from Max's usual station just outside the main entrance to Pomeroy's.

Penn Street newsies were a mixture of poor kids, some combative, some lazy, and others like Max who took the job seriously. Emotionally mature for his age, Max knew how to sell himself, which in turn was reflected in his newspaper sales. Short, dark, and good-looking, he attracted more than his share of regular customers on the main drag. *Telegram* management rewarded the diligent young fellow by promoting him to collector when he was 17. He now had the responsibility of gathering the day's receipts from other newsboys in his charge. In later years, he retained a close relationship with employees at the *Times* plant. The *Telegram* stopped publishing in 1919, but by then Max was so involved in other pursuits he barely missed his newspaper income.

After living at the Eighth Street address for a few years, Ellis Hassel moved his family in 1915 to a rental property at 736 Franklin Street. The following year he bought the adjoining house at 738 for $3,100 from the estate of Mrs. Annie Cressman. It was a brick row home with two full stories and an attic. The name Elias Hassel appeared on the deed, but he was now calling himself Ellis in other business and personal matters.

For the next seventeen years, 738 Franklin was the family home. After 1933 it changed hands a few times before becoming the Sportsman's Grill, a neighborhood tavern for several years in the 1950s. The building was extensively damaged by an unexplained explosion at 736 in 1997. The following year, 738 was torn down. When the demolition foreman was asked whether he knew that a notorious bootlegger worth millions had once lived there, he said "No," and with a so-what shrug went about his business.

It was a good home for the family of Ellis and Sarah. Max, always respectful of his parents would later conduct his bootlegging business away from the house. But while still in his teens he had other enterprises that he managed from home. He sold Larkin products door to door, then became supervisor of a crew of sales people. The Larkin catalog illustrated well over a hundred items ranging from soap and toiletries to food stuffs, furniture, and clothing. Mrs. Hawley Quier, in her nineties and still chair of the Reading Eagle Company board, recalled that as a child she accompanied her aunt, a Larkin's saleslady, to Max's house with orders she had taken.

"He was very polite, well dressed, and quite handsome," was Mrs. Quier's recollection of Max some eighty years after their brief meeting. Flattering descriptions were the norm from today's senior citizens who had even the slightest brush with Max.

Hassel's closest friend as a teenager, and for years to come, was Israel Liever. Together, this industrious pair became recognized as two of Reading's slickest operators during Prohibition. Izzy Liever was more adept than Max at avoiding legal scraps because he didn't reach as high as his adventurous partner. But Izzy often had a hand in Max's deals that helped expand his beer empire. And always there to advise these two young lions was Izzy's dad, Hyman Liever, probably the role model who Max most emulated.

While the lads were growing up, Hyman operated Berks County Bottling Works at 409-11 South Sixth Street where the Liever family lived. Max spent many hours in his buddy's house, which was directly across the street from the Americanization School. Max had been a top student there, learning English much faster than most of the students.

Apparently Max had no interest in following his father into the tailoring trade, instead soaking up business acumen from Izzy's father. Possibly it was Hyman who directed his son and Max into cigar making, a profitable vocation.

Reading, the seat of Berks County, had a long tradition of cigar production. At the time of the Civil War there were 163 cigar factories in Berks County. Industrialization greatly reduced the number of factories, but by World War I, several thousand men and women were employed as cigarmakers in the city. Local 236 of the Cigarmakers Union was the heart of the Socialist movement in Reading. It shared quarters at Reed and Walnut streets with the party. There were also many non-union shops, some employing mostly women and children. And still a third source came from small independents that made up possibly the city's largest cottage industry.

After leaving Pomeroy's the second time, Max took on Izzy as a partner to form one of the many local "buckeye" cigar companies. These were often family operations that were neither union nor sweatshop. Surprisingly, an obvious title was still available when the youths selected a name for their enterprise: Berks Cigar Company.

This venture probably could have been classified a sweatshop. In the beginning its only two employees were the partners. They rented a second-story room for $8 a month in a private house at 735 Chestnut Street next door to Ellis Hassel's tailor shop at 733. It is likely that Max employed his brothers part time. In the confines of one room with little ventilation, Max and Izzy certainly sweated for their hard-earned profits.

Most freelancers of that period bought Lancaster County tobacco as filler and used Connecticut shade-grown tobacco for wrappers. Most likely the young partners utilized molds which were available by then, rather than attempting the more difficult hand-rolled method. Union apprentices took three to five years to become skilled in that technique. Making cigars was a time-consuming process. The tobacco stems had to be stripped, a job often delegated to women in nonunion shops. Next, the leaves had to be soaked, dried, then moistened again so they could be worked. Finally the cigars had to be made, banded, and boxed. Whether Max and Izzy bothered with the final two steps is not known. One skilled cigarmaker, working eight hours, could turn out 300 to 400 a day. One can only imagine the toil involved for these teenagers in their cramped quarters. As a bootlegger, Max always insisted that his breweries make the best beer possible. So, it's not unlikely he believed quality cigars were also the easiest to sell.

A division of duties was agreed to: Izzy was in charge of production while Max, the more experienced salesman, was out hustling their product door to door and bar to bar. Although Max was no extrovert, he was no shrinking violet either. Whether it was newspapers, cigars, or beer, Max loved the challenge of making a sale, or swinging a deal.

There was a federal tax on cigars that legitimate companies paid weekly at the courthouse. The Reading district collected $1.5 million a year from Berks County cigarmakers. The buckeyes, however, were noted for not bothering with tax formalities. We don't know whether Max and Izzy met their tax obligations, but bootleg cigars were plentiful in Reading, especially in bars where cheap stogies were sometimes part of the free lunch package. Max proved he was never queasy about ignoring his income tax, so it's not likely he worried about paying the few-penny levy on a box of cigars.

Cigar sales were booming in 1919, allowing the young partners to form a second company, Universal Cigar Stores. They rented larger quarters on the second floor at 402 Penn Street to expand their operation. With Max's organizational skills, in all probability he now had a steady workforce turning out cigars being sold in various sections of the city.

A brief explanation about his early ventures was revealed many years later when he answered questions presented by an Immigration and Naturalization examiner:

"At the age of 16, I was in the wholesale tobacco business for three or four years: the Berks Cigar Company, and the Universal Cigar Stores," Max stated.

When asked whether Universal was a chain of stores, he said it was.

"Did you at that time have well-established credit at the bank?" the government attorney asked:

"I certainly did."

"To what amount?"

"To the amount of approximately $30,000."

With a $30,000 line of credit it is understandable he could afford rental properties for a small chain of stores. And with so much borrowing power it is understandable that he moved into the higher income brackets quite fast.

With the surge of ethnic groups migrating to Reading during the World War I decade, the neighborhood gangs were a natural refuge for poor teenagers. Peer pressure in gangs led to fights, vandalism, and theft. There's no evidence that Max needed that kind of excitement to fulfill his goals. He was more interested in providing income for his family. Although he enjoyed team sports, it was always business before pleasure, especially after his father began ailing and the family became more dependent on him. His early maturity kept him out of trouble. Certain ethics he learned in his structured family life became ingrained, even helpful when dealing with dishonest peers in his chosen trade.

From his father, Max learned that with a trade and a good work ethic you could provide for your family. From Hyman Liever he learned that with hard work and considerable imagination you could become financially secure. Max's own close friends were not the young roughnecks who never looked past the next fight or overlooked a chance to steal a bicycle. His pals were exposed to religion and ethics through Rabbi Yood as they studied the Torah. There certainly were no bad influences in Hassel's immediate family.

As Max and Izzy continued their partnership, they bought a corner house/store at Tenth and Perry streets for $3,500 in 1920 from Moses Schlecter. They agreed to assume payment on a mortgage held by John Barbey, with a stipulation not to sell "women's or men's furnishings, shoes or clothing" for five years. Possibly Max's affiliation with Larkin products concerned Barbey for some reason.

Izzy bought Max's share in the property for $1,000 the next year. By then, the partners had disbanded the cigar companies to examine other opportunities. Izzy got married and formed Union Realty Company with Leon Wise. The company would eventually be involved in several brewery transactions as Max continued to spread his wings.

Still in his teens, Max had already become an entrepreneur: buying, selling, taking risks, always looking for new opportunities. In 1919 he opened a cigar store on the southwest corner of Ninth and Penn streets. The place became the main office of Universal Cigar Stores. Brother Calvin sometimes clerked in the store, in addition to helping his father in the tailor shop.

At the Penn Street smoke shop, Max made new acquaintances. There he met the type of sidewalk philosopher who had strong opinions about Prohibition. Max listened more than he talked as the easy-money crowd decried the terrible fate that awaited since the government banned alcoholic beverages. Some of Max's customers were merely blowing smoke, but others made sense. He listened and digested the best ideas of the most sensible prognosticators about ways to profit from the moral dilemma that was about to be forced on the American public. By the time he was 19, Max had 20/20 vision regarding Prohibition. There would always be a market for booze and he jumped at the chance to strike it rich. Many bootleggers would turn out to be little more than street fighters, but from the beginning, Max took aim at the heavyweight crown.

It is interesting to ponder what Max's destiny might have been if Prohibition hadn't presented him with a fork in the road. In 1919, the first cigar-making machine was introduced in Newark, New Jersey. Within a few years, these $20,000 labor-savers were turning out millions of cigars a week in Reading factories. With his fearless approach to business, it is conceivable Max would have gone into hock to quickly join the vanguard of automated cigarmakers.

Instead of becoming known as Prohibition's Millionaire Newsboy, might he have turned into a tobacco tycoon? But when the 18th Amendment was passed, he decided to test the theories of his smoke shop visionaries who predicted Americans' thirst for alcoholic beverages would continue unabated.

He chose to forgo cigars for a much more lucrative pursuit.

2

First Steps Over the Line

As an alien, Max was not drafted to serve in World War I although he turned 18 in April 1918, almost seven months before the war ended the following November. Another battle being fought on the home front was reaching its conclusion. State after state was passing anti-liquor laws. The moralists were primed for the big day when they could celebrate their great victory with passage of the 18th Amendment.

President Woodrow Wilson signed the War Emergency Act right after the war, paving the way for a premature start of Prohibition. This temporary legislation's purpose was to help the country work its way through a worldwide grain shortage caused by the war. The production of beer and liquor was banned until demobilization, possibly a year or more in the future. It appeared the extended fight between the wets (the anti-prohibitionists) and the drys (the prohibitionists) was over even before the 18th Amendment became law. White, Anglo-Saxon, Protestants, the WASPs, for years had waved the Puritan flag to rid America of that evil caricature, John Barleycorn. Their time in history had arrived.

The breweries and distilleries gave public notice that they would adhere to the War Emergency edict, but their cooperation was short-lived. The government, which was relying on the honor system to preserve its grain supplies, quickly found out drinkers and suppliers alike were doing business as usual.

The government didn't expect immediate acquiescence, but it did not foresee that almost complete disregard would be the alternative.

After the thirty-sixth state, Nebraska, passed an anti-alcohol law, the 18th Amendment was ratified by Congress on January 16, 1919. It would not officially go into effect for one year. To let the public ease into untested dry waters, Congress set July 1, 1919, as Bone Dry Day. It hoped six months would be long enough to wean tipplers off the bottle. Pennsylvania was one of the states that did not pass a law banning alcoholic beverages until after the 18th went into effect.

Bone Dry Day came and went with little ado as the boys at the bar hoisted a few to the futility of trying to ban their favorite pastime. In the fall of 1919, Congress passed the Volstead Act which set the rules and regulations by which Prohibition was to be enforced. The big issue during the Volstead debate was the amount of alcohol to be permitted in near beer. This small loophole in the ban on alcohol meant very weak beer still could be produced. Congress, in its infinite wisdom, decided beer with no more than .05 percent alcohol was allowable.

The federal government would now control quotas of industrial alcohol to companies that needed it for manufacturing purposes. Also, alcohol for medicinal use could be sold by licensed pharmacists if prescribed by a doctor. The government also controlled the amount of wine that could be purchased for religious ceremonies.

Three months after Prohibition officially began on January 16, 1920, Reading and Berks County barmen showed their disdain for the Volstead Act by renewing their city or county liquor licenses. Elected officials joined the party by issuing licenses, falling back on the excuse that taverns needed local authorization to sell near beer. The $140,000 in licensing fees Reading and Berks County shared each year inspired politicians to retain the permit system as long as possible. This subterfuge for circumventing national law ended in 1923 when Pennsylvania Governor Gifford Pinchot pushed through legislation permitting the sale of near beer without a license by all retail outlets. The following year, local licensing of breweries, bottlers, and beer distributors ended.

Hebrew culture discouraged heavy drinking and smoking. Jewish immigrants viewed Prohibition as a foolish restraint forced on the public by Christian moralists. For Jews, homemade wine was an intricate part of religious worship. Freedom of religion was a staple of American democracy, so how could they accept a law that tampered with a tradition from antiquity.

The many stills in low-rent apartments throughout Reading did not shut down, nor did most of the breweries. Many Italian and Polish immigrants were in the hotel business. They saw Prohibition as an experiment that would quickly fail. From their experience abroad, most aliens were suspicious of government. They resisted this dramatic reversal of a personal freedom. When Prohibition provided an irresistible opportunity, many of the young newcomers from Europe answered the siren's call. Bootlegging quickly burgeoned into a social phenomenon that would leave a scar on the nation's history second only to slavery.

Max Hassel never followed the pack; he was always well out in front. As he assessed the public's early reaction to Prohibition, he knew beer and hard liquor would never go out of style. If there's a market, a good salesman will find it. At 19 he was already a veteran in commerce. He was not afraid to take chances, the classic attitude of young men all too eager to match wits with the authorities. As a Jew, he was not saddled with the WASP belief that alcoholic beverages were Satan's gift to the weak. Let others engage in the moral debate; he was too busy looking for ways to secure his family's economic future.

While building a nest egg for new ventures, Max began smoking his own cigars. Later he would buy only the best Cubans, a grade somewhat above those he and Izzy sweated over. Alcohol had little appeal to Max. Intimates claimed he had no taste for beer, the drink of choice since Cleopatra's day. As Max became established, his circle of friends included hard drinkers and gamblers. To be one of the boys he tippled, but always under control. Drunkenness was a sign of weakness that Max accepted in others, but personally guarded against. As for gambling, he soon tested those waters, and for the rest of his life enjoyed matching his poker, pinochle, and gin rummy skills against all comers.

One associate said he never saw Max down on the floor rolling dice with the boys.

In 1919, the newsboy/cigarmaker/cigar store operator/property investor/Larkin Products manager was carrying quite a plateful. The budding businessman was juggling all these enterprises and still looking to expand. So, when Prohibition loomed, he listened to the debate, and absorbed the best of opinions being cast about. If it meant crossing the line to take advantage of this golden opportunity, he did not hesitate. It was a dangerous playing field and he was obliged to develop character flaws that conflicted with his family's tradition of honesty, honor, and religious devotion. He might have avoided the wrong path if ambition and ingenuity had carried him to the top in another field of endeavor in another era. Instead, he became a product of his time.

Benjamin Sher was a 50 percent owner of the building at Ninth and Penn where Max ran his cigar store. This elderly gentleman liked his young tenant. It is not known what brought them together in business, but judging from the arrangement that developed, it would appear Max did most of the talking. About the building at 102-104 Schuylkill Avenue, Max said years later, "The property was in Sher's name but he gave me a blank assignment of half interest."

It was late in 1919, several weeks before Prohibition officially began that Max and Sher started working out plans to form a business called Schuylkill Extract Company. Using his adopted name, Max Hassel filed an application to withdraw federal alcohol from a local warehouse. The government allotted alcohol to eligible manufacturers. Max's application indicated his company would use industrial alcohol in the production of various food extracts. He was also licensed to buy wine for ceremonial purposes. The permit was granted on May 7, 1920, after Max posted a $20,000 bond. The bond was required to ensure that the alcohol would be used for legitimate purposes. The amount of alcohol he was allotted is not known, but the size of the bond indicates he could withdraw several thousand gallons each month.

Max learned early that the newly created Prohibition Agency was made up of political appointees who were more interested in supplementing their meager salaries than enforcing the law. At first there was practically no enforcement, then when agents did come around he developed a cooperative relationship with them as they checked his product line and gave him clearance to continue. Schuylkill Extract business records are long gone but the mythical extracts were sold in bulk to customers who were equally lax about filing records of transaction.

Not satisfied with reports from its field agents in Reading, the Philadelphia Prohibition office sent investigators to track Schuylkill Extract shipments. One led to a Market Street address in West Philadelphia, a small basement leased to M. Wiener. Hassel's records showed that Max had sold 21,000 gallons of Horke wine, or approximately 3,000 cases, to Wiener. But by the time the investigators arrived at Wiener's store, he hadn't been seen for more than two weeks and there were no facilities to bottle the wine. The building owner claimed there had never been any large shipments there even before Wiener broke his lease.

On the advice of attorney Charles Matten, Max surrendered his permit on January 24, 1921. Claiming ignorance of the law, Max said he did not realize an alien was not eligible for a permit when he applied. The federal agency was lenient, and returned his $20,000 bond.

One acquaintance he made during this period was Fred Marks, a supervisor at the local government. Charles Siedel, the Berks County Republican Party chairman, had recommended his friend Freddie for the federal post. During their long association, Marks became one of Hassel's principal aides. It is likely that in addition to Max's alcohol quota, Freddie made available extra gallons on which they split the profits.

With a sizable stake by the time his permit was cancelled, Max went into the financial business, making loans and venturing into real estate. But the big money was in bootlegging and he soon was moving in that direction again. Not many people were aware of his first setback except the bootleggers who were buying his alcohol. By 1922 he was involved in the same racket under an assumed name. When the phony operation was uncovered early in 1923, Max told a tale about having been approached by a fellow who said he was Stanley Miller hunting a site for a chemical company. Miller proved to be the first of many ghost owners of Hassel companies. Together, they formed Berks Products Company, which should not be confused with the latter-day local leader in building materials. The company's familiar address was 102-104 Schuylkill Avenue.

Max later admitted he forged Miller's name on the application for special denatured alcohol, on authorization of the company president, Stanley Miller. A permit was granted to Miller the summer of 1922 and the company was up and running in the same building previously used by Schuylkill Extract. The fictitious Miller was also licensed to buy and sell whisky permits to druggists. When the feds caught up with Max, he couldn't remember where Miller lived or the name of the company chemist, or the formula used to make chemical products. He did remember the formula was kept in a safe, but unfortunately the safe had disappeared. At 22, he already was unshakable under questioning, a courtroom style he developed that made him an excellent witness the few times he was interrogated in public. For this second offense, Max received a citation, and his permit was again revoked on October 25, 1923.

There's a trace of evidence that Max Hassel and Abe Minker were associates in an early bootlegging adventure. For a few years they had lived in the same Eighth Street neighborhood, but when the Hassel family moved to 738 Franklin, they went their separate ways. Abe's North Eighth Street gang engaged in open warfare with the South Seventh Street gang. Hijackings, brawls, and abductions marked 1922 as Prohibition's bloodiest year in Reading. While the two gangs fought, Max Hassel stayed on the sidelines quietly building for the future.

After Minker was arrested for perjury in April 1922, Hassel, using the alias Max Hasson, posted bail for him. Under the assumed name,

Max was called by District Attorney H. Robert Mays to testify at Minker's preliminary hearing. Mays intimated that Max and Fred Marks, known associates, were in cahoots with Minker in an illicit alcohol business. Max denied they were and there's nothing on the record proving the DA's charge. However, the same day Minker was convicted of perjury, his 16-year-old brother Isadore was arrested during a police raid on a Philadelphia warehouse. A large stash of distilled alcohol was confiscated. Investigators did not reveal where the alcohol came from, but Max Hassel was illicitly selling alcohol at the time.

The loss of his alcohol permit in 1923 was but a mere bump in the fast lane where Max was traveling as Reading's foremost bootlegger. By now he had made deep inroads into the illegitimate beer business that had so-called legitimate brewers running scared.

3

Amber turns to gold

If Max Hassel was a millionaire at 24 as the government claimed, it is possible he reached that milestone as soon or possibly sooner than most of his much more famous underworld contemporaries. Lucky Luciano and his pals, Frank Costello, Bugsy Siegal, and Meyer Lansky, raked in really big bucks at a tender age, but they edged into bootlegging under the sponsorship of Arnold Rothstein. The legendary New York gambler financed their early ventures in rumrunning—and took a big slice of the profits. Al Capone in Chicago faced stiff competition for several years before attaining the seven-figure status. Waxey Gordon possibly matched Hassel's early take during those first years of Prohibition, but he was a dozen years Max's senior, and he was in other rackets besides booze. Dutch Schultz wasn't a major player until the last five years of Prohibition. Nobody can be precise regarding the wealth of racketeers. Their accounting systems were geared to hide profits, not expose them.

The WASP goal of banning alcoholic beverages was primarily directed at the retail level to destroy the tavern system. The reformers were less fanatic about beer, but they lumped it in with hard liquor in their proposed legislation because it contained, generally, between 3 and 4 percent alcohol. The distilleries and wineries that made the stronger beverages came under closer scrutiny than the breweries when the government set up its Prohibition Agency. Had an attempted plot to form a Pennsylvania beer cartel succeeded in 1897, the prohibitionists would have faced a much better organized opponent when they waged their war.

When monopolies were in vogue at the end of the Nineteenth Century, the most influential brewers in Philadelphia and Pittsburgh developed a plan to gain control of Pennsylvania's beer industry. The State Legislature was about to push through a bill with a universal license fee of $10,000 for all breweries. This would have driven small breweries out of business, allowing the big ones to become dominant. Soon, a cartel would have gained control of the $35-million-a-year beer industry, which in turn would have increased the price of beer at the tap.

But the real hidden agenda in this plan was that the small breweries were in on the ruse. They were being promised stock in the new combine, providing them substantial income if they closed their plants. The scheme, if successful, would have left thousands of workers outside the metropolitan areas unemployed as the big city breweries operated at full capacity. Before the proposed legislation came to a vote, Phillip Laurer, a Pittsburgh brewer, admitted to the press that he was in on the scheme. Public reaction frightened rural and small town legislators, and the bill that was enacted continued to prorate license fees according to the size of a brewery's production.

At the beginning of Prohibition it took only a few years before legitimate beermen were edged aside by racketeers. The brewers made near beer, but they made more real beer until they were caught. When that happened, they sold out. The beer industry was quickly consumed by a new breed of businessmen, lawless characters who rationalized that they were only giving the public what it wanted. Their methods of satisfying supply and demand, as bad as they were, never really turned the public against the racketeers, and organized crime was born.

The new Prohibition Agency was ill-prepared to track the liquor and beer profiteers. When the great moral experiment started in 1920, the government assumed it would need fewer inspectors in breweries to check the outflow of taxable near beer. But through that loophole in the Volstead Act poured millions of barrels of strong beer for the next thirteen years.

The Volstead Act was Prohibition's enforcement tool. Instead of banning beer completely, Congress was duped by brewers into allowing the production, distribution, and sale of beer that contained no more than one-half of one percent alcohol. This watery version looked like beer, had the smell of beer and was called beer—but it wasn't even close to real beer. It was the near beer clause in the Volstead Act that gave the brewers an excuse for staying in business.

So, beer was produced in the normal manner, then watered down to satisfy federal inspectors. Unfortunately for the tax collector, much of the real beer was being smuggled out of breweries before the final step of the near beer process. There had always been inspectors, known then as gaugers, who could be bought by brewery tax cheats. But with the advent of Prohibition, bribery zoomed. Not until 1923 did either the state or federal agencies bring any pressure to bear on the beer makers of Reading.

Always known as a beer town because of its large German population and its brewing talents, Reading had eight breweries at the turn of the century. When Prohibition commenced, only four were still operating. The town's beer drinkers enjoyed a wide choice: stout, porter, lager, and ale. Bar flies of that era would have cringed at the thought of light beer and did not take kindly to near beer. The breweries were predominantly owned by men whose lineage was only a short trip back to Germany.

Reading Brewing Company at South Ninth and Laurel streets was the biggest, turning out 125,000 barrels annually. Fisher Brewery at 1600 North Eleventh Street was the newest and smallest, but its owner closed down because of the War Emergency edict in 1918—then resumed production about 1922. The oldest company was Lauer Brewing with its recently built plant at North Third and Walnut streets. Deppen Brewery, just above Elm on North Third, was a Lauer neighbor. The fifth and least active during Prohibition, was Barbey Brewery at West Elm and Gordon streets.

The production of illegal beer in Reading proceeded practically unhindered the first three and a half years of Prohibition. Only a few incidents involving Fisher shipments, plus the seizure of a Deppen truck, and a hearing at which Reading Brewery was cited for selling porter to a Maryland distributor caused a ripple of inconvenience. Max Hassel would eventually control three of the five beer plants.

Reading's bars, taverns, hotels, and clubs had a shorter respite before the federal government clamped down. Many of these places operated openly because they had city liquor licenses. Others without permits required identification before allowing patrons to enter. These unlicensed establishments were known as speakeasies or blind pigs.

The honeymoon ended in February 1922 when the feds arrived on an early-morning train from Philadelphia. Several flying squads knocked off dozens of speakeasies. Tons of hard liquor and wine were confiscated, fines were levied against owners and bartenders, but no strong beer was hauled away. Other similar raids that year left local drinkers with the impression that there was a psuedo legality attached to beer. But that would change.

While still in the alcohol business, Max Hassel began negotiating to take over the beer industry in Reading. His first major target was the Fisher Brewery just outside the city in Muhlenberg Township. Unlike other family breweries in Reading, Fisher had a history of short-term ownership. John G. Stocker and his brother-in-law, John Roehrich, built the brewery in 1891. August Scheider bought the plant in 1907, and for a time it operated under the name Fairview Brewery. Then its name was changed to Augustiner Brewery. It became the Mt. Penn Brewery in 1912 with F. G. Ligued as company president. William Fisher was the next owner in 1916, but he operated only a short time before halting production during World War I. Fisher sold the company to his son, Harry, while it was closed. The new owner let the plant sit idle when he went into the hotel business.

It appears Max Hassel approached Harry Fisher in the later part of 1921 about buying the dormant plant, but only on the condition that the deal include a brewery license. Since Harry hadn't renewed his license for four years, this stipulation couldn't be met until April 1922 when the county issued brewery permits. That didn't stop Hassel from pushing through the purchase in November 1921. Using a rather bizarre name, Brazilian Aramzem, Max incorporated the company in Delaware as the new owner of Fisher Brewery.

At the 1922 licensing hearings, Harry Fisher's application to renew his beer permit led Judge Gustav Endlich to ask, "Why?" Harry said his father closed down during the war because materials and ingredients were in short supply. But Harry said he wanted to reopen the brewery to make near beer. This hardly seemed to be a good business move. But Harry claimed his few years in the hotel business led him to believe there was a good market for near beer. Whether the judge believed him or not, Fisher was granted a license. What Harry failed to mention was that Brazilian Aramzem already held title to the plant.

Max completely refitted the brewery and had the kettles bubbling even before Harry paid $250 to have the Fisher license renewed. William Abbott Witman Sr., president of Brazilian Aramzem, proved to be little more than caretaker of the deed until the license was obtained. Now began a maze of title changes that tax lawyers would have to wade through whenever they came after Max Hassel.

In August 1922, Max introduced another straw buyer, Maurice Muchnick, a Realtor. Although Harry Fisher had sold out to Brazilian Aramzem in 1921, he was again listed as the seller when Muchnick put up $14,000 to buy the property. Muchnick took title to the three-story brick brewing building, the ice plant and ice house, stables, bottling plant, machinery, engines, boilers, and everything else connected to the business. In addition to the bargain price, another convenience was the Philadelphia and Reading Railroad spur line that ran right by the Fisher complex.

The ink was barely dry on that transaction before Muchnick got a $15,000 mortgage from the Union Realty Company, owned and operated by none other than Max's old buddy Izzy Liever and his partner

Leon Wise. In a real estate index in the Recorder of Deeds office, there's a vague reference to Union Realty giving its own partners a $50,000 mortgage in connection with the Fisher Brewery. Then, in March 1923, Union Realty was the seller, Fisher Brewing Company the buyer of the brewery property. Another bargain—$1. Now comes a surprise signer. Max Hassel usually stayed behind the scenes in the many major purchases he made, but the property now came under his name as he paid Aramzem $6,000. Another month flew by before Max sold out to William Abbott Witman Jr., for $25,000. That would seem to be a $19,000 profit for Max, except it was all his money supposedly being passed about. The only purpose of this last transaction, we can speculate, was to get Hassel's name off the title. Sometimes only parts of the brewery complex allegedly changed hands. Just when the Reading Home Ice Company came into being cannot be documented, but that company sold the ice plant and ice house to Max in January 1924. Somewhere down this twisted road of exchange, William P. Moeller, the company's brewmaster, gained a $7,000 interest in the bottling plant. Quietly, with no formal announcement, the brewery was operating under the name of the Fisher Brewery Company again in the early months of 1924. But it wasn't long before Hassel's first brewery was in the headlines as the federal government hauled William H. Hart, the alleged president of the company, into court. That case became something of a *cause celebre* for the Prohibition forces. (See Chapter 4)

For the next couple of years the brewery was closed more than it was open after a series of raids. Then in August 1926, the Fisher Brewing Company sold the property to the Hyde Park Development Company. After the plant was padlocked and dismantled near the end of 1926, it stood idle for the next eight years.

At the end of this make-believe chain of ownerships there was a legitimate transaction in 1934 when Katherine Stocker, whose family founded the brewing company, purchased it at sheriff's sale for $100. Banks and private lenders and the county had written off loans, mortgages, and taxes that were long overdue. Later in the 1930s the plant resumed operations as Woerner Brewery. Over the years companies not in the beer business have occupied the property.

The old brewery building is currently owned by Jim Williams, president of Keystone Interior Systems, Inc. which occupies the first floor. There is little left on the upper two floors dating to the storied Prohibition years.

It is safe to assume that the Fisher Brewery was a gold mine that operated for more than a year without government interference when Max first owned it. The cost to produce a half barrel of beer was about $2.50. Wholesalers paid in the $8-to-$10 range, and the price to speakeasies was anywhere from $11 to $16. With such a huge profit margin, it is easy to see how Max became Reading's beer baron at such an early age.

He added to his wealth from the illegal beer produced in Lauer Brewery during Prohibition, but he never owned the property. At the time the 18th Amendment was passed, Lauer's was the oldest beer company in Reading. Having moved the business from South Third and Chestnut streets to a new, bigger plant on North Third Street above Walnut, Frank Lauer put his son Carl in charge about 1920. Carl began leasing the brewery to Max Hassel in 1923. Max paid $2,500 a month rent for the next two years. A month or two after leasing the property, Max took the precaution of subletting the property to an associate, Steven Gierot. Subsequently, the operating firm in charge of production and distribution was the Gierot Manufacturing Company.

Prohibition certainly produced unusual associates. It tells us something about the force of Hassel's personality that he could convince established businessmen to risk notoriety by helping him break the most controversial law of the land. The young immigrant was 21 when he talked Harry Fisher into selling his brewery. And less than two years later he convinced Carl Lauer that he had the connections and financial backing to run a major brewery, despite the inherent risks of the time.

There's no record of exactly how Max presented his offers to the established brewers of his day. From all reports, he was no high pressure salesman. In his quiet manner he made them offers that would benefit both parties. Did he have a grand scheme to take over all the breweries in Reading? Or was his success with Fisher's so great that he needed Lauer's to meet the demands of his customers? Max was prepared to take all the risks, set up a distribution system, and be his own purchasing agent. He knew something about marketing from his early ventures. He understood the importance of customer service from his newsboy experience, his cigar business, and his Larkin Products enterprise. Max's mentor, Hyman Liever, possibly advised him how to approach the brewers. Carl Lauer and the other company officers must have been impressed with this confident, well-organized, polite young man who had answers for all their questions. Max's resume was far less impressive than the image of the entrepreneur he projected. Just how that scenario played out would have been interesting to observe, but the end result was that Max Hassel was a wealthy man in his early twenties.

A clearer picture of how Max Hassel took over the Reading Brewing Company presents itself because of his close relationship with Hyman Liever. If Hyman was a role model, Max learned at the knee of a man who also winked at the Prohibition laws. To keep his bottling works on South Sixth Street profitable as long as possible, Hyman was one of Reading Brewery's best customers during the first few years of Prohibition. He continued to bottle the strong stuff long after the law said he shouldn't. By the time the feds started bearing down on Reading's bootleggers in 1922, Hyman had decided real estate was a less risky business.

Hyman was well acquainted with Lambert Rehr, president of Reading Brewing Company. Rehr had established his reputation as a major builder in Reading for decades. Many of the row homes in East Reading were built by his construction companies. He was also president of Reading Hardware Company and Vice President of Reading Trust

Company in 1920 when he became president of Reading Brewery. Rehr was known as a hard-driving businessman who invested only in moneymakers. So he must have realized when he took over leadership of a beer company at the start of Prohibition, that near beer alone was not going to add to his already substantial wealth.

In the summer of 1923, Judge Endlich held a hearing regarding a federal complaint against Reading Brewery. Dry agents reported finding a couple barrels of real beer sporting Reading Brewing Company labels in the warehouse of a Hagerstown, Md., distributor.

At the hearing, Lambert Rehr testified he knew nothing about 3.2 beer being shipped to Hagerstown for $16 a barrel. Rehr said his production managers had been instructed to make sure no real beer slipped out of his brewery, and whenever some did, he discharged the guilty party. It was a hollow boast. A few months earlier a truck that had picked up ten halves at Reading Brewery was stopped by state police. Beer from two of the barrels was tested at 3.7 percent alcohol.

Reading Brewing sales ledgers were located in the old Reading Hardware building in 1997 when William McShane bought the property and opened the Neversink Brewery. The dusty old records of the first three years of Prohibition show that C.M. Baer of Hagerstown was a steady buyer of Reading Brewing porter and near beer. Rehr evidently played it safe by keeping the records in his Reading Hardware office.

Judge Endlich let the 72-year-old Rehr off with a warning following the hearing. Whether Lambert approached Max Hassel, or Max reached out to him through Hyman Liever, is anybody's guess. But Hyman cannot be ruled out as the middleman who brought them together.

The licensing board eventually renewed Reading Brewing's permit that year, but Rehr decided it was time to get out of the business. Even before the Maryland embarrassment, Rehr and his board of directors had begun unloading the numerous saloons the company owned.

The Lievers were in on the ground floor of this activity. In 1922, Hyman and Izzy bought ten hotels or barrooms from Reading Brewing. They later sold all of these properties, most continuing to operate as speakeasies.

Rehr and his board of directors voted to sell the brewery, bottling plant, ice house, racking room, and other buildings in the plant's large complex at South Ninth and Laurel streets. It was about this time that the Philadelphia Prohibition office released a report that a syndicate was buying up southeastern Pennsylvania beer companies. It is known that Max Hassel was a close associate of Max "Boo Boo" Hoff, the kingpin of Philadelphia beermen, so it is reasonable to believe that Max became a member of the syndicate which operated for several years. This cartel was one of the early cooperative illegal ventures that grew into a business octopus that one day would be labeled *organized crime*.

The first chapter of the Reading Brewery story under the ownership of the Hassel family began on December 5, 1923. That day, George W. Green, a Mount Penn Realtor, bought Reading Brewery at South Ninth and Little Laurel Streets for $100,000. The next day in two further transactions Green bought additional company buildings and land on the west side of South Ninth, paying $10,000 and $70,000. The total cost of the brewery property was $180,000. Green was just the front man for Max Hassel. For a 23-year-old with considerable debt obligations, who still lived with his family at 738 Franklin Street, Max was able to find the financing to pull off the deal. It is difficult to ascertain whether Max Hassel ever actually satisfied any large mortgage debts during his lifetime, but the brewery remained in the family for twenty-three years.

For the original purchase in 1923, it appears Max took out a mortgage with Berks County Trust Company, and received loans from both Reading National Bank and Northeastern Trust Company. George Green was the first of several strawmen Max employed for the next ten years.

It seems likely that Hassel stepped up production immediately because he was never one to dally. The philosophy of bootleggers has always been to run illegal stills and breweries at maximum capacity because the life expectancy of such operations is quite short. By the time Max started rotating false ownerships of Reading Brewery, he was bringing supplies in and shipping beer out by the rail carload. All three breweries he now controlled had Philadelphia and Reading Company sidings or spur lines either on or running by the properties.

The second "owner" of Reading Brewery was Bill Moeller, who came to Reading to be brewmaster at Fisher's. He worked in the same capacity at the Reading and Lauer breweries, too. Moeller held the Reading Brewery title for only three days before it was transferred to August Manufacturing Company in July 1924. In addition to being in charge of turning out a good brand of beer, Moeller also was listed as president of August.

Corporal Realty Company was the next straw buyer as Max added one more deadend to the paper trail that federal investigators were trying to follow. This was in December 1926 and the purchase price was $175,000. Corporal Realty, in addition to gaining ownership of the productive brewery, also agreed to assume two mortages totaling $140,000. By July 1929 the brewery had been dismantled and padlocked for more than six months, so Berks County Trust Company picked up the title for a few days, then deeded the property to Kathryn G. Sauer for $1. She was a secretary for Charlie Matten, the attorney who represented Hassel in criminal and civil matters all through Prohibition.

In this never-ending game of *deed deed who holds the deed?* very little money changed hands. Kathryn Sauer held title for a couple of months before handing it to Paul A. Matten for $1, the usual fee in these clandestine transactions. Paul was Charlie's brother.

By September 1931 Charlie Matten officially jumped on the merry-go-round by signing his name on the deed. Three months later, Max's tailor entered the game. Sam Lunine ran a haberdashery in the 300 block of Penn Street.

"So Sam, would you be interested in owning a brewery for a while?" Max might have asked. Max was forever buying new hats at Lunine's store, then giving them away. And Sam never made the pants too long for his favorite customer. "Well, if that's what you want, Max, I think I can handle it," Sam might have answered. It was Lunine's name that still graced the deed when the refurbished brewery reopened in 1933.

Lunine remained the caretaker owner until Laurel Realty Company, formed by Calvin and Morris Hassel, became the deed-holder from 1934 to 1938. Morris Hassel, by now a veteran in real estate and manager of the family finances, put the brewery, now called Old Reading Brewing Company, in a trust under the stewardship of Herman H. Kreckstein, a Philadelphia attorney. It was Kreckstein, representing Calvin and Morris Hassel, who sold the brewery on the last day of 1946 to Harry Fishman and family who operated the plant for another 30 years as the Reading Brewing Company.

The Fishmans sold the company name and its beer formula to Schmidt's of Philadelphia in 1976. The following year the brewery was demolished, but other buildings in the complex on the west side of South Ninth Street are still in use today.

4

Streets Awash with Beer

Gifford Pinchot, an arch prohibitionist, became Pennsylvania governor in 1923. He immediately ordered his state police to start arresting offenders of the Volstead Act. If the federal government wasn't going to enforce its own laws, then he was only too happy to give them a helping hand. In April, the state police made their first catch in the Reading area—two beer trucks moving north on Eleventh Street a few blocks from the Fisher plant. The young drivers, Harry Snyder and Roy Aronsfield, were fined and thirty-four halves were seized. There was no action taken against the brewery because the truck was unmarked. From then on, however, it was a constant cat and mouse game for the bootleggers trying to sneak beer past the state or federal agents.

Although Max Hassel could laugh off the small fines he anonymously paid for the arrested truckers, a second incident in August hit closer to home. His 17-year-old brother, Morris, was his most trusted driver. Hijackings and betrayals were commonplace in a racket infested with fast-buck artists with shifting loyalties. Morris could be counted on not to reroute a delivery into the enemy camp, then claim he was held up.

By mid-summer, Max Hassel was aware that dry agents were lurking near Fisher Brewery. It was an early August afternoon and 17-year-old Morris Hassel was about to leave the plant to deliver sixteen halves to a customer. But two dry agents were spotted hiding in a weed-covered field, the former Reading Fairgrounds site across Eleventh Street from the brewery. The delivery was postponed until the feds crawled away.

Spotters in the city phoned to report the drys were seen motoring towards Philadelphia.

But agents Frank Tibbetts and Daniel Rankin doubled back, arriving in the city in time to nab Morris and his truckload at Eleventh and Union streets. At his brother's arraignment, Max posted $1,000 bail. The teenager, claiming he was 19, had a hearing before U.S. Commissioner Henry Maltzberger two weeks later with prominent local attorney Robert Grey Bushong as his counsel. This was the first of several hearings at which Max and Bushong would appear before Maltzberger. The agents testified that the confiscated beer had tested at 4 percent alcohol. The commissioner ordered Morris held for trial.

There was no trial, and court records do not indicate why. Possibly it was learned that Morris was a minor, and the case was handled as a juvenile matter. To no one's surprise, the case disappeared with no record of its disposition. Morris continued to work with his older brother for the next several years. There's no evidence that Calvin was ever involved in Max's nefarious adventures.

A Prohibition Agency report stated Fisher's was not operating on the day Morris was arrested, but lots of strong beer was stored in the plant. The place was padlocked, and guards were assigned to prevent further shipments. The U.S. Marshal's office hired guards locally at $5 a day for eight-hour shifts. Hassel's lawyers won a court battle in which the feds were prevented from removing or destroying the plant's supplies, equipment and machinery.

Subsequent events revealed that the guards were easily bought. Many were uneducated out-of-work drifters, hardly Pinkerton-trained types. A fifty or hundred dollar bill for looking the other way when a truckload of real beer left the grounds was easy money, hard to refuse. Since much of the beer was moved in the early a.m., *night blindness* was an occupational hazard among these worthies. Without close supervision from the Philadelphia office, the hired watchmen were more interested in making sure the coast was clear than bagging bootleggers.

In time, stronger locks were installed and the guards were withdrawn. Now the stream of beer swelled to a river. It wasn't until the following spring, however, that the feds made another attempt to close down Fisher's for good.

Five weeks after Morris Hassel's arrest, three dry agents sent from Philadelphia to check on the Fisher plant decided to drive into Reading to snoop around Deppen Brewery on North Third Street. They witnessed an autotruck (a car in which the rear seat was removed and rebuilt into an extended pickup truck). This allowed more space to transport beer. The vehicle was being loaded from the Deppen racking room where barrels were filled. The agents seized the vehicle and arrested two men who were taken to the City Hall lockup. Later the marshals confiscated another loaded beer truck parked in front of the brewery on Third Street.

When the agents tried to enter the brewery, workers blocked their path. The city police were called. With some reluctance, the cops restored order before things got out of hand. This was the first of several incidents in which local men in blue made no effort to hide their disdain for the feds. They weren't crazy about the state police, either.

The sometimes comical skirmishes between bootleggers and dry agents excited the literary talents of *Reading Times* columnist Elmer Pickney. Li'l Elmer, as the satirist called himself, waxed poetic one morning with a few verses about a team of agents who took extreme measures to block illegal rail shipments out of the Reading Brewery.

> Two little "revanooers,"
> Sitting on a rail,
> Stopped the mighty brewers
> Shippin' beer for sale.

Two U.S. "revanooers"
   Eatin' of their lunch
Stopped them shippin' out the booze
   To make our neighbors' punch.

They quit the job to go to bed,
   When daylight 'gan to fail,
Two others came to take their place,
   And sat down on the rail.

The agents carried out their blockade, each pair working twelve-hour shifts for two weeks. It effectively stymied rail deliveries from the brewery, but beer hauled via motor vehicle continued to meet holiday demands. For reasons unknown, the quartet was ordered back to Philadelphia after a fortnight of hard rail time.

Reading Brewery was a gusher for the first four months Max Hassel owned it in 1924. As the district Prohibition office concentrated on closing Philadelphia breweries, the Quaker City's speakeasies became more and more dependent on beer from the Pennsylvania Dutch counties.

Max installed alarms, erected fences, reinforced doors, built false walls, and took other precautions to make Reading Brewery raid-proof. A Philadelphia and Reading Railroad siding led right up to a shipping platform on the west side of Ninth Street. Boxcars could be shifted onto the siding that passed into the loading yard through heavy steel gates. Loaded cars, if destined for shipment to Philadelphia, would be released down a slight incline and once outside the fence were coupled with an eastbound freight.

Local deliveries were carried out by having boxcars shunted to any of the city's several rail yards, where the load was parked at an out-of-the-way area. In the dark of night, deliverymen from local distributors or speakeasies would back up their trucks or autotrucks to the boxcar, load up their quota of kegs, then hastily depart. Transactions were not impeded by paperwork or price dickering. The honor system worked, but if a driver took more than his boss had paid for, that blind pig owner could look for a new supplier. When trucks were seized by agents, the owner could be counted on to claim the vehicle had been stolen that very night.

Two brothers, Joseph Green, 21, and Theodore Green, 22, of Northmont, were the unlucky lads who saw the system break down when two loitering state policemen grabbed them in the act of loading their truck from an unlocked freight car on April 16, 1924. The car stood on a siding at the Spruce Street yard near Reading Brewery. Corporal John Robbins and Trooper Reese Davis waited till the brothers had hoisted fifty-seven halves onto their truck, then pounced. After taking the Greens to Berks County Prison in City Park, the staties, using rudimentary testing equipment, determined the "ebullience" of the beer was well above the legal limit. About three decades later, Reese Davis became commander of Troop C in Reading. After retiring from the state police, Davis was elected Berks County sheriff for four years.

Instead of being lauded for enforcing the Volstead Act, the staties were reproached by local authorities. Corporal Robbins claimed he and his partner just happened by the rail siding at midnight and saw some strange activity that needed investigation. They were stationed in Pottsville at the time.

This incident added fuel to the smoldering dispute about jurisdiction. Governor Pinchot had declared war on all bootleggers, ordering his state police to go wherever necessary to enforce the law. Pennsylvania municipalities perceived the state police as storm troopers who should be limited to fighting rural crime. Reading Mayor William Sharman huffed that his own police department was quite capable of finding law-breakers without any outside help. But he, like all other Reading mayors during Prohibition, never ordered his officers to initiate a brewery raid.

A few days after the Green brothers were arrested, Sharman attended a conference of mayors the governor assembled. The mayor did not agree with Pinchot's call for solidarity in the war against bootleggers. Sharman nixed the governor's suggestion that cities exchange detectives in order to increase arrest rates in areas where they were not so recognizable.

"I don't see," Sharman said, "how we could send our detectives to other cities to secure evidence against bootleggers. Our men are paid to work here. I can't see how we can have them on our payroll here and have them work elsewhere."

Although railroad companies were warned of prosecution if caught transporting illegal beverages, freight lines all over the country did not turn away customers who shipped near beer and real beer. The railroads claimed it wasn't their duty to test the contents of every barrel they hauled. Like brewery guards, railroaders were happy to supplement their salaries with easy money. And there was plenty of that being passed around. The P&R was no better or worse than most other railroads in trying to help or hinder the government's efforts to curb illegal traffic. Hassel was never charged with influencing any rail executives or lesser minions, but too many freight cars were seized with his beer in them to let us believe his connections with the railroad were not well established.

May Day 1924 and the federal agents were back in town anxious to verify rumors that the breweries in Reading were supplying not only its local customers with real beer, but Philadelphia and South Jersey speakeasies to boot. Agents lurking at the South Eighth Street P&R freight yard observed a truck sidling up to a boxcar. They watched as the transfer began. The trucker and his helper moved nine kegs before they were tipped by a sentry that the drys were moving in. The pair abandoned the truck, fled the freight yard, and returned on foot to their speakeasy. The feds seized the truck and the boxcar with its 150-keg cargo. There were no arrests, but this time Max would suffer more than a minor adjustment in the loss column.

Reuben Sams, director of the Philadelphia Division of the Prohibition Bureau, was determined to block the steady flow of high-test beer from Reading. According to Sams, he was acting on direct orders from President Calvin Coolidge and Secretary of the Treasury Andrew Mellon. As Max Hassel's notoriety spread, so did Reading's. Within a week of the freight car seizure, Sams' agents returned with warrants to search the Reading and Fisher breweries.

Two Fisher employees were arrested inside the plant on May 8 by federal agents. Tests revealed beer in several vats was far above the .05 percent limit. A boxcar on a nearby P&R siding was also found to contain numerous barrels of high powered beer. Although the Reading Brewery was also searched by the feds, no further action against the owners, now identified as the August Manufacturing Company, was taken immediately.

When Fisher's was awarded a federal permit to produce near beer several months earlier in 1924, it had posted $50,000 to guarantee there would be no further violations of the Volstead Act. The government now warned that the bond might be forfeited. Joseph Hoverth and Joseph Stunhofer, the two employees charged with making illegal beer, claimed they did not know who their employer was. But the government identified William H. Hart as president of the Fisher Brewing Company.

Defiant, arrogant, clever—Hassel and his cohorts had all the traits that so angered and frustrated honest government enforcers. These few good men had not only the known enemy to fight, but also the enemy within—crooked guards and government attorneys who delayed prosecutions and allowed cases to disappear. Time after time breweries that were padlocked continued to produce the liquid gold that made Hassel and the select few very wealthy.

In June, Director Sams again assigned another crew to Reading with orders not to come back without a good case against the bootleggers. A P&R boxcar on a siding near the Fisher Brewery was being loaded when the drys arrived. Sure enough, it was high voltage stuff. Sams announced this raid on June 8, at the same time revealing that a Camden Cereal Company truck carrying eighty barrels of beer had been seized. Whether Hassel had an interest in that New Jersey brewery at that time is not known, but a few years later he definitely did.

Hassel also had more than a passing interest in a case that was being tried in Philadelphia that summer. The Green brothers from Northmont, who were drivers for the Hassel outfit, had to testify in a case involving the Columbia Brewery near York, Pa. Eventually, the Columbia Brewery and plants in Lancaster, Lebanon, and Easton also came under the Hassel umbrella through his involvement in the Southeastern Pennsylvania syndicate with Max "Boo Boo" Hoff as its nominal chief.

Sams, before turning his attention to Reading, had closed down almost all the Philadelphia breweries producing real beer. As his campaign heated up against the Hassel breweries he stated that most of Philly's beer supply that summer was coming from Reading.

The Fisher Brewery case involving the April and May seizures of strong beer was to be argued at a hearing in early June. Up to that time, practically all cases involving liquor violations had been settled at hearings, either before U.S. commissioners or federal judges. Hassel, fearing his plant might be dismantled, ordered his lawyers to petition the court for a jury trial. It was a bluff that did not dissuade the government. This would be the first liquor case tried in U.S. District Court in Philadelphia in which a jury would be employed. Because of the high profile lawyers involved, plenty of fireworks were anticipated.

On June 1, Federal Judge Dickinson empaneled seventy-five jurors, from which eleven men and one woman were selected. Both sides had a formidable array of attorneys: Philadelphia Congressman Benjamin M. Golder headed the defense team; Assistant U.S. Attorney Francis B. Biddle led the government forces. But before an anticipated showcase trial could begin, Golder announced his client was ready to plead guilty. An hour-long conference led to an agreement that was acceptable to both sides.

All beer at Fisher Brewery would be confiscated and destroyed. The brewery would be padlocked for a year and the building could not be used for any business purpose. Hops, barley, sugar and other materials valued at $25,000 were ordered confiscated. The Fisher Company was fined $1,000, and its president and "owner," William Hart, was fined $1,000.

Max Hassel's name was not mentioned during the surprise legal proceedings, but behind the scenes he was already laying the groundwork to expand his growing empire.

The federal drive continued in late July when a P&R freight train bound for Philly was halted before it left Reading. Another 139 halves and 25 kegs of real beer were seized after the drys broke into the sealed car. On August 1 federal agents arrived at the Reading Brewery to announce that it had been operating without a license. The machinations of the government were about as curious to the public as was Max Hassel's ability to continue his brewery operations after each seizure. Just who was responsible for licensing breweries seemed to be a continuing point of contention never completely resolved in the courts. The August Manufacturing people claimed they had a city license—or was it a state license?

Six brewery employees were working at the time of the latest raid, the thirty-eighth credited to the Prohibition Agency's Eastern Pennsylvania division. There were no arrests, but Sams reported that he would seek a federal order to dismantle and padlock the brewery.

A few days after the raid, agents returned with a temporary injunction to padlock the place. They also opened the valves on all the beer vats. And from that first amber stream that flowed out of the brewery into the streets of south Reading a tradition was started that would be celebrated several times in the next few years when a city brewery felt the wrath of the government.

A pail and bucket brigade quickly formed outside the plant as beer came pouring into the street on its way to sewer grates. The gusher quickly overwhelmed the capacity of the storm sewers. As the underground lines filled, two manholes on Ninth Street blew, and geysers of beer added to the frenzy. Streams in the gutters soon became curb-to-curb lakes. Kids and adults frolicked ankle-deep, scooping up beer in whatever vessels were handy. Some would rush home with their booty, pour it into the bathtub, then return for refills. The real tipplers just stayed put, dipping, then hoisting their mugs in a toast to whoever opened the floodgates. It was the city's biggest bash, with thousands of gallons, if slightly tainted, of free beer. From that warm August day in 1924 and for the next several years, containers of all types were dragged out whenever rumors started about a pending padlocking. The memories of streets awash with beer are among the most vivid for survivors of the Prohibition era who lived near the breweries.

Hassel had gotten the government off his back by making an accommodation to settle the Fisher case. But he was determined to put up a tougher fight to retain control of the far more productive Reading Brewery. His lawyers fought the government writ to have the brewery dismantled, giving Max time to regroup and keep the facility operating.

With Hassel's crew constantly stirring up trouble at the Fisher and Reading plants, the feds decided to pay closer attention to the Lauer Brewery, too. On August 4, two agents caught six fellows unloading kegs from a freight car on North Third street near Lauer's. The bootleggers escaped but three trucks and two hundred halves were confiscated. The license on one of the trucks had been issued to Morris Hassel and William Moeller. The license of a second truck was registered under the name of James Hart, a relative of the Fisher Brewery straw owner. Regardless of the names on official records, the chief dispatcher in charge of all these illegal movements of beer was Max Hassel.

Although Sams and his agency were getting the headlines, Mrs. Agnes B. Stallings was quietly building a case against Max. She was head of the Internal Revenue's beer and wine division. For six months her investigators had been nosing around Philadelphia and Reading. Her people were checking bank accounts, talking with brewery suppliers, and putting a lot of twos and twos together. Not until 1926 did Mrs. Stallings come down on Max.

The booze and beer federal agents had seized in the city or county was stored at Berks County Prison in City Park. Every so often the sheriff received a court order to destroy the contraband after legal actions against offenders were completed. In the instance of the Green brothers' escapade at Spruce and Front streets, the grand jury heard their case and shrugged. It ignored the bill of indictment against them because there was no evidence to prove the suspects knew the kegs contained real beer when they were hired to pick them up. So Sheriff John Esterly got the call to dump the beer along with many gallons of booze that was filling his storage area. When the bungs on some of the casks were popped, the beer shot out, spraying nearby trees with suds. The sheriff saw the positive side of his destructive task: "The saturation is good for the blight."

The intoxicating beverages were dumped into the sewer system. At the other end of the line, a Schuylkill River fisherman noted that the carp and sunnies he caught were unusually flippy. Then he realized that a stream of happy hour refreshment was gushing from a nearby sewer outlet.

On the last day of August 1924, the government issued warrants against seventeen Pennsylvania breweries that had been raided. The names of 63 people who were to be prosecuted as officials of those breweries were released to the press. The Reading companies charged were August Manufacturing Company, Deppen Manufacturing Company, and Lauer Brewing Company. The locals who received warrants were:

William C. Haberle, Carl F. Lauer, Mrs. Florence Landis, Max Hassel, William Moeller, and Steve Gierot. The latter two were known associates of Hassel's. The others were officials and shareholders of Lauer Brewing Company stock.

August Manufacturing: Frank A. Caheen Jr., George G. Meads, I. Raisch, Max Hassel, and William Moeller.

Deppen Manufacturing: Louis E. Wiswesser, W. L. Diffenderfer, and R. D. Nevin.

Bail was $5,000 apiece, with Hassel and Moeller ordered to pay $10,000 because their names appeared twice on the list.

After more than four years of illegal alcohol and beer activities, Max Hassel for the first time was publicly linked to an illegal brewery. Although he had been rumored to be THE big bootlegger in town, until the Lauer raid he was still a shadowy figure to many of the townsfolk.

The government now changed the rules of the game regarding prosecutions. Up this point, most liquor and beer violations had been handled locally, usually resulting in fines and short jail sentences. Because of the heavy bootlegging activity in Reading and Philadelphia, major liquor cases would now be tried in federal criminal court, with heavier fines and sentences promised.

The Deppen and August cases were settled rather quietly with relatively small fines, but the Lauer/Gierot case dragged on for four years as Lauer, Haberle, and Mrs. Landis claimed they had no idea the company leasing the property was making and selling strong beer. Finally, in 1928, federal Judge William Kirkpatrick accepted the defense argument that the government had failed to prove that the beer seized in a freight car outside the brewery had been manufactured inside the brewery. This was another victory for Congressman Ben Golder, once again hired to represent Max Hassel and the other Lauer defendants. The judge's decision was a boon to the racketeers as it set a precedent that further saddled prosecutors in their attempts to link seizures to the racketeers.

With all of Hassel's Reading plants buttoned up by the government by the fall of 1924, the average beer drinker in the city probably imagined Max was yesterday's news. It appeared his meteoric rise to notoriety in his hometown had burned out.

The raids that year might have slowed Hassel's cash flow but only temporarily. *Audacious* might best describe his attitude as he continued to ignore all the legal restraints under which he now had to operate. Since he paid far better than the government, his August Manufacturing was soon back in business. The double-dipping plant guards shrugged and looked the other way, hoping the home office had forgotten about them. But, by the middle of November, Reuben Sams' agents were again posted near the Reading Brewery to find out what was going on.

C. J. Fennessey and John Geiger spied on the plant from a shed across the P&R tracks west of the Reading Brewery. On November 19 they observed the rail siding leading into the courtyard on which a number of boxcars were situated. The agents watched as beer barrels were muscled into the cars at the loading platform. The siding was located on an incline. Eventually a large group of huskies put their weight to the rear car and a brakeman loosened the brake at the front of the line for its descent out of the yard. Once past the steel gate, the freight cars were pulled by a shifting engine to another siding where a locomotive was waiting. As the brakeman coupled the beerman's special to the engine, the agents made their bid to block its getaway.

The brakeman ignored the shouting agents, completed his chore, and yelled to the engineer to take off for Philadelphia. When the engineer also disregarded their cries to stop, the agents ran to their automobile, then sped down Ninth Street following the rail line. They reached the Klapperthal station in time to stop the train. The belligerent brakeman scuffled with Fennessey and Geiger before being placed under arrest on a conspiracy charge. Fifteen boxcars loaded with beer were seized. The feds said the beer was destined for Philadelphia and Atlantic City.

The P&R had been specifically notified not to accept shipments from the Reading plants. Further investigation indicated beer being made at Lauer's and Deppen was also in the cargo. Added to the intrigue were reports that Fisher Brewery had been reorganized and was also turning out real beer again. Other belated rumors had the agents engaging in a running gun battle with bootleggers near the P&R freight yards, but Reuben Sams denied that.

In early December, a federal grand jury convened in Philadelphia to probe the disappearance of large amounts of confiscated liquor being held by the Prohibition Bureau in its Eleventh and Market headquarters in Philly. The grand jury was also informed that in recent weeks, another twenty beer-laden boxcars originating in Reading had been seized.

The U.S. Marshal's office decried the shortage of well trained and better paid guards. At $5 a day, the quality of watchmen would not improve, declared W. Frank Mathues, the U.S. marshal in charge of hiring Reading guards. He fired the four sentries at the Reading Brewery after the train seizure, but claimed the new men he hired were no better.

"One particular case," Mathues stated, "was that of the appointment of a man recommended by an official of the Anti-Saloon League. I was forced to discharge him because of intoxication." There were reports that in addition to bonuses for ignoring shipments, the guards were offered all the beer they could drink. Mathues went on to report that the Reading breweries had caused his marshals far more trouble than any other plants in his territory.

Assistant U.S. Attorney James Biddle blamed the U.S. Marshals office for losing control of its employees. Three marshals were indicted. In an injunction bid to padlock Reading Brewery, the officers of August Manufacturing were listed as John H. August, president; Charles C. Bennett, treasurer; and Edwin R. Early, secretary. Listed as workers who would face charges were Max Hassel, William Moeller, and Charles Rhine. Previously, the Prohibition Agency had claimed Moeller was owner of Reading Brewing Company. William P. F. Moehler was the company's brewmaster. In other future documents involving August Manufacturing, Charles Rhine was listed as president. The government puzzled over titles, but had no doubts that Max Hassel was running the whole show.

Another temporary injunction to padlock the plant was issued by a federal judge. But getting authorization to dismantle a plant was often a lengthy affair, depending on the judge handling the case. Finding a friendly judge who would drag his feet was the surest way to slow the process. Until dismantling was ordered, the padlocks were little more than an inconvenience to the Hassel forces. Beer continued to be brewed and secreted out of the plant to a surplus of customers.

Reuben Sams kept his agents hustling as they bagged another upstate bootleg operation in December. The Liberty Brewing Company in Tamaqua was seized by the government for making strong beer. Later events would indicate that Hassel had an interest in that plant, too.

Despite his huge losses in 1924, substantially more of his beer was eluding the Prohibition agents than the shipments that were confiscated. A 1925 production graph of Hassel's beer enterprises would have again shown far more peaks than valleys.

On the other side of town, Lauer Brewery was under close scrutiny since August 1924. A writ to dismantle was stalled, and Gierot's application for a federal near beer license had not been approved. However, the guards were under orders to allow near beer to be shipped out. These watchmen complained to superiors that neighborhood toughs and truck drivers picking up near beer were threatening them. Dry agents, in town to keep an eye on all the breweries, also said they were constantly being tailed by suspicious characters. On one occasion, a brawl broke out when the harried agents confronted their stalkers.

Despite the government presence, real beer was being smuggled out of Lauer's, so the Prohibition office obtained a search warrant.

On February 20, 1925, a team of eight agents entered the brewery and arrested four men working as engineers and firemen. Laboratory tests of the beer taken from certain vats proved it was in the 3.5 percent range. In addition to the quartet arrested, Carl Lauer, Isaiah Dennis, and Jacob Bechtel were charged with manufacturing and selling an illegal beverage. They denied they had anything to do with the operation.

In its bid to obtain a permit to make near beer, Gierot Manufacturing had posted a $50,000 bond. Hassel and friends were now threatened with forfeiting it. But it was never announced that these threats were fulfilled.

At Reading Brewery there was a 10-foot-wide alley running off the west side of Ninth Street. The racking room, where barrels and kegs were filled, was located along Little Laurel Street. In this alley, a contrivance similar to a drawbridge used to span a medieval castle moat was erected. A steam winch was used to raise and lower the bridge to allow trucks to pass through the alley. When the heavy metal floor of the bridge was raised to a vertical position it blocked entrance to the alley at Ninth Street.

U.S. Deputy Marshal Charles Mink explained that a system had been worked out by the bootleggers to release trucks over the bridge during the brief lapses during changing of the federal guards. In that short span, as many as ten loaded trucks could pass out onto Ninth Street to make deliveries. Then the bridge was quickly raised again. Mink claimed the device had been installed because the bootleggers in recent months found it impossible to get any beer out of the complex by means of the railroad.

U. S. District Judge J. W. Thompson eventually issued an order to have Reading Brewery dismantled and padlocked until the following December. Materials were seized and sold for $310. Forty bales of hops, two hundred bags of barley, and two hundred bags of cereal preparation were hauled away by the buyer, Samuel Cohen, a Hassel handyman who handled a variety of jobs for the boss. Before machinery could be taken apart or destroyed, there was enough beer to fill three thousand barrels to be disposed of.

When the public got wind that another beer letting was imminent, whole families rushed to Ninth and Laurel lugging receptacles of all shapes and forms. But the feds proved to be party poopers by restricting the flow to avert another flood. Valves on the vats were regulated to slow down the disposal. Sewers didn't back up, the amber stream was a mere trickle, and only the very patient were rewarded with a pailful. The beer Forty-Niners would have to wait till another day to strike it rich. It took more than two days to empty the seventy-nine wooden and steel vats that were located on the second and third floors of the brewery.

Machinery and equipment were either taken apart or destroyed. The big tanks were not damaged but the "heads" were removed, rendering the vat useless. Heads were steel ports on the side near the bottom of the storage vats. Valves and other essential parts were removed from boilers and stored in a room sealed with special locks. The entire dismantling took nine days. Government observers called the August plant one of the largest and best equipped breweries in eastern Pennsylvania. The officers of the company were listed as Max Hassel, Bill Moeller and Charlie Rhine. They were served with papers enjoining them from ever again participating in a brewery enterprise or any enterprise that could be construed as in violation of the national Prohibition laws.

With Reading Brewery disabled and out of commission, supposedly, for the next ten months, Rhine and other August officials offered guilty pleas before Federal Judge Dickinson. Somehow, Hassel had been dropped from the defendant list. The judge went easy on August, leveling only a $1,000 fine.

The phoenix mentality of Max Hassel repeatedly shocked and frustrated federal authorities. Time after time when they assigned his breweries to the ash bin, he revived them to profitability. Only a month after putting August Manufacturing on ice for the rest of the year—supposedly—the government returned Fisher Brewery to its hit list. The refitted brewery had been shipping out strong beer for several months. On March 27, 1925, armed with a search warrant, the feds uncovered seven hundred cases of bottled beer and thirty barrels of the same strong brew at the Northeastern Bottling Exchange. The NBE was an arm of whatever name Fisher Brewery was operating under at the time. It was located in a structure adjoining the brewing building.

Enforcement officers guarding the Lauer plant were used to reinforce the Fisher raiding party. NBE was using the latest bottling machinery, and had been operating for some months, the feds reported. The Volstead Act forbade the bottling of real beer.

Not all of the raids that year were conducted by the authorities. It was a Saturday night in late June 1925 when a boxcar loaded with 250 halves was parked on a siding near Sixth and Canal streets. A city hotel proprietor and his helper were waiting in two trucks to pick up fifty kegs. The two thirsty trainmen who had parked the boxcar got huffy when their request for a half barrel donation was rejected by the consignee.

The somewhat heated debate had drawn a small audience before the hotelman loaded up, resealed the boxcar, and left. So did the angry train crew. Word quickly spread that a large cache of real beer was there for the taking. Within minutes, a large crowd was cheering a few brave men who pried open the freight car door. The scramble was on. South Reading streets were alive with beer barrel rollers going in all directions. Some pushed their loot into the nearby Schuylkill Canal to be retrieved the next morning.

Of course there was no police investigation although railroad detectives who arrived late Sunday reported they found only one keg hidden in a bush. Cellars in the neighborhood were overloaded with beer, but not for long. Folks looking for bargains scurried about South Reading to find strong beer priced at $3 to $5 a keg the next several days.

Except for the great barrel roll, the summer of 1925 was generally quiet on the beer front, but plenty was going on behind the scenes. Governor Pinchot, well informed about Reading's reputation as a wide open town, decided to move his troops closer to the city. He had a running battle with Mayor Sharman about the state police making liquor arrests in Reading. Now James Maurer, the Socialist firebrand, joined the fight to keep the state police out. Maurer, president of the State Federation of Labor, personally appealed to Pinchot not to move Troop C to the former Eckert mansion in West Reading. The State

Board of Public Grounds and Buildings was on the verge of signing a lease to house the staties in the stylish structure across the Schuylkill River from Reading.

Major Lynn Adams, superintendent of the state police, supported the move. Troop C was currently headquartered at Pottsville, but Adams was riled about the performance of Schuylkill County grand juries that persistently refused to indict liquor law violators. The commander saw better opportunities to uphold the Volstead Act in Reading. The lease on the Pottsville barracks ended April 1.

All through March, the proposed move was kicked around in Harrisburg. Maurer sought a second audience with the governor, and when that failed he stated, "It is a mistake. Pottsville doesn't want the troopers and now state officials are trying to foist them on Reading."

Max Hassel was acquainted with Maurer and surely supported Jimmy's stand on this issue. The feds were giving him enough trouble without having the staties breathing down his neck. He anticipated that Governor Pinchot would pressure Troop C to turn up the heat on the breweries in Reading, as if things weren't hot enough already.

The troop occupied its new quarters in April and for several months they made no waves while settling in. But Max was preparing. Trying to extend his early warning system, Hassel made contact with Trooper Paul Chambers and a clerk, James O'Neill, at the new headquarters. This action turned into a bribery case that wasn't settled for two years. (See Chapter 5)

All three Hassel plants had been padlocked in the spring of 1925, but it would have been uncharacteristic of Max to just let them sit idle. And the command at Troop C's new quarters was not fooled by the apparent inactivity. Federal guards had been withdrawn, so troopers were assigned to make sporadic checks. In early September, Captain Samuel W. Gerhart reported to his superiors in Harrisburg his suspicions that something appeared to be stirring in the Fisher and Lauer buildings. Both had ice plants that continued to operate, but possibly some of the ice trucks were taking out more than ice. It's quite possible that Gearhart also had information that the bootleggers had infiltrated his barracks with a couple of spies. Rather than risking a leak by using Troop C to stage a raid, the state command ordered Troop D in Butler to make a surprise attack.

September 25, a Saturday afternoon, two troopers from western Pennsylvania and Private Reese Davis of Troop C, watched from a distance as several men loaded kegs into a freight car on the Fisher rail siding. The staties drove into Reading to get a search warrant from Alderman Henry Mayer, then returned to the brewery. The loaders quickly scattered as the lawmen approached, but two workers inside the plant were taken into custody. Although no strong beer was found in the vats, beer in the boxcars was tested with a bulameter. The beer's alcoholic content was close to 4.0.

This was the first of another round of raids that unmasked the tenacity of Hassel's crews to continue to produce beer regardless of the roadblocks thrown up by the enforcers. The big problem for government agencies was how to really…really close down the breweries without blowing them up. Hassel had the means to replace damaged equipment and the mechanics to reconstruct whatever was dismantled. Max's profits were so huge that they far outweighed whatever his losses were. Incursions by the enforcers were factored by the racketeers as a normal business expense.

The new padlocks at Fisher Brewery were barely secured before Gearhart's guerrillas sprung into action on North Third Street, where the vats at Lauer brewery were brimming. Hassel's spies, Chambers and O'Neill, were not earning their $75 a week. October 5, 1925, was the date of the most notable bust Hassel experienced at one of his breweries. The fifteen freight cars of Reading Brewery beer seized the previous year might have had a higher value, but this Lauer foray got far more public exposure. The staties had obtained a search warrant, having observed large amounts of mash being hauled out of the plant. Towers of steam billowing from the plant's smoke stack suggested the brewmaster was working long hours. The assumption that where there's steam there's something cooking proved solid beyond the cops' fondest hopes.

The raid got underway that Monday afternoon as a single trooper scaled a wall and unlocked a gate for eight of his cohorts. After using pickaxes to break through heavy doors, they discovered dozens of full storage tanks and working vats. Tests of beer from twenty-four vats were taken. All showed the alcoholic content exceeded 3 percent.

Unlike federal Prohibition officials, who went pretty much by the book when making arrests and following up with proper padlocking and dismantling procedures, the staties assumed a vigilante attitude toward beer runners. Their boss, Governor Pinchot, the consummate Prohibitionist, did not authorize them to play rough, but he didn't criticize them when they did. There was no better example of their law-be-damned mind-set than on that afternoon when seven workers were arrested. These employees were told to notify the plant owners to come forward and claim their beer. The workers couldn't, or wouldn't iden-tify their employers. As the afternoon wore on, Lt. William Plummer, the raid commander, waited for somebody to admit ownership, but nobody did.

Without court authorization, tank valves were opened; barrel bungs and bottles were smashed. The staties added to their reputation of act-ing first and asking questions later. Three troopers were trapped on the third floor by the foaming torrent gushing from numerous vats. By wading hip-deep in suds to the safety of higher ground, they escaped a bubbly death. Beer cascaded out windows, and down stairs, through air vents and elevator shafts, and eventually onto Third Street, where the bucket and pail brigade was waiting. Hundreds of neighborhood youngsters and adults wallowed in a river of whipped amber, enough to fill ten thousand barrels. It was the biggest flood of beer the city had ever seen. In addition to the army of scoopers, hundreds of others gath-ered to watch. New Year's Eve never offered such a wet celebration. The last tanks weren't drained until after 9 p.m.

The state police rationalized their drastic action: since the brewery had no federal license, why were court orders needed to destroy outlawed property? Were the brewery owners going to sue, thereby admitting they were engaged in an illegal enterprise? If 3-point beer was illegal, Troop C decided to cut out the middle man and save the taxpayers money. The state police command had no faith in federal guards. Harrisburg headquarters feared the well-organized bootleggers would find a way to smuggle out the beer if it wasn't disposed of immediately. On other occasions that had happened.

The state police estimated the loss of ten thousand barrels of beer was worth $130,000 in potential profits to the bootleggers. At that time the price to truck drivers was $22 a barrel. Hotels, clubs and speakeasies then paid $28 to the deliverymen.

At 6 o'clock that evening, while beer was still being drained from Lauer's, a detachment of troopers added to the excitement by entering the Deppen Brewery across Third Street and one block north. Rumors about a raid were rampant on Penn Street hours before it happened, so possibly Louie Wiswesser, the Deppen president, made an emergency dumping. The staties drew a blank when they examined his vats and searched the plant. A little near beer was found, but none of the strong stuff.

The feds, possibly hoping Hassel's workers at Fisher's would think the commotion was over for the night, went crashing into the North Eleventh Street plant at 1 a.m. the next morning. They found a quartet of young men and several vats of strong beer, but the racking room was quiet, as was the bottling department. The employees were arrested. It had been a busy twelve hours, but only at the Lauer Brewery had the enforcers really scored.

The next day, Wiswesser filed for an injunction to restrain the state police from damaging Deppen equipment or materials in the event of another raid. When Lt. Plummer told the court no more state police raids were contemplated in the near future, Wiswesser withdrew his request.

Three troopers guarded Lauer's that night. The next day security was turned over to federal authorities, the usual procedure after state flying squadrons conducted a successful action. Troop C officers did not identify Max Hassel as the operator of Lauer's, but they did mention that the main suspect was also the boss at Fisher Brewery and several others.

Although the staties had completed their brewery raids for the year, there were a few more incidents in 1925 when beer that was smuggled past plant guards failed to exit the city. On October 20, another of the Marks brothers on Hassel's payroll made the headlines. Jake Marks was nabbed loading a truck with beer barrels removed from a freight car in the Spruce Street rail yard. His white truck was prominently labeled with the name of a laundry company, who reported to the state police that the vehicle was sold several weeks ago. When questioned, the buyer denied he owned the truck. This was a typical situation in which all types of trucks were borrowed, loaned, or rented to haul beer but rarely did anybody 'fess up to ownership.

Shortly after Jake was hauled off to jail, the state police received another tip about two boxcars on a siding in the freight yard near Oley Street. The cars were sealed. While two troopers remained to guard the cars, a third went to obtain a search warrant. In the meantime, railroaders came to couple one of the cars to a locomotive over the protest of the cops. The engineer said he was taking his cargo to Port Clinton. Without any authority to halt the train, the troopers hopped aboard, unwilling to let their prize get away. Trooper No. 3 returned with a search warrant but had trouble finding his cohorts who were riding around the large freight yard. Once reunited, the troopers had a heated debate with the engineer to uncouple the boxcar. The lawmen won, and inside one car were three hundred halves of strong beer. The other contained seventeen 50-gallon drums of grain alcohol. The catch for that day was valued at $10,000 by the state police.

John Hyneman, a once and future gambling kingpin in Reading, was cutting his teeth in the rackets at the time and played a small role in this seizure. True to form, the staties drained all the beer taken from the two boxcars. The empty casks were released to the county commissioners, who sold them to Hyneman for fifty cents apiece. The casks came full circle when Hyneman returned them to his bosses, the bootleggers.

The final seizure and arrests that year were at a siding in the Northmont section of Reading. This was near the Fisher Brewery where the beer probably originated. On November 8 the state police grabbed James Hart, John Beckey, and George Wolf as they passed kegs out of a boxcar. Again, without bothering to obtain a writ to destroy confiscated property, the staties cracked the bungs and let the beer flow.

As 1925 ran its course, all three of the Hassel-controlled breweries in Reading were under U.S. Marshal guardianship. But more important to Max was a shocking development in December when he was arrested and charged with bribery.

5

The Fruits of Corruption

For the entreprenuer, Prohibition was a golden opportunity. The risk taker welcomed the chance to fill the vacuum created by the 18th Amendment. Brewers ostensibly stayed in business to make near beer, but seasoned drinkers wanted the real thing, not a pale imitation. The beer plants were quickly renovated to circumvent Volstead regulations. Near beer vats were prominently located when federal inspectors scheduled tests for alcoholic content. Less conspicuous, sometimes behind reinforced walls, were tanks in which 4 percent beer was stored in much larger quantities.

Ingenious precautions to evade detection were dreamed up. More often, however, beer bootleggers relied on that old standby, a less innovative method but a tried and true scheme to protect their interests—graft. They paid government inspectors to turn in false reports about how much and what type of beer was being manufactured. They paid guards to ignore shipments of real beer that were loaded on trucks and trains.

Max Hassel relied heavily on payoffs and bribes to thwart officials at the Prohibition Agency's division office in Philadelphia. His early warning system included a network of lookouts along delivery routes, plus paid spies in the state police.

Surprisingly, it appears he was a hands-on operator when canvassing law enforcement people to work for him. As crafty and cautious as he was about hiding his ownership of breweries behind layers of deed transfers and phony names, he dealt face to face with any number of lawmen, some of whom testified that he tried to bribe them. Was it

Max's power of persuasion that drove him to deal directly with these guardians of the law he meant to suborn? He wasn't reckless, but all too often he did his own dirty work when he had plenty of soiled hands at his disposal. Possibly he needed to face the potential betrayers to be convinced they would bend to his will.

Although court records show that Max was suspected of "influencing" federal agents when he operated the Schuylkill Extract and Berks Products companies, no charges were filed. Twice cited for making illegal sales of government alcohol, he repeatedly denied he had tampered with agents assigned to his plants. That happened early in Prohibition before the agency realized how easily the low-paid, mostly untrained appointees could be corrupted. The only lesson those early citations taught Max was that bribery was the cheapest and best method of protecting his interests. So he gave of graft freely throughout his career, willing to spend thousands more in legal fees to escape conviction each time he was caught.

Max always had a semi-believable story ready when he was called to answer accusations made by agents. The first incident occurred on a chilly November afternoon in 1924. He strolled up to a pair of drys assigned to keep tabs on Lauer Brewery. As they stood outside a Third Street gasoline station, Max invited them to join him at a nearby bar to get out of the cold. Clarence J. Fennessey and R. D. Farlow would later testify that Max flashed a large roll of bills. Fennessey claimed Max offered them $700 to relax their vigil. "Not enough," was the agents' reaction. Max, they said, drove away in his late-model car, then returned and displayed several $1,000 bills. The pair showed nodding interest but refused to consummate deals individually as Hassel insisted. They wanted a package deal; Max wanted separate agreements so each agent could not witness the other's. Hassel left. Fennessey and Farlow discussed the matter with superiors. Although no money exchanged hands, the government charged Max with attempted bribery the following month.

At his hearing before U.S. Commissioner Henry Maltzberger, Max was defended by Benjamin Golder, the Philadelphia criminal lawyer and future congressman, and Robert Grey Bushong, a former county judge from Sinking Spring. He, too, would later be elected to Congress.

Golder and Bushong argued that Max was joking around, merely teasing the agents with his show of big bucks. Maltzberger declared that the scant evidence presented tended to indicate "a frameup" to get Hassel. The commissioner exonerated him, and the legend that Max was untouchable began to evolve.

For Fennessey, an honest agent who would build a long and honorable record with the Prohibition agency, it was a slap in the face he would never forget. He had any number of encounters with the Hassel gang over the years. A fews weeks after the bribery attempt, Fennessey was one of two agents involved in the capture of a freight train carrying August Manufacturing beer when the brakeman was arrested at the Klapperthal station. That escapade was compared to a silent movie chase by Prohibition officials. The frameup possibility offered by Maltzberger suggests he felt the agents were conducting a vendetta to get Hassel.

When the state police moved Troop C into the new barracks in West Reading in the spring of 1925, Max thought it best to extend his spy network.

A tall, good-looking trooper, Paul Chambers, soon came under the beer baron's influence. Chambers was assigned to general duty, sometimes investigating crime in rural areas or handling traffic problems. He agreed to keep Hassel informed about pending raids on Reading breweries, but often he was off on other assignments when enforcement squads struck. To add a bit more protective padding, Max drew the barracks clerk, who also served as telephone operator, into his web. Trooper Chambers was the go-between, setting up a meeting between Hassel and James Vernon O'Neill. O'Neill had passed the test for state trooper in 1920 and served in that capacity for two years. Then he switched to the office job. Later it would be debated whether he was under state police command, or served as a civilian on the Troop C payroll. Max Hassel was not interested in his classification. All he wanted was tip-offs when Troop C was going to raid one of his plants, particularly the Lauer Brewery which at the time was running at maximum production. He believed the relocated staties would go after the North Third Street plant to establish their reputation in Reading. Subsequent events would prove him right.

This is the story O'Neill eventually would confess to his superiors about his brief but eventful association with Max Hassel:

In mid-July 1925 he was informed by Chambers that Max Hassel wanted to meet with him in Reading. A few days later, O'Neill said, he parked his red Jordan at Fifth and Franklin streets. Hassel arrived in a red Cadillac. Max invited the clerk into his car. They took a short drive over the Bingaman Street Bridge, Max offering to pay for information O'Neill could provide that would facilitate the safe removal of illegal beer from Lauer Brewery. Max proposed to pay him $150 a week, half of which O'Neill would give to Trooper Chambers. At that initial meeting, Hassel handed him $150, plus a $50 bonus. There were several more payments, all made by Hassel, totalling $1,500. O'Neill split the money evenly with Chambers. The payoffs were always in $50 and $100 bills.

On October 6, the day after the big Lauer raid by the state police, O'Neill received word from Chambers to meet Fred Marks at Tenth and Franklin streets. The former Reading cop and now one of Hassel's most trusted aides arrived with Chambers. Duck, as Freddie was known in racket circles, didn't write Chambers and O'Neill off Hassel's spy list, but for the time being they would no longer be paid unless their intelligence improved. Obviously, that payoff was not one of Hassel's better investments.

Captain Samuel Gearhart, Company C commander, called the unsuspecting O'Neill into his office the next day. Gearhart claimed to have proof about the bribery scheme. O'Neill caved in almost immediately. He spilled the complete story to his boss. A week later he was taken to state police headquarters in Harrisburg to repeat his tale to Major Lynn Adams, commander of the state troops.

A formal written confession by O'Neill was taken. Present around a large conference table when O'Neill laid out the conspiracy story were Adams, Gearhart, and Assistant Attorney General Louis M. Graham. Also invited to the party was Trooper Paul Chambers who had been stonewalling his accusers.

O'Neill was taken to Washington, D.C., where he was questioned by Mrs. Mabel Walker Willebrant, the Justice Department's top prosecutor of liquor cases. She already was familiar with the Hassel name, having read reports from the Philadelphia Prohibition office about frequent raids at three Reading breweries Max controlled. She encouraged the staties to push hard for convictions of Hassel, Chambers, and Marks.

The distraught O'Neill turned over most of his share of the bribe money he had stashed in his barracks footlocker. He admitted having spent a small amount for automobile repairs. He was assigned to the Harrisburg office and allowed to continue working with no loss of salary for three months. There was one very important stipulation: he would not be charged if he testified against the other suspects. Chambers had been fired after his continual denials following O'Neill's confession. In December the handsome ex-statie was arrested and charged with extortion. For the second time in his fast-paced career, Max Hassel was charged with conspiracy and bribery. Fred Marks was charged with conspiracy.

Max was preoccupied during the Christmas holidays with an even more stressful matter. His mother Sarah was in failing health. She died January 3, 1926, at the age of 60. This was the first great loss to a family that was very close. Just how much this immigrant woman understood about her middle son's sudden wealth is not known, but as she neared death her children did not further burden her with information about his latest arrest. She was buried in Kesher Zion Cemetery just east of Grill along Route 724.

The Prohibition Agency boasted about the big fish it had netted, sure that O'Neill's testimony would fry Hassel and his cronies. But it wasn't that easy. In the weeks leading up to preliminary hearings, O'Neill was kept under surveillance. However, it appears the bootleggers managed to present him with options. The Hassel forces teased him with money, the state tested him by threatening him with the loss of employment and possible jail time. It's not unlikely that some of Hassel's henchmen suggested bodily harm would be part of the equation even if the boss frowned on that type of extortion.

O'Neill was transported back to Reading for the preliminary hearing, Major Adams and Captain Gearhart confident O'Neill would stick to his story. But on the Friday morning of the hearing he told his lawyer, Harry Lee, he wasn't sure he wanted to testify. The state police got wind of his indecision and District Attorney David Mauger asked for a postponement, declaring his star witness was ill. Rumors were flying as the hearing was rescheduled for the next week.

A crowd jammed the Sixth Ward office of Alderman Henry Mayer the morning of January 23, 1926. Anxious to observe Max Hassel in court, the gawkers were disappointed when his hearing was pushed back to later in the day because the defense lawyers for him and Paul Chambers were busy with other cases. So the hearing for Fred Marks proceeded and James O'Neill rattled off his tale of bribery for the first time in public. Under cross-examination, O'Neill admitted he was in Mauger's office the previous Friday and was not sick. That refuted Mauger's reason for seeking the postponement. H. Robert Mays, a former D.A. and now defending Marks, was trying to show that O'Neill's testimony was tainted because of state police pressure.

During direct examination, the state police clerk testified about his contact with Hassel other than on the five Saturdays when he had picked up his weekly payoff:

"Hassel called me up half a dozen times and I gave him facts as best I could. I called him up a few times and told him everything was all right, or vice versa. I based my information on the troopers leaving. It was only my opinion. I didn't know actually whether they were going to knock off a brewery or get a burglar." He said Chambers really didn't know anything about troop movements concerning the Lauer Brewery.

Alderman Mayer heard O'Neill's story about receiving $1,500 in cash from Max Hassel, splitting the money with Chambers, and finally about the clerk's confession to the state police high command about his misdeeds. Marks was held for grand jury action on the conspiracy charge.

The main event started at 5:30 p.m. The alderman's office was again packed to the doors. Max was tastefully dressed in a dark double-breasted suit, but more noticeable was the large diamond ring he wore on his right hand. He did not testify and rarely spoke to his lawyer.

If the clerk was wavering a week earlier about accusing the bootleggers, he certainly stood fast to his original story on the witness stand. Defense attorneys Bushong and M. Bernard Hoffman could not shake him. He repeated his tale about receiving the $150 a week payoffs from Hassel that he split with Chambers, and the sudden halt of bribe money after meeting with Marks and Chambers. Hoffman, representing Chambers, grilled O'Neill but failed to expose any flaws in his tale. Bushong tried to show that the state police brass was attempting to frame his client. Without substantiation, he introduced a rumor that O'Neill had heard Major Adams and Captain Gearhart say they were going to "get Hassel and ship him back to Russia."

O'Neill denied ever hearing such a statement. About another tidbit Bushong threw at him, O'Neill stated, "I never heard anything said that Governor Pinchot would pardon me if I went to jail."

No witnesses, including the defendants, were called by the defense. Mayer ruled that the case against Hassel and Chambers would also go to the grand jury.

Desperate measures now were considered by the defendants. Free on $6,000 bail, Max must have talked long into the night with his associates about what to do about Jimmy O'Neill. Their first attempt to fix the case had failed, so this time the ante would have to go up to win over the vacillating witness. Just what kind of pressure—threat of physical harm or promise of a bigger payday—was not publicized. The bootleggers had unlimited funds to buy the witness, and several Hassel associates, with their investments and future at stake, were willing to dispatch O'Neill as a last resort. Would Jim accept their latest offer, only to succumb again to dire threats of perjury charges from the state police hierachy?

Just what happened to O'Neill has never officially been revealed. After the hearing he was reassigned to the Harrisburg office. Then he disappeared. During the ensuing search, it was rumored that Chambers had also skipped. Major Adams quickly launched a statewide alert to find the renegades who were giving his command a bad name. He assigned troopers to track motor registrations, check haunts of the pair, and send fliers to other law enforcement departments. The press ran stories that the fugitives had fled to Canada, or parts unknown. If Chambers had run he would have forfeited the $4,000 bail Hassel had posted for him.

District Attorney Mauger knew his case would be very shaky without O'Neill. But he presented it to the grand jury, using Major Adams and Captain Gearhart as his feature witnesses. The panel indicted Hassel, Marks, and Chambers. The trial was scheduled for the March term of criminal court. Chambers suddenly turned up, feigning surprise that anybody had been worried about him. He gave no explanation about his recent whereabouts.

Mauger stalled by placing the bribery case far down on the list of cases scheduled for trial in March, knowing it would not be held during that session. Barney Hoffman, playing the speedy-trial card, tried to get the district attorney to ensure that the case would be high on the

June court schedule. Mauger refused to do that and the stall continued through two more sessions.

Interspersed with the state's case against Hassel, whispers of another bribery attempt drifted back to Reading from Easton. Using a Reading pal, Louis Cohn, as the ghost owner of Seitz Brewing Company in Easton, Hassel operated the plant for some time before dry agents raided it on May 28, 1926. In an effort to drive out the invaders, Seitz workers sprayed them with ammonia. The agents survived the gas attack and closed down the place. U.S. Commissioner Frank Reeder in Lehigh County reported that dry agents turned over to him a large sum of money they were offered by somebody trying to make the Seitz Brewery prosecution go away. But Hassel's name was not mentioned and the case faded away, the government a few bucks richer from the extortion attempt that failed. Cohn disappeared, later showing up as a Hassel confederate in New Jersey. After being closed for several years, the Seitz property was sold to Hudson Realty Company of the Bronx. Some believed Dutch Schultz had an interest in the place.

Meanwhile, the search for James O'Neill continued, but at a questionably slow pace. When it appeared O'Neill was gone for good, maybe dead, Mauger was pressured by Judge John Stevens to put up or dismiss the charges. The DA decided to give it a try.

As the trial opened on March 20, 1927, Max, as always, was impeccably dressed. He wore a dark suit, but now with a jury studying his every personal effect, he did not have on the diamond ring so prominently displayed at the hearing. On entering the courthouse he was wearing a light gray fedora with a wide black band, the rim turned down on one side. During the trial he always focused on whoever was speaking, rarely addressed his attorneys, and listened with an arm resting on the defense table or over the back of a chair. There was another full house for the two-day trial.

Right from the start, District Attorney Mauger let the jury know that his star witness was among the missing, possibly for good. He then presented Judge Stevens with an all-important issue. He asked that notes of O'Neill's conspiracy confession and those of the preliminary hearing be admissible as evidence. Hassel's chief counsel was now Congressman Bushong, who was elected to the U.S. House of Representatives the previous November. Bushong vehemently objected to the DA's motion. He said the written word was no substitute for the actual witness who the jurors must hear and see in person to make a true judgment. Bushong lost that battle, Judge Stevens ruling that the complete transcripts of the confession and the hearing would be read to the jury. Court stenographer Stanford Cornelius, at risk of lulling the jury to sleep, completed his dull recitation of the hearing notes in slightly more than three hours. The confession was much shorter.

According to O'Neill's earlier testimony, the court was informed that Paul Chambers broke down and cried while the clerk was offering his confession in Harrisburg. When the tall, good-looking Chambers heard this in the courtroom he leaned back in his chair, laughing aloud. It was his way of conveying to the jury, "Do I look like somebody who would do that?" He wanted them to measure his macho appearance against O'Neill's "ridiculous" claim. It was no laughing matter, however, when Major Adams later testified about a conversation he had with Chambers:

"I asked Chambers whether he sold himself for $1,000. He hung his head and cried. He gave no reason for the weakness. He explained he spent the money. I took him to Harrisburg and had him there for two or three weeks. After he was discharged from the service I understand he went to work for Hassel."

Major Adams was grilled by Bushong and Henry Keiser, also representing Hassel, about state police investigative tactics. The attorneys tried to get Adams to admit that Hassel was targeted by the state police even before the conspiracy was exposed. Woven into the attorneys' questions were suggestions that Adams had assigned Chambers to "get Hassel." Adams firmly denied that, but added, "I was more interested in catching the men who corrupted Chambers and O'Neill than I was in punishing them. As concerns O'Neill and the fact that he was not arrested, I was acting under the orders of the attorney general."

The state called Leslie Talley, captain of the Reading Iron Company police. He described events of a September 1925 afternoon when he witnessed a convoy of several beer trucks leaving the Lauer plant, accompanied by a fleet of automobiles. The intersection at Third and Walnut streets was blocked by the cars to allow the trucks to pass and to prevent police cars from chasing the trucks. Talley said he saw Max Hassel and Fred Marks in different cars in the convoy.

An improbable witness for the state was Constantine H. Condos who identified himself as proprietor of the Colonial Hotel. Condos was the strawman for Hassel in the purchase of the hotel at Fifth and Court Streets the previous October. Although Condos managed the place, the building was owned by Max. Was his appearance in court a charade manufactured by Max and the boys, or did the manager have an ax to grind with the boss? The former seems the likely choice. This was C.H.'s story:

He was in the district attorney's office on a business matter a week before the trial started. When the bribery case became the topic of conversation, Condos said he just happened to recollect an incident that occurred on September 22, 1926. The district attorney listened with interest. The next thing Condos knew, he was subpoenaed as a witness. It should be noted that by September 1926, James O'Neill had been missing about eight months. At the trial, Condos was asked to repeat his tale.

It was about a noisy argument he recalled in Morris Hassel's Paramount Realty office at the rear of the Colonial Hotel lobby.

"At first they talked business and then they became louder and louder," Condos said. "I went to the office. One man, who was louder than the others, said that he must come out and tell the truth; that he lost his home, his business, his reputation and everything. Someone said, 'O'Neill sit down.' Hassel came out, and I said, 'We can't have any trouble here,' and he left." The witness smiled broadly as he pointed to Max when asked to identify him.

Under cross-examination, Condos admitted he didn't see who was in the room other than Hassel. About the name he heard, he then enlarged: "It sounded like O'Neill or Neill, I can't say exactly, but to the best of my recollection I believe it was O'Neill." He said he would recognize O'Neill if he saw him.

Another witness, a travelling salesman, testified he was in the lobby that evening and remembered the uproar but could not distinguish what was being said.

This story raised more questions than answers about the whereabouts of O'Neill. Did Max and his attorneys dream up this scenario to show that O'Neill was alive and well? Was it an attempt to show that O'Neill had been in Reading all along, so why hadn't the state police located him? But the words Condos recited also created the image of a frightened man who was being harassed by Hassel. Why would Condos want to add to the suspicion that Max was intimidating the missing witness? It didn't make sense that the hotel manager would risk telling a story that could add to the owner's problems. Bushong, who very well might have been a part of this pretense, said in his summation to the jury:

"If you were Mr. Hassel and had held such a conversation, would you hold it in front of seven or eight men? Why, they held a convention that night!" That bit of sarcasm inspired the only laugh of the trial. It was just one small chapter of a case that seemed so pat when the suspects were arrested, but was now showing considerable wear and tear.

When the prosecution rested on the second day, the defense said it had no witnesses and Judge Stevens ordered summations to begin immediately. In his closing argument Bushong harped about having no opportunity to question the man who accused the defendants of bribery. A. H. Rothermel, an assistant district attorney, reminded the jury that Max Hassel sought protection to guard against state police raids on his illegal beer enterprise. He said Hassel did not pay $60,000 on a two-year lease for Lauer Brewery "just to make soft drinks."

The jury began deliberations at 7 p.m., worked all night and took twenty-eight ballots before notifying the court at 10 o'clock the next morning that it could not reach a unanimous decision. The final vote was 10-2 for conviction. With a hung jury, the district attorney promised he would seek a new trial which Judge Stevens quickly agreed to. While the hunt for O'Neill continued that spring, Mauger pursued every avenue hoping for additional evidence to beat the racketeers.

Interest in the bribery case was overshadowed in the daily press that summer by the month-long adulation of Charles Lindbergh. His historic flight to France in May still continued to get top play by newspapers across the country when Hassel's second trial began on June 13.

The first surprise was Judge Stevens' announcement that the jury would be sequestered. Rumors of a jury fix at the first trial added to the growing belief that Max Hassel had too many friends in the right places to ever be convicted. The same array of prominent defense lawyers crowded the defense table as Mauger and Rothermel prepared to face off with them again. The judge had a parley with the attorneys who agreed to tone down their constant bickering on points of law so prevalent at the first trial.

Instead of a packed house, a *Reading Times* reporter describing the courtroom on opening day of the trial stated: "There was only a corporal's guard of regulars in the benches yesterday." Max, now attired in a light summer suit, appeared confident, always the proper, unemotional defendant who seemed to be just another disinterested onlooker.

The prosecution's witness list was slightly longer, but only the questions during cross-examination added some variety to the drama. Congressman Bushong drew an admission from Captain Gearhart that O'Neill was never given any information about Troop C movements. But, he continued, "He may have picked some up in conversation with other members of the troop."

But this was just a warmup by Bushong before delving into the main focus of his interrogation: to what extent had the prosecutors tried to locate O'Neill since he disappeared? From Major Adams he learned that pictures and circulars were distributed around Pennsylvania. Federal authorities had notified the Royal Mounted Police of Canada to watch for him. O'Neill's relatives were questioned in Philadelphia and Pottsville by state troopers. Berks County Detective Harry Hilzinger testified he had a subpoena when he visited O'Neill's brother in Philadelphia only two months ago, but was back in Reading by noon of the same day. Nothing came out of that trip. A federal inspector of breweries, Frank Evans, testified that on his first assignment as an agent he went to a dozen cities in eastern states, plus a trip to Canada looking for O'Neill—to no avail.

Bushong roasted Detective Hilzinger for not trying harder in the Quaker City. He later offered a blistering opinion about the several law enforcement agencies involved in the manhunt:

"Of all the idiotic exhibitions of detective work, that of the search for O'Neill takes the cake. We heard a state police detective testify that he went everywhere except to the hometown of O'Neill where he might have expected to find him." The clerk was from Bradford in western Pennsylvania. "We heard how a federal officer, with every expense paid by the federal government—per diem, hotels, railroad fares—traveled over half the country with a picture of O'Neill in his hand. He went to Niagara Falls, N.Y., and Niagara Falls, Ontario. He went to New Haven and heaven only knows where else. But he didn't tell us why he went to these places. It didn't matter to him where he travelled; his traveling was free."

Bushong and Hoffman continued to punch holes in the accounts offered by the police in their ineffective pursuit of the fugitive. Again, without the star witness to give a personal account of the bribery scheme, the jury was left to judge much of the case on written testimony. The reading of O'Neill's confession and the 27,000-word transcript of the preliminary hearing again consumed several hours.

The jury took three hours and forty-one minutes to reach a verdict by 7:30 p.m. on the second day of the trial. But Judge Stevens said he would keep the verdict sealed until the next morning. The Hassel camp, with its reliable spy network in the legal system, found out almost immediately that their boys were acquitted. The evening betting line in gambling circles after the jury began its deliberations was 2 to 1 for "not guilty".

With very reliable sources about the outcome, Hassel and friends and colleagues gathered at midnight in a local cafe to celebrate their victory. Hours before court reconvened the next morning, the trial story in the *Times* strongly intimated the defendants were acquitted, although it lacked official confirmation. Lindbergh, after being bannered the two previous days about triumphant parades through Washington D.C. and New York City, suddenly took second billing to Reading's folk hero. The four female and eight male jurors returned to the courtroom that morning as Judge Stevens opened the sealed verdict and had it read. None of the defendants, lawyers or small audience were demonstrative. In a case in which there were no defense witnesses, Max Hassel, Fred Marks, and Paul Chambers were found not guilty by unanimous vote. Silence was golden. Judge Stevens ordered the trio to pay $1,000 in court costs.

The lengthy ordeal that had dragged on more than a year and a half did not alter Hassel's mode of operation. If his breweries in Reading were padlocked from time to time, his income from plants in other towns was not interrupted. During the June trial the district attorney had tried to introduce a Lebanon minister who had led a community drive to have the Lebanon Valley Brewery closed down. At the time, Jake Kozloff was operating the plant for Max Hassel. The Rev. C. E. Liebegott was prepared to tell the court that he had been approached by a man in 1925 who said, "I am S. Bings of New York City, and I own a lot of valuable material at that brewery. Hops and stuff like that. Couldn't you let me get that out before the brewery is closed?" Judge Stevens ruled that the minister could not testify because his meeting with the stranger took place before the bribery case began. The minister did not testify but he did identify Hassel as the man who approached him.

The ownership of Lebanon Valley Brewery remained in the Hassel family for many years. When Max's brother-in-law, Julius Cohen, died in 1963, he left $175,000 in LVB shares to his widow, Lena. Julius was president of that brewery and vice president of the Eagle Brewing Company in Catasauqua when he died.

As Reading Democrats and Republicans were trying to stem the Socialist tide in late October of 1927, Max shared headlines with the parties—but it wasn't for the sizable election campaign contributions he had made. Although he dumped five-figure gifts into the political trough, it was for a lesser bit of giving that he was back in the news.

Colonel Samuel O. Wynne, who replaced Reuben Sams as Prohibition administrator for the Eastern District of Pennsylvania, was determined to knock Max Hassel out of business. The old Army man would have liked to drag his Reading nemesis in for a court-martial, but Wynne found civilian law somewhat more complicated. After the state police bribery case fizzled, Wynne was being pressured from Washington to take up the chase. So he dispatched two of his most trusted employees on a mission of solitary intent: get the goods on Max Hassel. A month later Wynne rejoiced when he thought they had accomplished what none before them could.

"At last we have apprehended the man we wanted most," the colonel trumpeted. "I made the declaration a month ago that I would round up some of the ringleaders on bribery charges. This is my first man and an important one."

The pair he selected for this top priority job was Meredith Kerstetter and Paul Hurley. Kerstetter was a veteran dry inspector with a clean record. Hurley also brought strong credentials to the job. During World War I he had received the Congressional Medal of Honor and other citations.

Fueling Colonel Wynne's determination to corral Hassel was the recent loss of another case against Fisher Brewing Company. A federal judge dismissed charges because the federal agent who had entered them failed to appear at the trial. "Another payoff!" Wynne roared.

Wynne was sure Kerstetter and Hurley could not be bought when he sent them to guard the Fisher Brewery in late August 1927. The first few nights they occupied lookout posts in the brush, but realized they had been discovered by spotters. So they moved into the open.

They were seated in their car in front of the brewery on August 26 when Morris Hassel arrived in a large sedan. When they admired his new car, he offered to take them for a ride. They refused, so he came to their car. The agents gave indifferent answers when Morris questioned them about their duties. He drove away, but came back a few days later in a roadster. Morris boasted that his car had more power than theirs, so Hurley agreed to let the 20-year-old show him. As they rode, Hurley would later testify, Morris offered him $500 for "goodwill." On their return to the plant, Hurley discussed the offer with Kerstetter. Morris gave them Max's phone number in Philadelphia when they said they wanted to talk with him.

The agents drove home the next day to report to Alexander McPhee, the deputy director of the Philly office. McPhee ordered them to return to Reading and get as much extortion money as they could from either of the Hassels. Hurley's testimony at a later hearing:

"The next night we met Morris and Max Hassel in front of the brewery. Both did the talking. They agreed to give us $1,000 to allow the shipment of two carloads of beer from the brewery. We told them it was worth $1,500 for our reputations. We compromised and took $1,250.

"Arrangements were made at that time for us to drive across the Penn Street Bridge and turn left at the first road in West Reading. We stopped about one hundred and fifty yards down the street and waited. In about five minutes a car pulled in with lights out. I could not see the person in the car. He handed me a bag and then drove away. I took the bag to our car and under the dash light saw it was a bag of pears. In with the pears we found $1,250. I told Kerstetter that we had better leave that community or we might get hit over the head with so much money. We drove to Third and Penn streets, where we stopped under the light and counted the money. Then we wrapped it, sealed it, placed our names on it and the next day we took it to Philadelphia."

Two days later, the agents stated, they again met Max and Morris outside the brewery. The offer this time was $4 a barrel for each shipment they allowed to pass. Morris gave Hurley $800 which he slipped into his pocket and took to his home office the next day. They left the brewery about 1:30 a.m. After a phone call to Philadelphia, other agents raided the plant before dawn.

The Prohibition agency waited almost two months before filing bribery charges against the Hassels. Alex McPhee came in person to appear at a bail hearing before U.S. Commissioner Maltzberger, who by now was well acquainted with Max and Morris. Izzy Liever posted $3,000 bail for each of them. The following day, Colonel Wynne declared to the press: "The man we wanted for brewery violations—now we have him and I hope we have him right." But his trusted agents had been up to some strange business during the two-month lapse between the money exchange and the arrests of the money men.

Once again Max tugged at the strings of influence by bringing a former congressman and state senator aboard as his defense counsel. John R. K. Scott was regarded as one of Philadelphia's top criminal lawyers. He would occupy the first chair at the defense table, supported by Barney Hoffman. At the arraignment hearing before Commissioner Maltzberger, U.S. Attorney Henry B. Friedman was the prosecutor.

Hassel's drawing power forced Maltzberger to take the hearing to a bigger room in the Baer Building to accommodate the crowd. The two agents gave practically identical versions of how they received more than $2,000 from the Hassels in two payments. But Scott grilled Hurley about his murky actions after the two deals were completed. Scott's cross-examination:

"Where did you go after you reported the case to Philadelphia?"

"On my vacation"

"Where did you go?"

"To Buffalo, N.Y."

"Didn't you intend to go abroad?"

"Yes."

"When you told McPhee about this matter, had you intended to go abroad?"

"Yes."

"Did you tell Morris and Max Hassel that you intended to go abroad?"

"I told them the money would come in handy for the trip."

"When did you change your mind?"

"On September 3."

"What did you do with your ticket?"

"I gave it to another man."

"Were you suspended?"

"No."

"Are you sure?"

"I heard rumors I was temporarily suspended."

This exchange was never thoroughly explored but it appears Hurley was up to something right after he and Kerstetter completed the job they were sent to do.

The agents appeared sheepish when they were asked what happened to the pears that were in the money bag. They said they ate a few, then threw the rest away, along with the bag.

"You knew you were getting evidence, so why didn't you save the pears and bag?" the prosecutor asked.

"That I don't know," Kerstetter mumbled.

Nine days after the arraignment, Scott filed a brief with Maltzberger claiming the government was guilty of entrapment. Citing Colonel

Wynne's jubilant reaction to Max Hassel's arrest in October, the attorney charged it was obvious the government's intent was to frame Max. He said no money was exchanged until after the agents bargained for a higher payoff. But Maltzberger ruled that the case would go to trial.

In December, U.S. Judge J. Whitaker Thompson upheld Scott's appeal. On dismissing the bribery charge against Max, the judge stated, "The law will not stand for the conviction of a man who is lured into the commission of a crime."

On the same day, District Attorney Mauger gave up the long fight in the earlier state police bribery case. He said he didn't want to burden the incoming district attorney with other indictments he still held against Hassel, Marks, and Chambers. He withdrew all charges so there could be no third trial in that case.

Morris Hassel, however, was not included in Judge Thompson's decision. Max's younger brother was ordered to stand trial for bribery in the "pear" case. The following May he made a deal with the prosecutor: he pleaded guilty to possession of illegal beer seized during a Fisher Brewery raid, paid a $500 fine, and the bribery charge was dismissed. After that, Morris pretty much dissassociated himself from bootlegging to concentrate on his profitable real estate business.

Hassel's lawyers had a very good year in 1927, professionally and financially, and their heavy workload continued in 1928 as their well-heeled client would spend a lot of time and money warding off several branches of the United States government.

6

The Inner Circle of a Large Ring

The company that Max Hassel kept was an array of personalities in just about all walks of life. His associates during Prohibition ranged from adventurous teenagers looking for a fast buck to established businessmen willing to risk notoriety for the big bucks. He certainly became well acquainted with the legal community, and his benevolence when charities came asking was legendary. Many local policemen and politicians were under his sway and not just for the money. His quiet demeanor, self-confidence and good looks added to the romance that endeared him to women. His defiance of the Volstead Act made him a pop hero to the drinking crowd. As a fashion plate, his imitators were many. Unlike the typical bootlegger, he inspired an aura of respectability. Being on the wrong side of the law just added to his mystique.

Let's look at those who helped Max become the *Millionaire Newsboy.*

When the Marx Brothers were big in vaudeville during the Roaring Twenties, Reading had its own Marks brothers who gained a measure of local fame. Fred, Charlie, Isaac, and Jake weren't comedians, although some of the tales about them had a touch of humor. They had the dubious distinction of being faithful followers of Max Hassel, and sometimes were caught in the glare of publicity when things went wrong.

Charlie was Reading's first political appointee to the post of federal Prohibition Agent for Berks County. With little schooling but well connected, he had been hired as city clerk under Republican Mayor Ira W. Stratton. Charlie, a close friend of GOP County Chairman Charles Siedel, then moved up to the lucrative federal job that was worth a lot more than its $2,500 a year salary—if you knew how to use your authority. And Charlie was very good at that. He became, literally, a standing joke to the residents at Third and Walnut streets. Often posted on that corner, Charlie was always peering in the wrong direction when the Lauer and Deppen beer trucks rolled by.

When federal dry agents conducted their first major raid on Reading speakeasies in February 1922, Charlie was one of the last to know. His superiors in Philadelphia had learned that Marks was taking payoffs from Berks barmen, so he was left out of the planning loop before the enforcers arrived. The raid began before 7 a.m. He was roused from bed two hours later by a barman who complained about a breakdown in the protection he was paying for. The next day, Charlie was suspended. Six months later the suspension was lifted, but by then his political friends had helped him to become a U.S. Customs inspector in Philadelphia. He later fed at the public trough as a state inheritance tax appraiser for many years.

Freddie Marks had the highest profile of the brothers. "Duck," so called because he waddle-walked, had a checkered career but was definitely a survivor. When Prohibition started, he was on the Reading police force. Charlie the Republican and Fred the Democrat believed that a family that covered all bets regarding political affiliations was a smart, safe family.

In 1922 Duck was appointed supervisor in charge of a government alcohol warehouse in the Berks area. He was not a judicious choice. Working for the government did not stop Duck from testifying as an alibi witness for a young racketeer during a trial involving warring Reading bootleg gangs. While doing his job of doling out approved allotments of alcohol to medical people and industrialists, he came in contact with Max Hassel. It didn't take long for the home office in Philadelphia to realize that Freddie was releasing substantial amounts of alcohol that weren't accounted for. Like Charlie, Duck was soon looking for other employment.

The following year, Freddie was a passenger when Stanley Kozak outdistanced state police pursuers during a booze run. The troopers later located Kozak's car in a garage and arrested the pair. Kozak pleaded guilty to a liquor charge, but Duck waited out the prosecutors by gaining three hearing postponements before the charges were quietly dismissed in 1924. Gradually he was becoming one of Hassel's top lieutenants. As a defendant in the 1926 bribery case involving state policemen, Fred beat the rap when the prosecution's top witnesses disappeared.

After Prohibition he was a county detective, eventually being promoted to chief detective. Despite his unsavory record, Duck was elected to the State Legislature for one term in 1941.

Jake Marks was arrested for hauling illegal beer in a truck. Before his trial he left for parts unknown. Later he showed up in Detroit where he became a well-connected bookie. It was generally believed Jake provided refuge for James O'Neill, the state police clerk who became a fugitive rather than testify in the bribery trial of his brother Fred, Max Hassel, and Paul Chambers.

Isaac Marks ran the Colonial Cigar Store on Court Street. His backer was Max Hassel, who used the store as a message center. If you wanted to contact Max, you left your name and phone number at Ike's smoke shop. The place was a front for Reading's biggest bookie joint. In a large, well-equipped room behind the store, tote boards with horse racing results from tracks all over the country were displayed. The betting parlor was on line with a national wire service for up-to-the-minute postings. Operated by a New Yorker, Jack Bassing, its craps and poker tables were busy day and night. If Hassel didn't actually run the place, he certainly had an interest in it. Rumors lingered long after the gambling house was gone that Frank Costello had visited there in the early 1930s. The notorious Manhattan mobster was said to have visited Reading to sell slot machines. When the old Post Office at Fifth and Washington streets was replaced by a bigger one in 1935, Ike's cigar store and the gambling establishment were moved to 440 Washington Street across from the Abraham Lincoln Hotel.

In 1941, Ike Marks and his old cohort, Jack Bassing, were among ten men who pleaded guilty to operating a horse parlor at 120 Madison Street. Ten years later, Ike was questioned by investigators for the U.S. Senate Committee on Organized Crime. Ike wasn't called to testify at the Kefauver hearings that summer in Washington, but some of the information he provided was used against Abe Minker's outfit that eventually ruled Reading politics in later years.

A fifth Marks served Max Hassel well but not in the same illicit manner as did his father and uncles. Ed Marks was 12 years old when Ike put his son to work in the cigar store. Ike was no role model. He forced his son to toil long hours without pay through his teen years. In addition to selling cigars and tobacco and lottery tickets, the lad answered the phone. Many of the calls were for Hassel. Ed passed messages to Max whenever he came by for his daily supply of expensive 25-cent cigars. Max's generous tips kept the job from being completely nonprofit for young Ed.

In the rear of the store, Max kept a good supply of booze. When he wanted to entertain, Ed would be summoned to deliver a few bottles of the bonded stuff to the boss's top-floor suite in the Berkshire Hotel. Ed, now well into his eighties, didn't have many kind words for his late relatives. Jake was the best of the bunch in Ed's eyes.

As a youth, Ed was an outstanding swimmer and cross-country runner at Reading High School. Working at the store, he became friendly with Calvin Hassel, the poor soul of the clan, and offered to teach him to swim. Since he lacked coordination, the sink or swim technique didn't work for Calvin. He repeatedly sank.

Another family that was even more productive than the Marks brothers in Hassel's organization were the Moellers.

William Peter Frederick Moeller and his sons William Peter Moeller, Carl Frederick Moeller, and A. Robert Moeller, all became brewmasters.

When Max bought Fisher Brewery at the end of 1921, he hired an experienced brewmaster who devoted his life to improving the quality of beer he made. That was William P. F. Moeller, the immigrant son of a brewmaster who owned a brewery in Hartz, Germany. This Bill Moeller had worked in Brooklyn, N.Y., when he first came to America. From 1915 to 1919 he was brewmaster at a York, Pa., brewery until it closed down. For the next couple of years he practiced his trade at Fountain Springs Brewery in Schuylkill County.

Max Hassel always wanted the best, and Bill Moeller, who had patented a new system of fermentation and maturation of beer in 1910, was of a similar cast. He accepted Hassel's offer and moved into a big house on the southeast corner of North Eleventh and Exeter Streets. Fisher Brewery was only a few blocks north on Eleventh.

In the basement of his house, Moeller set up an extensive laboratory where he was continually experimenting to develop new beer-making techniques. His grandson, Fritz Moeller, remembers the maze of glassware that fascinated him as a child.

Moeller's oldest son, William Peter, became a brewmaster in 1920, so he contributed his talents at Fisher's, too. A few years later he became the brewmaster at Seitz Brewery in Easton when Hassel added that plant to his growing collection. William M. Moeller, William P.'s son, remembers living in Easton and hearing stories about how real beer was smuggled past the federal inspectors. A hose was run from the riverside brewery across the bottom of the Delaware River. The hose terminated in a garage "filling station" on the New Jersey shore where the beer was barreled and trucked away. This was a variation of the same system used to move beer in several of Hassel's landlocked breweries.

There's some question whether it was Bill Moeller the elder or his namesake who sometimes was called on to serve as the strawman when

Max wanted to change the title on one of his properties. But it definitely was Bill the First who was in charge of brewing at Fisher, Reading, and Lauer breweries when Max Hassel controlled them.

Devoted to his job, unlawful though it was, Moeller often took Sunday morning walks out Eleventh Street to make his rounds at Fisher's. On one occasion he was accompanied by Max, the name he'd given his black German shepherd. Possibly the brewmaster was thinking about the last, or next, raid at his plant, but for whatever reason when he left, he locked up the building with Max still inside. The family pet sniffed around, found an open window on the second floor and jumped out. He made a safe landing and returned home not too long after his master arrived.

His heirs remember that old Bill referred to Max Hassel as a visionary. Max formed the second half of their mutual admiration society because the beer Bill produced was so highly sought throughout the southeastern Pennsylvania area. Much of the strong brew produced by other bootleggers was not quality beer.

Bill's younger sons, Carl and Robert, worked for their father, and in turn for Hassel in lesser capacities, but carried on the family tradition by becoming brewmasters after Prohibition. A fourth-generation beermaster is William M. Moeller, the son of William Peter, who, in later years, became a consultant for micro breweries.

William Hart was one of the many ghosts whose name was used to hide ownership of Hassel properties. Samuel Cohen often showed up in the Hassel camp to handle white collar jobs, sometimes as a notary public.

Of all the old Reading bootleggers, Jake Kozloff endured the longest and climbed the highest. While working with Max he managed the Lebanon brewery that Hassel controlled. After Prohibition, Jake headed up one of the early casino operations when Las Vegas began to flourish. He ran the New Frontier Hotel, often rubbing elbows with some of the top entertainers in the country. He later had gambling interests in the Caribbean.

Tiny Hoffner was something of a favorite of Hassel's. Although pretty much of a flunky in racketeering circles during Prohibition, Tiny put on some good shows in the boxing ring at the Armory at Walnut and Rose Streets. Max was usually there to cheer him on. In 1928, Tiny, weighing 220 or more pounds, twice fought 185-pound Bill Peters for the city heavyweight championship. Bill had the lumbering Tiny's number both times. Whenever Boo Boo Hoff brought a boxer from his stable to Reading, he sat with Hassel at the matches—and they weren't always discussing the fight racket.

Hoffner's biggest claim to fame happened when he ran Tiny's Chateau in the Black Bear Inn just off the Philadelphia Pike in Reiffton, first as a speakeasy, then as a nightclub after Prohibition. By chance, he hired 19-year-old Jackie Gleason to perform at the Chateau for a week in 1935. Gleason always cited that gig as the launching pad for his long and illustrious career. Jackie admitted he was a miserable flop at his maiden performance. But when Tiny encouraged him to have a few drinks before the next show, Jackie followed that advice that night—and forever.

When Jake Kozloff headed west seeking his fortune in the Las Vegas casinos, Tiny Hoffner went along. He became Kozloff's trusted aide from then on.

A couple of other managers of Hassel-controlled breweries were Louis Cohn and Harry Reichlein, a pair of Reading men who often worked out of town during Prohibition. Cohn was the central figure in a bribery case that eventually fizzled at the Seitz Brewery in Easton. In the 1930s he managed the Harrison Cereal Company brewery in Harrison, N.J., for Hassel, and Reichlein was the main man at a Niagara Falls brewery controlled by the North Jersey syndicate. After Prohibition, Reichlein, better known as "Tosky", became a popular figure running sports teams in Reading.

Attorney Charles Matten was with Max from the beginning to the end. The first time Max got into trouble with the government for dealing in alcohol, it was Charlie who got him out of that jam with a slap on the wrist. Matten was an assistant district attorney at the time. He was an announced Democratic candidate for district attorney in the 1923 primary, but at the last minute stepped aside to assure David Mauger's victory. Did Charlie make a sacrifice for party unity, or did he have the vision to build a private practice in which he could do much better financially with clients like Max Hassel? The last time Max appeared at a legal proceeding, Charlie was there to argue that his longtime friend and client deserved to become a U.S. citizen.

When Max went shopping for defense lawyers he not only looked for those with superior legal talent, but also for men with political connections. Three attorneys in particular met those qualifications.

In the first of Hassel's three bribery cases, Congressman Benjamin J. Golder defended him. Golder served three terms in the U.S. House of Representatives. He certainly knew his way around the halls of Congress and was available for advice when Max went to Washington, D.C., seeking a brewery license.

Employed by Max to work with Congressman Golder in the first bribery case was Robert Grey Bushong of Sinking Spring. RGB was a former county chairman of the Republican Party, and also a state-appointed judge to fill a vacancy on the Berks County bench. He was the lead attorney when Max again faced bribery charges several months after the first case was dismissed. By that time, Bushong had been elected to represent the Reading-Allentown district in Congress. Evidently his involvement in Hassel's well-publicized cases did not deter voters on election day. More likely, the anti-Prohibition vote, which was considerable in 1926, helped Bushong win.

With an even more formidable record was John R. K. Scott, a leading Philadelphia criminal lawyer whose political resume included terms as Pennsylvania State senator and a U.S. Congressman. He defended Max in his third bribery case and later during his income tax battles.

All of the above had an abundance of clout in political backrooms where Prohibition deals abounded. It is reasonable to assume that Max called on them for information and influence when he sought govern-

ment-associated favors. It was not uncommon for legislators to continue their private law practices, although most avoided defending
notorious offenders.

M. Bernard Hoffman's legal work for Hassel was the foundation on
which Barney built his reputation. In later years he was regarded as the
dean of Reading criminal attorneys. He was at the defense table for
Max in two of the three bribery cases.

Emanuel "Manny" Weiss was more than just a legal counsel to Hassel. He was a friend and adviser, and also represented Max during a
somewhat ridiculous civil suit they suffered through in 1931. During
Hassel's income tax problems in 1928-29, Hassel had Weiss and Scott
in his corner.

A close and loyal associate of Hassel's for many years was Harry
Rhode. This hard-drinking, hard-driving roughneck was thought by
many to be Max's bodyguard. But Max always insisted that Harry was
merely his chauffeur. According to mob legend, Harry had no equal as
a wheelman. And he wasn't always sober when he negotiated the two-
lane, crowned roads that were often in disrepair. Max, however, had
complete faith in Harry's ability to reach their destination in the short-
est possible time. Young Ed Marks moved in with Harry and his girlfriend in the mid-30s to get away from the parental strife he had
endured for years. Ed recalled that Harry's domicile was no model of
domestic tranquility either.

Of course two of Max's closest intimates were Izzy Liever and his
father Hyman. Especially as teenagers and during the early years of
Prohibition, Max and Izzy were always together. Hyman's influence at
various stages of Max's career was unquestionably strong.

When Max was in Reading, he received his weekly hair trim from
Sol Nigrelli. Although Hassel was careful about which records to retain
and which to discard, Warren Diefenderfer, an accountant, was known
to have performed work for him.

There were dozens, possibly hundreds of racketeers, who would
claim to be close friends of Max's, but those who knew him best

vouched his inner circle of intimates was quite small. He had complete control of his emotions, seldom showing elation or anger. His immediate family knew the personal side of Max better than others, but for the most part, only Morris was exposed to his business (illegal) side as well.

7

1928—Under Siege

By 1928, the Socialist Party had changed the face of Reading politics. The voters elected J. Henry Stump mayor, and James H. Maurer and George W. Snyder councilmen. For the next twenty years the Socialists were major players in Reading government. From the sidelines, Max Hassel probably helped Jimmy Maurer's party break the stranglehold of the two-party system. A close associate claimed Max always made five-figure contributions to both Democrats and Republicans during election campaigns.

When the Socialist candidates ran in 1927, if Max played true to form he would have covered his bets with a contribution to the third party. His principal interest in politics was influencing people in positions of authority. He understood the American election process, but there's no evidence that he had definite ideological leanings. He certainly fancied himself as an advocate of free enterprise, but in a town like Reading he was exposed to the unionist movement and proved sympathetic to it. Although he was an independent cigarmaker, not affiliated with the cigar union, his tendencies to help the needy carried over to the workingman. He was never accused of being stingy with his own employees.

It doesn't seem likely that Max Hassel developed much interest in politics per se. As a Russian-reared immigrant, he was familiar with life under Tsarist rule. Alien Jews in America hoped the Communist takeover in 1917 was the dawning of racial equality for those left behind in their homeland. Jewish intellectuals, however, were not so sure the Reds were enthusiastic about religious equality. Socialistic dogma spread rapidly in U.S. metropolitan Jewish circles, but in Reading most of its leaders were Protestants or Quakers or those indifferent to religious faiths. In all of America, Reading was one of the true hotbeds of Socialism. Although Max was too busy with his bootlegging activities to join the movement, it's quite possible he agreed with the party's goals. He became more than just nodding acquaintances of Mayor Stump, Councilman Maurer, and other Socialists in the 1927 election landslide. Charlie Dentith, who was appointed a city detective by Stump, was a Socialist. The diminutive Charlie, already closely aligned with Hassel, became the racketeers' liaison man in City Hall.

Hassel probably admired the Socialists for beating the odds. On the campaign trail, Jimmy Maurer, the party's spiritual leader and foremost spokesman, ridiculed Governor Pinchot's use of the state police to harass Reading's brewers and barmen. When Norman Thomas was chosen as the Socialists' presidential candidate in 1927, with Jimmy Maurer as his running mate, Prohibition was a hot issue. Campaigning in Reading, Maurer had this to say about the governor:

"Pinchot said that Coolidge had broken his oath of office in not enforcing Prohibition." Then he drew a big laugh from a Lauer's Park crowd when he quoted Pinchot as saying that Pennsylvania was dry although in the past he insisted it was impossible to enforce the Volstead Act.

Women on the Socialist platform committee who favored Prohibition, stalled debate for several hours at the national convention. Finally the committee voted to ignore the issue, much to the chagrin of the male majority opposing the 18th Amendment.

Between the success of the Socialists and Max Hassel's rise to the front rank of eastern bootleggers, Reading had an image problem in Washington and Harrisburg. Although Herbert Hoover became president in 1928, Republicans were still trying to divert attention from the Teapot Dome scandal that was running its course. Why not target the Reading Socialists and their bootleg-ridden city?

Mixed signals were coming out of Philadelphia. Alexander MacPhee, assistant Prohibition officer in the Philly office, announced in September 1927 that Reading was practically "bone dry" of strong beer because of recent brewery padlockings.

A few weeks later, Max Hassel was being referred to in print as "a thorn in the side of the government," by Colonel Wynne, MacPhee's boss. As 1928 began, the feds were batting .000 against the Reading beer baron. Lots and lots of his beer had been confiscated, but the government had yet to convict him on any charge growing out of his interest in numerous breweries. Three times he had been charged with bribing Prohibition agents or state police employees. Three times he had walked.

In Reading's collective mind, Max was becoming something of a legend. Except for the WCTU and other proponents of Prohibition, he was seen as an artful dodger whom the government could not corner. To the wets who opposed Prohibition, this meant he was not only winning his own battles, but achieving victories for them, too. But the worst was yet to come.

In February 1928, a campaign to bring down Hassel began in earnest. Captain Gearhart was determined to revive the good name of his Troop C in West Reading after the O'Neill bribery fiasco. So he began working closer with the feds to collar the man who had embarrassed his command.

In June 1926 the state had set new regulations governing licenses to produce near beer. Neither Fisher nor Reading breweries were issued permits. But that didn't slow production one bit. Time after time, raids failed to achieve the anticipated end result because prosecution witnesses would fail to appear at hearings.

From December 1926 to February 1928, Fisher Brewery was raided eight times. The score for Reading Brewery for a ten-month period, April 1927 to February 1928, was five raids. Padlocking orders in federal cases were handled by the U.S. Attorney's office. Continually, when the Prohibition Bureau recommended padlocking and dismantling, court orders to that effect were slow in coming. Local courts could order the destruction of illegal beer, which they usually did, but in equity proceedings that followed, the wheels turned very slowly.

On Feb. 15, 1928, the state Alcohol Permit Department ordered a raid on Reading breweries. Captain Gearhart and Lieutenant Plummer with several troopers used sledge hammers and crow bars to break into Fisher's at 9 p.m. The vats were full and three workers were arrested. Meanwhile, Sgt. Douglass Zeek was leading a squad that entered Reading Brewery. Three more workmen were arrested. The beer found in vats at both places was of high-test quality.

The feds were back in town to check on the two plants five days later. The vats were still full but there was no evidence of any worker activity. Alex MacPhee noted: "From the silence that greeted our men and the appearance of the places, it might well be that phantoms are operating the breweries. But with no one around, our hands were absolutely tied. There was not a thing we could do other than to place a guard over each plant. The raids were the most unusual we ever made, finding conditions like that." McPhee said they were two of the most troublesome beer plants in the East. He guaranteed that none of the beer would get past newly hired sentries. None did.

The next day the state police returned to the two plants with court orders from Berks County Judge Paul Schaeffer to dump all the beer—10,000 barrels worth more than $100,000 dollars retail. Five vats at Fisher's were drained, and fifteen at Reading Brewery. The controlled dumping did not bring out the usual salvage crews wading through beery "snowdrifts" with their containers. The beer trickling out of the breweries did not clog the sewers, thus no lakes from which to scoop. Although the court order did not include destruction of the plant's equipment, Captain Gearhart's boys also battered and bruised tanks and lines and destroyed materials.

The state Attorney General's office filed equity proceedings in Berks County court against the owners of the breweries to restrain them from operating for one year. Named as defendants in the Reading Brewery action were Corporal Realty Company, Abe Serisky (a.k.a. Al Kline), Mendel Gassel (a.k.a. Max Hassel), Israel Liever, William Moeller, and Herbert Goslin, individually and as partners trading interchangeably as Reading Brewing Company and Prudent Products Company.

Named in a second suit as partners of Fisher Brewing Company or Hyde Park Development Company, whichever claimed to own the brewery at that time, were Harry Fisher, Lewis Fisher, John Ryan, Wray C. Arnold, Michael Levin, James H. Hart, and Max Hassel.

By the end of February it seemed just about every state and federal enforcement agency had its sights set on Max Hassel—except, possibly, the U.S. Attorney's office in Philadelphia. As events would suggest, Hassel might have been doing business with federal prosecutors, because that office was accused of sitting on cases involving him. Despite this cloud of suspicion raised by Colonel Wynne, the U.S. Attorney now made a show of joining the scramble to bring down the *Millionaire Newsboy.*

It's now the end of March and Colonel Wynne is getting information that Reading Brewery is again bubbling. So he rounds up another raiding force and it's off to Reading again. By now the dry agents need no maps to locate what have become the most infamous of breweries in southeast Pennsylvania..

If we are to believe the assistant Prohibition administrator in Philly, it was just by coincidence that the Reading Brewery was raided again on March 27. With a carload of agents headed for a destination other than Reading, according to Alex MacPhee, they were passing through the city several blocks north of the brewery. When the odor of beer drifted through the open car windows, they followed their noses to South Ninth and Laurel streets. Prearranged, a state police team was headed in the same direction.

The gates to the fenced-in plant were locked, the doors and windows barricaded with two-inch planking and reinforced cement, so the drys finally lowered one of their own into the plant on a rope through a skylight. An alarm system had warned all those inside to flee except two men in the engine room. The pair wasn't arrested. What followed was the discovery of seven full vats of finished beer, and five more still brewing.

Despite the heavy damage inflicted on the plant by the state police only five weeks earlier, MacPhee's joint federal-state police crew found new and repaired tanks brimming with strong brew awaiting delivery. Although the place was supposedly locked tight, it was again fully repaired, refurbished and rerunning. There's no way of knowing how much beer was shipped out during that month, but this was a good example of how quickly Hassel's team could recover from any knock-out punch the enforcers thought they had thrown. Colonel Wynne exploded:

"Who is this Max Hassel who so openly defies the United States Government? I'm going to demand immediate action on all cases pertaining to violations by the Reading and Fisher breweries."

Well, Max Hassel wasn't somebody who backed away from legal adversity. He knew the staties' record of dumping seized beer without written orders to do so. Acting as quickly as he could—but not fast enough—Max started the wheels turning to get an injunction to prevent his beer from being drained or letting the state police wrecking crew move in.

Usually when Max defied the law his fans rooted for him, but on this occasion they saw him as something of a party pooper for disrupting their fun. The state police opened the spigots the next morning and the beer was flowing into the streets where kids and adults were waiting with pails and bottles and buckets. The scooper crowd was in full dip when Sheriff Victor L. Goodhart crashed the party. He handed the state cop in charge a court injunction blocking the destruction of the beer.

"Shut the valves," Lieutenant Plummer ordered, but with beer two feet deep swirling on the vat room floor, troopers claimed they could not reach the spigots. Before the river of "real stuff" was finally dammed, $32,000 worth of it flowed out for home consumption or down the sewers. This was computed at $32 a barrel. The valves on the three remaining full vats were not opened, thereby preserving untapped beer worth $24,000.

Taking liquid loot after a beer raid had become a favorite pastime in brewery neighborhoods. On this occasion the thirsty public was well advised that the staties would be draining the tanks. The scene was gaiety at its best. Free beer, the thrill of getting even with Prohibitionists, and the parties that followed were intoxicating in more than the usual sense. How had Max managed to plug the dike? That's what everybody was asking, not the least of whom was Colonel Wynne, soon to be fuming again in his Market Street office 60 miles away.

This is the story behind the story:

Thomas Betz had his fifteen minutes of fame on March 27, 1928, when he was conscripted to become the Reading Brewery lessee of the month. Tom, a Reading native, was an insignificant worker at Seitz Brewery in Easton. The following is pure fiction, but it's conceivable this scenario is not too far off the mark. It is a conversation between Tom Betz and a delegation of Hassel associates who have just arrived at Seitz:

Tom: "What?"

Freddie, Jake, or Tiny: "We want you to testify that you're leasing the Reading Brewery."

"When?"

"Today."

"Where?

"In Reading."

"Why?

"So we can keep them from draining the beer."

"Who?"

"The drys, state cops and feds. You're coming to Reading with us NOW! We'll fill you in on the way."

Foreseeing what might happen, Max had dispatched his boys to Easton on a ghost hunt. As soon as it was learned the cops had opened the spigots, and Ninth and Laurel streets were awash with brew, Hassel's attorney, Charlie Matten, rushed to the courthouse to obtain an injunction to stem the flow. Judge Schaeffer was informed that Tom Betz was the current lessee of the brewery and he would be arriving to state his claim very shortly. When Tom was rushed before the bench, Judge Schaeffer listened, probably with some skepticism, as Betz claimed he leased the plant prior to the February raids. Without any notice to him, he said, 10,000 gallons of near beer were unlawfully destroyed and machinery was damaged. Was that about to happen again? he pleaded. Matten informed the court he was filing an equity case for Betz.

Judge Schaeffer issued a temporary injunction. Sheriff Goodhart hustled down to the brewery in time to save three vats of beer that had not yet been tapped. Kids in knickers and aproned housewives with containers continued to fill 'em up while guzzlers with mugs chug-a-lugged from the gutter. "Last call," shouted a comedian when the stream dwindled to a trickle.

As for Betz, he became the butt of Elmer Pickney's humor the next day when the *Times'* columnist joked about Tom's startling revelation: somebody had finally admitted operating the Reading Brewery. Li'l Elmer said Tom's claim was about as believable as Mayor Stump's promise there would be no political favoritism during his administration. Pickney was the right man in the right place to ridicule the fodder served up almost daily by racketeers, their lawyers, and jaded politicians during the "Roarin' Twenties."

Adding to the farce was Betz's failure to appear at a hearing of his own equity case against the state police a few days later. For his forgetfulness—likely for self-preservation—Judge Schaeffer ruled that Betz be added to the list of defendants named in the commonwealth equity case against Reading Brewing Company. Tom, the would-be corporate executive, faded into anonymity. The hearing gave Matten the opportunity to lay into the state police for the illegal destruction of property. Raymond Hoffman, an engine room worker in a building adjoining the brewery, testified what happened the night of February 21 when the vats were emptied:

"Later I made an inspection of the place. In making my rounds to oil the machinery I found that beer was poured away, the racking machines were ruined, hose was cut, and the kettles were dented. Many bags of sugar were cut open and the contents strewn on the floor. The spigots to the machines were broke off."

Like a true Hassel soldier, the brewery worker said he didn't know Tom Betz, who claimed to be his employer. He said he got the oiler's job after meeting a fellow named Ned who sent him to the brewery to apply. Since the boiler room was in a building separated from the brewing building by an alley, Hoffman said he knew nothing about what was being produced next door. That set Judge Schaeffer on edge:

"Do you mean to tell me you don't know what they were making at the plant?"

"They were making near beer," the young man replied. He denied knowing whether any beer had been produced between February 21 and March 26. During his lengthy stretch on the witness stand, Hoffman was nervous and sometimes his answers were evasive. He claimed that the day after the demolition when he returned to work, gauges had been broken in the engine room. As for who paid him, the reluctant witness chose the names Bill Miller or Pat Murphy, two members of a relief crew.

A different story was told by state witnesses. The February 21 raid had been authorized by James Shinkle of the State Permit Board. He testified to having visited the brewery after the beer was drained and he did not see any damage. Sergeant Zeek, who led the raid, agreed, but he pointed out, "This was a huge building, and it was bewildering as you went from one room to another."

Matten introduced the theory that the beer found in the vats on March 26 was the same brew discovered a month earlier. Corporal Carl Scupp, who supervised the runoff, scrubbed that idea. He said ports about six inches from the base of the vats were opened the previous month and he personally saw the beer flowing out. He estimated only enough beer to fill a barrel or so was left in the bottom of each tank.

Matten provided photographs of the ransacked brewery and a list of damaged or destroyed items prepared by Hoffman. After chastising the state witnesses for "trying to stop the making of a little beer," he tried to obtain from Judge Schaeffer a guarantee that in the future the state police would need a writ before going on a rampage. The judge refused to put himself on record as to what might happen the next time.

The good news emerging from this hearing, at least for the bucket and dishpan brigade, was Schaeffer's decision to lift the restraining order that had halted the disposal of beer in midstream five days earlier. Within the hour after the judge's ruling, spigots on the three remaining vats were opened. The city's beer hounds arrived, armed and ready. The revelry that Saturday extended well into evening, long after the gutters ran dry.

Reading tipplers probably drank as much at its numerous run-off parties as some towns consumed in a year.

Still another federal hearing in April seeking to padlock the Fisher Brewery brought a few more names close to Max Hassel out in the open. From the brewery's records it was learned that Max Abramson was listed as president of the company, and Samuel Cohen its vice president. Abramson was Hassel's brother-in-law. Cohen was one of Max's close associates charged with attempting to bribe a federal agent in Easton. Although the government frequently suggested that Hassel owned the Seitz Brewery, it never actually proved it. Also, during a tax case that year, the government claimed that another partner of Hassel's was Stephen Bell, president of Superior Beverage Company in Lancaster. With this array of breweries all over southeastern Pennsylvania, plus others in Jersey, Max was hardly suffering financially.

Any hope of reviving Fisher Brewery ended in April. A federal judge issued an injunction barring Hassel, Abramson, and Cohen from operating Fisher's for one year. The padlocks were applied. Some months later when the place was about to be dismantled, a Prohibition official admitted the locks were hardly strong enough to keep out intruders—or brewery workers. But there were no more raids.

While Colonel Wynne stewed about Hassel's continued evasive moves to avoid prosecution, the old Army man was also going public with his complaints about U.S. Attorney George W. Coles in Philadelphia. Coles was lethargic in handling seventy liquor cases the Prohibition office had submitted for legal action, Wynne declared. Applications to padlock the Fisher and Reading breweries were among the stalled actions. He then applied to Pennsylvania authorities to allow a Philadelphia judge, Harry S. McDevitt, to sit in those cases. The colonel was pulling out all the stops.

The brass in Washington decided it was time to visit Philadelphia to find out firsthand what all the fuss was about. Dr. J. M. Doran, federal Prohibition commissioner, brought with him U.S. Assistant Attorney General Mrs. Mabel Willebrandt, and William Knauer and Robert Ewing, deputy attorneys general. This high-powered quartet heard Wynne's complaints against the Philadelphia U.S. Attorney's office. They authorized him to file padlock actions against Fisher and Reading breweries before Judge McDevitt. The judge scheduled a May hearing in Reading.

It was music to Wynne's ears that same day when he learned that $250,000 in confiscated booze, beer and bootleg equipment and materials had been destroyed in Pottsville and Bethlehem. The next day his agents seized a 1,000-gallon still on a Bucks County farm. Wynne was on a roll, and he wasn't about to wait until May to settle the Hassel problem. In the past eleven months Reading Brewery had been raided five times, but still the padlocking proceedings dragged on.

Somewhere along the line, Morris Hassel had been charged with perjury regarding federal income tax evasion. Max agreed to drop his appeals seeking to prevent the padlocking of his two Reading breweries in exchange for a plea bargain for Morris. Morris pled guilty to possession of an illegal beverage, paid a $500 fine, and the perjury charge was dismissed. The press prematurely trumpeted that this was a sweeping victory for the government in its crusade against Reading's beer baron.

But Max and his brain trust had yet another booby trap left in its arsenal. Izzy Liever, who was charged as one of the owners of the Reading Brewery in the February 15 raid, entered the picture by contesting that charge. He claimed to have no interest in the Reading Brewing Company, Prudent Products, or Paramount Realty Company, other defendants in the equity case. So the padlocking process was stalled again, this time for months. There were no more raids for a few months but Alex MacPhee stationed his agents around Reading all summer.

"Reading right now is consuming a great deal of beer," MacPhee observed, as if this was something new. "We are going to find out, if it takes us two months or so, where it is coming from. We not only closed but dismantled all of Reading's breweries some time ago. But the gang, the clique, is still operating by bringing beer in from outside."

The deputy chief of the Philly office was correct about the outside sources, but he lied about the breweries being dismantled. The buildings had been padlocked since May 1, but the federal courts had not yet issued orders to remove all the equipment.

Hassel had been trucking in beer from New Jersey breweries that he now operated. Instead of making beer at Ninth and Laurel streets, he was storing it in a warehouse at Ninth and South on the Reading Brewing Company property. The feds finally caught on in late August when four hundred barrels were seized. As usual, nobody was around when the agents chopped their way into the building. MacPhee announced this was the first activity in a general cleanup that was to follow. None did, because Max by this time had had enough of the steady harassment regarding his Reading operations. The focus of his business now shifted to New Jersey.

The same day of the August raid, Federal Judge William Kirkpatrick in Philadelphia ruled for the defendants in the government's 1924 case against Gierot Manufacturing Co., better known as Lauer Brewery. This action had dragged on for more than four years. Max Hassel, one of six defendants, again was represented by Congressman Benjamin Golder. The judge ruled that the government had not supplied sufficient proof that the defendants were involved in the production and distribution of high-powered beer. Charges dismissed.

The Philadelphia grand jury had been in session since August. District Attorney John Monaghan was compiling corruption evidence against police officials and city politicians by the dozens. At one point, Max Hassel's name appeared on the grand jury witness list, but the subpoena servers never quite caught up with him. He was the only one of eighty-two suspects who was not indicted by that grand jury. From time to time during the investigation, Hassel's name surfaced, only to be lost in the melange of crooks on both sides of the law. As more and more documents were confiscated from government offices, businesses, and other sources, the usual reports were circulated that a major expose of prominent citizens who had dealings with bootleggers was imminent.

Judge Edwin O. Lewis joined the crusade by threatening to form a commission under the Philadelphia charter that would "have the power to subpoena any witness no matter what his station to testify." The cleanup continued into 1929 with the police department taking the hardest hits. The probe's feature victim among the bootleggers was Boo Boo Hoff. The one-time fight manager eventually declared bankruptcy and soon faded from the Prohibition scene.

By the beginning of October 1928 the state finally won the long court fight to dismantle the Fisher and Reading breweries. Although the main buildings of the two plants had been padlocked since springtime, a dozen legal roadblocks were thrown up by the Hassel forces hoping to salvage whatever equipment or machinery still usable. Judge Schaeffer had authorized dismantling back in May, but appeals to higher courts prevented further internal damage to the two plants.

Finally in November, a federal judge upheld the Berks decision and bids were put out to find the right demolition company.

State Deputy Attorney General Knauer came to Reading to attend the gutting. Too often he had seen Hassel breweries rise from the ashes to become big moneymakers in a very short time. Knauer and Sheriff Goodhart toured the plants that still smelled of stale beer, and made notes about how the wrecking crew should do its job. "I guess we covered everything. This certainly was a modern plant," Knauer said about the Reading Brewery. The large wooden fermenting vats on the third floor were showing signs of deterioration from lack of attention. Other enameled vats were in better condition, but they, too, would be ripped apart. More than five hundred beer barrels and kegs were ordered smashed.

The highest bidder for the demolition project was Alex Rudolph who set a price of $1,746 to do the job with an eleven-man crew. Nine other contractors offered lower bids and probably were glad they lost out after Rudolph's workers struggled almost a week cleaning out the two plants. A holiday air swept through the Reading Brewery neighborhood when the news came down that the old plant was about to be "buried." Spectators were angry when state police barred them from the premises. They had hoped to tour the vacated and dilapidated brick building. Without electricity, workmen used lanterns and flashlights to dismantle machinery.

Max Hassel did not attend the funeral of this dear friend that had made him a millionaire. There was only a short period of mourning. His fertile mind was filled with grandiose plans. The Beer Belt of North Jersey was beckoning. He sought counsel from other bootleggers about the advisability of making the big leap. Louie Wiswesser, the Deppen Brewery president who had been even more elusive than Max in regard to dodging raids from the state police and the feds, issued a warning: better to be a big fish in Reading's little pond than trying to swim among the sharks.

This advice proved prophetic. Louie's youngest son, Earl, recalled his father telling how he and others had tried to warn Max about the dangers of competing in the big time. It tells us something about Max's ambition that he was willing to mix with the toughest criminals in the country to keep moving upward. He had his finger on the gold ring and couldn't let go.

8

Tax dodger swings a deal

The Max Hassel tax hassle came to a head in 1928. For years he waged a war of attrition in which the government eventually won a costly but inconclusive victory. Costly, because Internal Revenue officials certainly must have felt cheated in the end. Inconclusive, because the settlement did not change Hassel's attitude about paying his income taxes. What started out as a $1.24 million lien against him by the U.S. government was settled for one eighth of that amount.

For the first five years of Prohibition, Max paid income taxes, undoubtedly fudging on his income, as did many others had since the 16th Amendment was ratified in 1913. The U.S. Treasury's Bureau of Internal Revenue accepted his annual tax returns, not bothering to investigate their accuracy. Following are the net income figures he reported on his tax forms:

1920	$6,000
1921	$3,000
1922	$2,384
1923	$8,100
1924	$21,534.71

These figures represented his alleged net income from legitimate businesses: retailer of Larkin Products, real estate, and a loan company he started in Philadelphia in 1924. Hassel didn't originate the theory that bootleggers shouldn't have to report illegal income because the 5th

Amendment supposedly protected them from providing self-incriminating evidence—but he certainly practiced it.

Officials at the Philadelphia Internal Revenue office couldn't help but hear about the young rising star up in Reading whose beer was supplying many of the speakeasies in the big city. It wasn't until 1926, however, that a government tax expert, Joseph E. Kelley, was dispatched to the Berks County seat to find out exactly what kind of money the 26-year-old upstart was making. After reviewing Hassel accounts in several Reading banks, Kelley came up with figures that indicated Max's yearly earnings had leaped from five figures to six figures and into the seven-figure bracket by 1924. Following are the yearly totals listed in Kelley's report:

1920	$15,375.61
1921	$94,117.81
1922	$29,147.81
1923	$113,003.80
1924	$1,089,579.77
1925	$1,076,423.81

Max claimed he made slightly more than $21,000 in 1924, while the government agent placed his income that year at more than a million dollars. In 1925 after his breweries were padlocked, Hassel acted as if the government should help share his losses. Kelley fixed Max's net income in 1925 at more than $1 million for the second straight year. As the result of Kelley's investigation, Hassel received notice that he owed $1.24 in unpaid taxes. His earnings for 1925 were not included in the suit because Max had not yet filed a tax return for 1925.

Hassel was given a hearing to explain the huge discrepancy in his and Internal Revenue's figures. Max stuck by his accounting which eventually led to a perjury charge. When he eventually got around to filing a tax return for 1925, he added insolence to insult by claiming his earnings that year totaled $9,358. The return form, notarized by

Max's buddy, Sam Cohen, was accompanied by a check for $58.13. Imagine the reaction of the IR boys when that token check was passed around the office. It was an audacious taunt.

The government filed a $1,240,000 lien against Hassel in October 1926, claiming he owed that much in unpaid income taxes for 1920 through 1924. It was the Internal Revenue's biggest tax lien against an individual, up to that time, filed in the Federal Court's Eastern District of Pennsylvania. The Philadelphia press, after looking deeper into Hassel's background, began calling him "The Millionaire Newsboy" in print. That epithet followed him the rest of his days.

Investigators were sent back to Reading to pore over more bank records. According to their figures, he earned at least $161,000 in 1925 and owed the U.S. $31,355. This was a drastic drop from the $1 million figure Kelley had submitted, but just as drasticly above the $9,398 in earnings Max claimed. The government was indeed generous in its latest estimate, considering the huge amounts he had spent to stay in business. So why did Max fudge his own figures to such a minimal amount? Does his bold action lend credence to the tales that he enjoyed taking the government right to the edge? He certainly couldn't claim deductions for graft and salaries for literally hundreds of politicians, police, drivers, and brewery workers he paid, nor the cost of equipping and supplying breweries, and not least, his high style of living.

It was no secret Max was doing very well, what with his Cadillacs and sports cars, tailored suits, expensive jewelry, and his generosity to friends and charities alike. Readingites now realized they had a home-grown millionaire racketeer adding to the notoriety of their wide open city. The government admitted it didn't expect to extract a million dollars from Max. It was willing to negotiate with his attorneys, but in the event no settlement could be reached, a civil action would be filed.

During his investigation of Hassel's 1925 tax return, Joe Kelley learned that Max declared a $75,000 loss resulting from the Reading Brewery being sold at sheriff's sale. This was certainly an admission that he owned the brewery. According to Hassel's legal team, this was the reason his 1925 income sagged. A search of Hassel's real estate transactions failed to reveal there had been a sheriff's sale, but if it did occur, the brewery quickly reverted to Hassel ownership.

Kelley uncovered a 1923 check for $150 drawn on Reading Liberty Bank made out by Max Hassel for deposit in the Reading National Bank. A notation written on the check said *Graft*. At a later legal proceeding when the check was introduced, a government attorney asked Kelley what he thought the notation meant. The investigator intimated the check probably was a payoff, to whom he couldn't say. Charlie Matten, representing Hassel, suggested, possibly, *graft* was merely miswritten by the author who meant to scribble *draft*.

After almost fifteen months of negotiations, Internal Revenue backed off from its original $1.24 million lien but apparently not enough to convince Max to settle.

Finally, in early 1928, numerous Reading associates of Hassel were subpoenaed to appear before the federal grand jury in Philadelphia. Among the witnesses called to testify were Samuel Cohen, the Notary Public who stamped Hassel's tax returns; Israel Liever, Max's longtime friend and business associate; attorney Herman H. Krekstein, who advised Max in tax matters; William P. F. Moeller, beermaster at Hassel's Reading-controlled breweries; and Morris Hassel. Joe Kelley testified for the Revenue agency. Max Hassel was indicted and charged with perjury and attempting to defraud the government of $86,999.

A minor sensation developed in mid-March 1928 when the Revenue bureau declared Max Hassel was a fugitive. Two U.S. marshals were in Reading trying to serve Max with arrest warrants. They checked many of Hassel's haunts to no avail, so he was placed on the fugitive list. It must be remembered that all through 1928, Hassel was also at war with the Prohibition Agency and the state police, who were trying to close down, once and for all, his breweries in Reading.

As the income tax probe heated up, Barney Hoffman made light of the marshals' failure to locate Max, "He's laid up with a cold." The attorney said he talked with the two marshals earlier in the week, claiming they said nothing about warrants to be served. Barney denied Max was missing; he was just taking medication for a nagging cough. His stall so annoyed the Prohibition bigwigs in Washington that they leaked a threat through the Philadelphia press that Hassel faced deportation if he didn't come out of hiding. The state police had tried for a little PR mileage by talking deportation in their bribery case two years earlier. Few, if any, of the major immigrant bootleggers during Prohibition, were ever shipped back to the old country. But it was a tool of intimidation police and prosecutors often used to worm information out of small fry in the trade. Hassel's alleged sniffles took only three days to dry up.

Max finally appeared before Commissioner Maltzberger who scheduled a preliminary hearing on March 29. His clandestine financial affairs would now be exposed for the first time. It was a twisted money trail that reluctant local bankers mapped out for government prosecutors. They were asking hard questions about the origin of large deposits and just who deposited them. Now eight years into Prohibition, the dirty money Max had spread around was coming back to haunt some of Reading's prominent financiers. Hassel's practice of using phony names failed to cover his tracks this time.

Commissioner Maltzberger was charged with determining whether the case should go to federal court. Assistant U.S. attorney Henry Friedman might have expected to have an easy time with the local yokels, but the witnesses proved to be as evasive and forgetful as Max himself. Friedman was taking on a local hero who had been generous to the little and big people alike. Bank employees passed the buck around like a slippery football, nobody admitting it stopped with them. Sent from Washington to assist Friedman was Eugene Meacham, special counsel for the income tax bureau.

Before getting into the dollars and cents of the matter, attorney John Scott made a motion to have the perjury charge dismissed because of lack of evidence. He also claimed a 1927 law that reduced the statute of limitations from six to three years in federal cases was applicable in the Hassel matter. An Internal Revenue attorney argued that the law did not apply to revenue cases. Maltzberger delayed his decision about the statute until later.

The government then went on to present a mind-boggling accounting of bank deposits and withdrawals Max Hassel made in 1924. Sharing the wealth of business Max directed their way were Reading National Bank, Reading Trust Company, Farmers National Bank, Colonial Trust Company, and Northeastern Trust Company. Max, along with several others in the southeastern Pennsylvania beer syndicate, also dealt with the Corn Exchange National Bank in Philadelphia. Obviously he had no trouble obtaining loans to finance his illegal enterprises.

During the daylong hearing, Max sat unperturbed between his attorneys, but he listened intently to witnesses who often were less than candid or cooperative. Scott tried to block testimony by claiming the relationship between bank employees and clients could be compared to that of doctor and patient—confidential. That didn't work. Charles Smith, teller for Reading National Bank, was the first to testify Max Hassel's accounts weren't always listed under his adopted name. In addition to his Max Hassel account, Smith said, Max used the names M. J. Cook and M. J. Case on other accounts. He had accounts under his own name and R. S. Kantner at Northeastern Trust.

Of the $630,000 Hassel deposited in 1924, $467,000 went to Reading National. Northeastern Trust showed Hassel deposits of $154,469. From these totals alone, the government figured his income that year was considerably more than the $21,534 earnings he declared. With five-figure deposits and withdrawals being tossed around the courtroom, the government had trouble pinning down just who was handing out money to whom. Tellers passed the buck to bank managers who denied authorizing payments or had memory lapses or pleaded ignorance of the transaction in question.

Harry Rahn, Reading National Trust officer, waged a murky exchange with Friedman about a $40,000 cashier's check issued against Hassel's account in July 1924. After it was established that Rahn endorsed the check, Friedman asked:

"Whose endorsement is on that check?"

"Mine is one," Rahn replied.

"What was it made in connection with?"

"I don't know."

"Why was it made?"

"For accommodation purposes, I judge."

Friedman then showed Rahn a $50,000 trust certificate made out to R. F. Rahn.

"Whose money is represented in this transaction?"

"I wouldn't be able to answer directly; the money was handed to another party."

"To whom?"

"To Mr. Witman of our bank."

A heated debate between Scott and Friedman erupted over the latter's attempt to introduce an affidavit signed by Rahn. Friedman backed off but continued to question Rahn about other transactions. The trust officer, except for denying he kept any of the money he received for cashing various certificates, was unable to say who ended up with the cash. Proof that Hassel had laundered bootleg money was hard to come by. After a full day of haggling about the cozy relationship Max appeared to have with local banks, Maltzberger ruled the hearing would be continued for further deliberation.

Even the Secret Service entered the picture by releasing a story to discredit Max. The late Harry McVaugh supposedly committed suicide because he was shortchanged in several deals with Hassel. McVaugh reportedly went to a Philadelphia hotel in August 1927 to collect $150,000 he said Max owed him. When his demand was rejected, he came back to Reading and turned on the gas in his Arlington Street home. Harry had been in a sanitorium with tuberculosis for some time before his death. The Secret Service got this tale from Harry's brother Peter, who said he would testify the next time Hassel appeared before Commissioner Maltzberger. Secret Service said it was investigating Max for a year and learned that he controlled three New Jersey breweries in addition to several others in Pennsylvania. Nothing came of the McVaugh tale.

Before a second session of the tax hearing got underway on April 16, Friedman withdrew the perjury charge against Hassel. After Maltzberger rejected the statute of limitations motion made by the defense, the Hassel team appealed to the federal court. Another month passed and another hearing went in the books as U.S. Judge Dickinson upheld Maltzberger's ruling and Max was ordered to stand trial.

During the summer of 1928 there was no movement in Max's tax case. It appears by some matter or means the suit was held in abeyance as a second case against Max was developing. Internal Revenue continued the chase when the federal grand jury again indicted Max for perjury and tax fraud for falsifying his 1925 tax return. It was alleged that Max swore to a district deputy tax collector that his net income that year was $21,534. However, he now claimed his net income was $221,207. (These figures had changed from Hassel's tax return claim of $9,383, and Kelley's original $1 million estimate.) According to prosecutors, Hassel owed $68,074 in taxes, somewhat above the $58.13 Max originally submitted with his tardy 1925 return.

Internal Revenue had broadened the scope of its campaign to collect Hassel taxes by filing a claim against younger brother Morris. Doing very well in real estate, Morris added to his wealth by failing to file income tax returns for the years 1924 through 1926. The government claimed his income for those three years was $120,000, so his tax bill was $16,126. At a preliminary hearing, Morris said he was unaware that persons under 21 were obligated to pay income taxes. He stated that when he turned 21 in 1927 he immediately took up the matter with his attorneys to rectify his error. The government said his ignorance of the law was "immaterial and irrelevant." The fact that Morris' income was in six figures before he had reached 21 shows that he, too, was an early bloomer.

By February 1929, Max decided enough was enough; it was time to move on. The tax guys, too, were getting worn down by the eternal stalling. So Max's lawyers and the Revenue Service's legal department reached an accommodation—$150,000 and everybody could go home happy. This was a remarkable drop from $1.24 million in the original claim, plus another $68,000 for 1925, plus Morris' tax debt that was wiped out. But then, this was Prohibition when stranger things were happening. The deal included a stipulation that none of the back tax claims would be held against Max or Morris in the future.

On February 5, Max appeared in federal court before Federal Judge J. Whitaker, who approved the tax agreement. When he levied a $2,000 fine on Max for defrauding the government and unlawfully attempting to evade income taxes, the judge said:

"The payment of this very substantial amount of $150,000 is a very severe penalty in itself. I do not feel that under the circumstances a jail sentence should be imposed."

Hassel's lawyer, John Scott, told the judge $60,000 had already been paid to Internal Revenue and Hassel had secured a bond for the $90,000 balance, which was to be paid in eighteen months.

Once again Max had avoided prison time. But lurking in the wings was another pursuer. Philadelphia County Detective Louis Raphael was waiting outside the courtroom to serve Max with a subpoena to appear before the Philly grand jury.

As Max walked through the federal building with Morris, Detective Raphael thought he was seeing double. "They looked liked twins," he remarked later. When he asked a Prohibition agent which one was Max, the federal man, also confused, pointed to Morris. The detective trailed Morris and John Scott to the clerk of criminal courts office where they were headed to pay the brother's fine. Max went in another direction and quietly left the building. Trying to serve the subpoena on Morris, the detective engaged in a heated debate with Scott before it

was substantiated that the big fish had gotten away. For whatever reason, the warrant was never served, and of the eighty-two suspects sub-
poened to appear before that grand jury, Max was the only one not
indicted.

In retrospect, Max survived his tax problems in much better shape
than did several top mobsters in years to come. The two most notable
offenders were Al Capone and Waxey Gordon. They served long
prison terms for ignoring their tax obligations. But Max bought an end
to his long ordeal at a bargain price.

9

Hotelier Expands His Holdings

From a distance, it would seem that Max Hassel did not have a very good year in 1928. With some predicting he was due for a fall, Max surprised the doubters by buying the Berkshire Hotel.

Just how the scenario leading up to this purchase unfolded is not known. But for those who don't believe in coincidence, the emergence of a group laying plans to build the city's tallest hotel, probably set Max to thinking. He owned the Colonial Hotel at Fifth and Court streets, but this place was aging and catered to the sporting and theatrical crowd. He wanted to buy the Berkshire Hotel but it was not for sale.

In October 1927, Conrad Klein, owner of the hotel, wrote his will with specific instructions: In the event of his death there should be no division of property among his heirs, or sale of the Berkshire Hotel until his youngest son, Phillip, completed his college education.

In September 1928, a series of events occurred that had a drastic effect on the hotel business in Reading. A list of local investors in a proposed $1.9 million hotel on the northwest corner of North Fifth and Washington streets appeared in the newspapers. Joseph E. Essick and W.A. Sharp, leaders of the group, attracted many civic and business leaders. A future mayor, Heber Ermentrout, and J. Stanley Giles, the man Ermentrout would appoint police commissioner, bought stock in this venture. Deppen Brewery President Louie Wiswesser was another shareholder. Max Hassel might have been invited to add his name to the list, but possibly he preferred sole-ownership deals where he could control all matters. He was not included among some eighty subscribers for stock in the proposed Abraham Lincoln Hotel. The Robert H. Meyer hotel chain, with headquarters in Birmingham, Alabama, was the driving force behind the project and would operate the seventeen-story skyscraper with three hundred rooms. The Abe would be in direct competition with the Berkshire Hotel located directly across Fifth Street.

Conrad Klein had been a hotel operator in Erie before moving to Reading in 1914. Klein recognized the opportunities Berks County presented. Reading was growing at a rapid rate, its industrial base was the envy of manufacturers and union leaders across the state. Klein fancied the city's reputation as a convention town. Some of the investors in the Abe Lincoln project more than a decade later had already laid plans to build a hotel before World War I. While they dallied trying to arrange financing for the project, Klein bought the property on the northeast corner of Fifth and Washington and erected his own seven-story, two hundred-room hotel.

The Berkshire Hotel opened on New Year's Eve 1915. As conventions and traveling salesmen increased, Klein built a $250,000, hundred-room addition in 1923. The new section extended the hotel east to Church Street. This five-month project was completed just in time for the city's 175th anniversary celebration that fall. Klein's brother, Peter, managed the hotel.

Just a week after the Abe Lincoln group announced in 1928 its plans to build, Conrad Klein committed suicide. He had recently returned from a New York sanitorium. The 58-year-old hotelman, in failing health for several years, shot himself in the basement of his Wyomissing home. Three days later the *Reading Eagle* revealed Klein's 1927 will which put restrictions on the sale of the Berkshire. The hotel's worth was estimated to be $630,000.

Max almost immediately made an offer to buy the hotel, despite Klein's explicit instructions. It is possible Klein had flashed the *not for sale* warning because he did not want his prize possession to end up in the hands of the town's notorious bootlegger.

Klein died October 7, 1928. On October 11 another will for Conrad Klein was filed in the county Register of Wills office. This second will had no restrictions about selling the hotel. It pointed out that there was a clause in the first will which cleared the way for the heirs to unload the Berkshire: "Wherein and whereby he (Conrad) directed, empowered and authorized, amongst other things, in case it deemed expedient and advisable by his said trustees to sell the whole or any part of his real estate on such terms and subject to such conditions and in such manner and in all respects as he or they might think fit…

Five weeks after Klein died, it was announced that Israel Liever's Union Realty Company was negotiating to buy the Berkshire for an unidentified investor group for $1.5 million. This princely sum worked magic. Klein's widow, Lucy; the eldest son, Frederick Hunter Klein; and the Reading National Bank and Trust Company, executors of the estate, talked things over. Despite Conrad's very clear wishes, the beneficiaries deemed the offer too good to ignore.

On the last day of the year, another ghost buyer, John G. Faber, entered the picture by negotiating with the bank to buy the hotel for $1.2 million, with a $1 million mortgage. Three days later, a new owner, The Berkshire Hotel Corporation, took over the deed and the mortgage. In the extended transaction populated with strawmen, ownership of the hotel eventually wound up in Max Hassel's portfolio.

Peter Klein was retained to manage the hotel. For his role in the sale, Klein was promised a $10,000 commission by Izzy Liever. When the money was not forthcoming after a few years, Klein filed a civil suit against Liever. In April 1933, a Berks County jury awarded Klein $12,246.

Max never worried about the size of mortgages. In the brewery business during Prohibition, there were no dreams of mortgage-burning parties twenty or thirty years down the line. Only $200,000 of Hassel's own money went into the purchase. After Max's death, the bank foreclosed on the sizeable mortgage, and the hotel no longer remained in the Hassel family.

Meanwhile, the estimated cost to build the Abe Lincoln Hotel was either grossly over-stated at $1.9 million, or the final plans were sharply cut back. In any event, Honky Conky Construction Corp. of Cleveland, Ohio, the low bidder at $919,158, was chosen to do the work. That name alone conjures up images of a silent movie with plank-wielding workmen knocking each other off scaffolds or spilling loads of bricks from five stories up.

Max immediately occupied the Berkshire's penthouse suite in January 1929 with his bachelor brothers, Morris and Calvin. Theirs was a good view of the Honky Conky aerial act right across the street, but Max was much too busy that year to sit around goggling. Actually, the top floor of Hassel's latest acquisition would soon become a fortress of sorts. Rumblings in the Philadelphia underworld sent temblors all the way to Reading. The big city's crime leadership was in a state of flux as the result of the spirited municipal grand jury probe that got underway in the fall of 1928. The indictments of gangsters and crooked policemen and politicians continued for several months.

Boo Boo Hoff, recognized as the beer baron of Philadelphia, was soon to fall from prominence and declare bankruptcy. Harry Stromberg (Nig Rosen) the New York mob's top guy in Philly, would emerge from the grand jury probe, as the top racketeer in Philly. He had shared that role with Waxey Gordon, but by the end of 1928, the former pickpocket was busy taking over the North Jersey beer industry.

Although his home base was Manhattan, Waxey always stayed connected to Philadelphia, keeping track of his real estate investments and other mob enterprises there. It was almost ordained that Hassel would drift into a close association with Gordon. They were among the top players of the Jewish racketeering heirachy in Philly. Soon, Gordon was taking Hassel into his confidence about his North Jersey invasion.

Hassel was too busy fending off the federal government attacks to join Waxey at that time. He wasn't quite ready to rush into an alliance with a gangster who made his reputation as a strike buster and enforcer. Advice Max was receiving from attorneys and Reading bootlegger colleagues was that he should steer clear of Waxey Gordon. The heavy traffic in North Jersey's "beer belt" was indeed perilous, his peers warned. But Max, confident of his innate ability to navigate through any tempest, had to do it his way. Reading and Philadelphia no longer held much promise.

As Hassel's hometown base of operations crumbled under the steady bombardment by federal and state drys, Hassel countered his losses by crossing the Delaware River. His principal acquisition in 1928 was the Camden County Cereal Beverage Company directly across from Philadelphia in New Jersey. Beer for the speakeasies of South Jersey couldn't be produced fast enough. To ensure as much protection as possible, Max Hassel plucked a soldier from the enemy camp to open the right doors. Yates Fetterman was a veteran dry official who finally succumbed to the lure of big money. An ex-Army captain, Fetterman was a deputy Prohibition administrator in Pittsburgh until he was transferred in March 1927 to Philadelphia, again as a deputy. Probably disillusioned over not getting the top Philly job, Fetterman resigned the next year.

He knew the Jersey territory and who the most reliable bootleggers were. Hooking up with Hassel, he became Max's contact man, making deals with roadhouses and clubs all over South Jersey.

Although Hoff took the biggest fall during Philadelphia's anti-corruption campaign, Mickey Duffy was badly damaged, too. What's in a name? Mickey Duffy picked a moniker that had *tough guy* written all over it. Actually, this mick was Polish. Born William Cusick, he battled his way to the top to earn the sobriquet, "Mickey the Muscler." Some thought of him as Philadelphia's Al Capone, a tribute to the tenor of violence resulting from his method of doing business. He was just as fearsome as "Scarface," more impulsive, and far less organized. Mickey was a renegade, rarely on good terms with Prohibition's other crime lords.

Duffy and Hassel both had offices in Philadelphia's Ritz-Carlton Hotel. Mickey was more into speakeasies, gambling, numbers, and extortion, so they really had no common bond. Although they knew each other, Max kept his distance, fully aware of Duffy's reputation for strong-arm diplomacy.

Philadelphia District Attorney John Monaghan's investigators had Mickey on the run, shutting down his drinking and gambling joints and leaving him scurrying for new enterprises. With Hoff bankrupt and forced to the sidelines, Duffy assumed he was the heir apparent to the beer throne in the Quaker City. It was during this transition period in early 1929 that he grew envious of the way Max Hassel managed to work his way through the rough times.

Hassel's method of doing business was exemplified by his opinion of violence, an everyday component of bootlegging commerce. Threat and force were tools of the trade. But Max refused to acknowledge certain codes of the underworld. He made no secret of his distaste for firearms. For many years he wouldn't ride with anybody carrying a weapon. Harry Rhode was his chauffeur, not his bodyguard, he insisted, but powerful associates who valued his ability to make them lots of money eventually provided him with protection, whether he wanted it or not. Mickey Duffy was the antithesis of Max Hassel. Mickey relied on guns and muscle to win his stripes. He didn't negotiate, he didn't capitulate, but he would decapitate if necessary. Max would soon find himself at odds with this loose cannon.

Although Hassel's Reading beer production was cut to a trickle after the 1928 series of raids, he was not hurting financially. During the Monaghan probe, authorities several times mentioned that Max was operating breweries in New Jersey. Camden County Cereal Beverage was the flagship of his beer interests at that time. Mickey Duffy, hoping to recoup losses he suffered during the anti-crime probe, cast a covetous eye at Hassel's Camden plant.

With an escort, Mickey drove to Reading, stopping at Isaac Marks' Colonial Cigar Store on Court Street to inquire about Hassel. Young Ed Marks, Ike's son and barely in his teens, was behind the counter when Mickey and his entourage entered. Ed didn't like the looks of

Duffy and his intimidating bodyguards. Asked where Hassel could be found, Ed got sassy with the visitors. The biggest of the gangsters slammed a large handgun on the counter. The feisty youngster knocked it to the floor. Duffy had to intercede to protect Ed from the burly thug. The lad refused to tell them that Max was living half a block away in the Berkshire Hotel.

When Mickey eventually caught up with Max, he offered to buy a share of the Camden brewery. No, Max firmly replied, he wasn't interested in taking on a partner. Max knew Duffy's reputation of using extortion to get what he wanted, but no amount of coaxing could change his mind. Max didn't realize it was an offer he couldn't refuse.

Papers obtained from Duffy's Ritz-Carlton suite in 1931, told of how The Muscler moved in on Hassel. Working alone one night in early 1929, Max was at his desk in the Camden beer plant. Two cars, loaded with Mickey's bruisers, pulled up next to the brewery. A dozen men gripping handguns climbed out and entered the brewery. There wasn't much conversation. A few of the huskies yanked Max from his chair, carried him outside and dumped him on the sidewalk. Mickey Duffy warned Max not to come back, the brewery had a new proprietor. Few people in Reading were aware of this episode, and those who were, knew better than to ask for details.

Instead of forming an army to recapture lost territory, Max played it safe in his Berkshire suite for several weeks, then negotiated a settlement with Duffy. Max didn't give up ownership of the brewery, but offered a profit sharing plan as Mickey's gang took over production and distribution. This was probably the low point in Hassel's career as a bootlegger. With his Reading breweries padlocked and for the time being his profitable operation in Camden in enemy hands, Max's string of bad luck continued. The federal government was gaining the upper hand in its tax battle, and the Philadelphia district attorney was determined to bring him before the investigating grand jury.

Even Hassel's legitimate business affairs were not going too smoothly. Two fires in thirteen months in the Colonial Hotel exposed

Hassel's name to the public, this time with no illegal undertones—at first. As usual, his ownership was hidden behind a dummy proprietor. The apparent owner of the Colonial Hotel was Constantine Condos.

The hotel building was a made up of the newer Colonial Hotel on the northeast corner of Court and North Fifth streets adjoining the original Belmont Hotel on the north side. A 1924 deed shows that Condos gained title to the property when he paid $45,000 to Jere Bare and Charles Dellinger and their wives who had inherited it the previous year. In 1925, a *Reading Eagle* headline tells us that "Max Hassel, Salesman, Buys $100,000 Hotel" from Harry Thornberg, who had purchased the property from Reading Brewing Company in 1915 for $5,000, with the brewery holding a couple of mortgages for $15,000 and $25,000. It appears the Colonial was a side deal when Hassel bought the Reading Brewery. The brewing company had a midtown office next to the Belmont in the early years of the century.

Regardless of who the buyers and the sellers were, when a February 1928 fire damaged the hotel, nobody doubted who controlled the place. This had been Max's business headquarters for three years. This is where he held high-stakes card games. This is where he tried to fix his state police bribery case. And this is where racketeers and traveling salesmen mingled with Reading Keystone baseball players and actors appearing at local theaters who roomed there.

Because of Max's reputation, early rumors circulated that a still had blown up, causing the 1928 fire. There were billows of smoke as damage was limited to the basement. Hotel guests were ordered out. Officially, the fire was caused by a short circuit in the main switchboard. It was a Saturday evening, drawing a large crowd and a big contingent of volunteer firemen who quickly controlled the blaze. Within a few hours, power was restored and all guests returned to their rooms. Despina Condos, wife of the alleged proprietor, collapsed from the excitement, but was revived outside. Prince Ali, at the Rajah Theatre that week with his juggling act, was among the evacuees.

On March 10, 1929, shortly after midnight, there was another explosion in the hotel. Although ten persons were injured, it was fortunate nobody was killed. The blaze broke out in the basement of the 75-year-old area of the building that had been the Belmont. Flames gutted that area, and there also was heavy damage to the newer Colonial section. Because the bottom part of an outside fire escape had been dismantled, several people were trapped on the upper floors. Two men, unable to use the fire escape, leaped from the third floor, suffering broken legs. All told, eight occupants and two firemen were hurt, and the blaze in this old firetrap stirred up plenty of political fireworks.

Condos, the hotel manager, took most of the heat, although he tried to pass it on to the state. He claimed there had been no fire inspectors in Reading for many months until he asked Harrisburg to send somebody to check his hotel. Several weeks before the fire, Inspector John M. Tezik dropped by, looked around and supposedly told Condos to have the missing section of the fire escape replaced. Tezik made note of several other needed repairs and filed his report. He even stayed at the hotel several nights while inspecting other buildings in town.

After the fire, the accusations started. Condos claimed Tezik said nothing about the faulty fire escape. Tezik's written report also failed to mention it, but he insisted he and Condos had an oral agreement to have it fixed. Mayor Henry Stump and city council blasted the state for not having fire inspectors in Reading for the past two years. Tezik claimed that Condos admitted ownership of the hotel.

Two other fire escapes were obstructed, according to firemen who fought the blaze. This, too, was missing from Tezik's report. Several rooms on the third floor lacked access to a fire escape, Fire Chief Neithammer said, another item Tezik failed to mention in his report.

Four days after the fire, the state had Condos arrested for failing to have the fire escape brought up to regulations. At an aldermanic hearing late in March, the entire scenario was reviewed, with charges and countercharges flying, witnesses blaming each other. Then defense counsel Charlie Matten asked Tezik whether he had proof of ownership of the building. With relish, Condos said he was just an employee. Then why was Condos being crucified? Matten wanted to know. The state had nothing to show that Condos was the owner, other than Tezik's claim that the defendant said he was. Now, Constantine said he wasn't. And he really didn't say who was.

After a few days of checking, the state learned the property was owned by Paramount Realty Company. Somewhere in the maze of confusion in which Hassel always managed to encase his holdings, it was determined that indirectly Max owned the hotel that suffered about $250,000 damage. Insurance would cover only $160,000 of the loss. Although the state indicated it would charge the hotel owner, the case quietly disappeared. The heavily damaged building was never repaired. The property was sold to the government to build a U.S. Post Office after Hassel died.

A good example of how Max did business came out during a civil suit resulting from his attempt to buy a Norristown brewery. Israel Liever was also a central figure, serving as middleman in a failed try to purchase the Adam Scheidt Brewery. This tale began in July 1929 when Max was extending his beer holdings as part of the cartel he would form with Waxey Gordon and Big Maxie Greenberg.

Liever arranged a meeting with Norman Wamsher, formerly of Reading but currently living near Norristown. Wamsher came to Reading, informed Liever he knew a Norristown lawyer who could introduce Max to Adam Scheidt. Wamsher returned a few days later with attorney Robert Trucksess , who told Liever he was well acquainted with Scheidt. Izzy told Trucksess that the buyer he represented had been trying for five years to meet with Scheidt, to no avail. Four days later the action moved to Trucksess' office in Norristown.

According to the Norristown pair, Liever brought along a $100,000 check as a down payment. Liever was then taken to the brewery to meet Scheidt. When Izzy stated his client was willing to pay $1.5 million for the beer plant, the owner laughed and said the offer was about one million shy of his asking price. This didn't discourage Liever. He asked if he could bring the proposed buyer to talk things over. "Why not?" Scheidt offered.

Liever reported back to Max. The boss indicated they were wasting their time, but Izzy convinced him to check out the plant himself. In August, Max accompanied Liever to Norristown. This time Hassel met with Adam Scheidt Jr. Max cut short a tour of the brewery, remarking, "I'm not interested in the equipment. Take me to the office, I want to see what's on the wall."

That's when Scheidt Jr. showed him a federal government permit to withdraw 17,000 gallons of alcohol a month. Max was disappointed: "You have nothing. This would just be a burden. If you get me 175,000 gallons I will be interested."

The beer baron had now exposed his real reason for wanting the brewery. He was well-schooled in the sale and distribution of government alcohol. That was how he broke into bootlegging in the early '20s. Despite the government's several tax, bribery, and brewery actions against Hassel, there had been no mention of recent involvement in the movement of hard liquor or government alcohol. But it is clear that he was prepared to deal in alcohol if Scheidt could provide licenses to withdraw large quantities. Scheidt Jr. said obtaining them would be no problem. He told Max the chair in which Max sat as they talked, often was occupied by the government administrator who could secure the licenses.

But Scheidt Jr. was unable to produce the big-quantity alcohol permits needed to close the deal. Finally, Max told the Norristown people to forget it, he had more important business to attend to in North Jersey. He would have liked to close the deal, thereby impressing the big boss, Waxey Gordon. The Norristown episode might have been forgotten as one more minor setback in his grand scheme had Norman Wamsher and Robert Trucksess also accepted it as just another lost opportunity, but they didn't.

Finders fees are often a questionable link in the negotiation chain leading to a final transaction. According to Wamsher, when he first met Liever in the president's office of Reading National Bank, Izzy said, "I and my associates tried to get Adam Scheidt to sell us his brewery, but we failed. If you can get him to agree to sell and arrange for an interview with him, I will give you $50,000." Wamsher couldn't believe the offer. "Did you say $15,000?"

"No," allegedly Liever assured him, "$50,000."

That was the crux of a civil suit filed by Wamsher and Trucksess. It reached trial in October 1931 because Hassel refused to pay $50,000 commission that the pair claimed they were promised. It seemed like a frivolous suit at best because the brewery deal was never finalized. The plaintiffs went through with their threat to sue, believing Max would make a settlement to hide his not-so-secret criminal activities rather than go to trial. Hassel fooled them, confident his lawyers would show that his accusers were nothing more than bare-faced extortionists.

For the first time in open court, Max testified in his own defense. His lawyers, John Scott and Emanuel Weiss, had a field day with the plaintiffs when they grilled them on the witness stand. Wamsher and Trucksess had nothing in writing to back their claim that Liever offered them $50,000 to open the door to Adam Scheidt's office. Trucksess testified that Liever said at their second meeting, "$50,000 will be nothing to us if we get the brewery. We can make at least $100,000 a month." "If we get the brewery" were the key words that Hassel's lawyers stressed. Since they didn't get the brewery, there could be no deal, although both Max and Izzy testified that no promise of a finder's fee was ever made. Wamsher testified he heard Hassel say to Liever after touring the Scheidt plant, "That's a pretty fine brewery. Izzy, you close the deal. But don't give more than $500,000 cash. I don't care how much you make the mortgage."

The plaintiffs introduced a copy of a $100,000 check they claimed was made payable by Liever to Adam Scheidt. An interesting exchange followed:

"Do you have the original of that check?" John Stevens, lawyer for the plaintiffs, asked.

"Not dated 1931, like that is," was Liever's smiling reply.

"Did you make out a check in 1929 like that?"

"Not that I remember."

"Do you remember offering a check for $100,000 to Adam Scheidt for his brewery?"

This time Liever was more emphatic: "I do not."

Trucksess was recalled to the stand to explain the 1931 date on the check. He said he sat down at a typewriter in his office to make a copy of the check and must have made a typographical error because he was in a hurry that day in 1929. Adam Scheidt testified that he had not seen the check, although he recalled Liever waving a piece of paper that he claimed was a $100,000 check the one time they met in 1929.

The trial ended abruptly shortly after the check matter was thoroughly examined. John Stevens addressed Judge Forrest R. Shanaman:

"At this time we will suffer a voluntary non-suit."

Nobody was more surprised than John Scott, who quickly conferred with his clients and Manny Weiss, co-counsel. Then he asked the court to impound the check with the fictitious date for "further proceedings and possibly another court." When Scott asked for the check, Stevens said he didn't know where it was, "you had it last." Edward Trexler, co-counsel for the plaintiffs rifled through his papers and finally found it. The check was impounded by the prothonotary's office, but never was put to use again.

Weiss denied reports that a settlement had been reached before court opened that day. He did not say whether a countersuit would be filed with the $100,000 check as prime evidence. In the end, the voluntary non-suit turned out to be just that. But it did expose Max Hassel as more than a beer baron as his apologists tried to paint him. His interest in selling large quantities of government alcohol took something away from his reputation as a beer-only racketeer.

There was another hint that Max might have been involved in illegal alcohol. A still operated by a Philadelphia gang was raided by the state police in October 1932. The 50,000-gallon still was in a farm building near Friedensburg, not far from Reading. There was speculation during the investigation following the arrest of eleven men that possibly the murder of Ben Myers, an acquaintance of Max Hassel's, might be related to the still case. Myers was a local bootlegger since the early days when he was in Abe Minker's gang. His body was found along the Philadelphia Pike in Exeter Township a few months before the Friedensburg raid. Another report that came out of the investigation was that a prominent beer bootlegger had a financial interest in the Friedensburg still.

Many years later a prominent woman in the Jewish community offered third-hand information to a friend that Max Hassel's gang had murdered a bootlegger on North Thirteenth Street during Prohibition. If that happened, it was never proven or even investigated by local police. If Max had a hand in Ben Myers' death, that, too, turned out to be hearsay with no documentation.

10

The Evolution of Organized Crime

The South Jersey shore was crawling with rumrunners during Prohibition. Secluded coastal inlets and back-bay areas were busy ports of entry for liquor being smuggled in from Canada, Europe, and the Caribbean.

Some historians have identified Atlantic City as the founding place of organized crime. The first major interstate assemblage of underworld leaders was held there in May 1929. They called themselves "The Seven Group." These were the established bootleggers from New York City to Kansas City. Charlie "Lucky" Luciano was credited with bringing together this convention of hard-core criminals for an express purpose. It was his vision to assimilate the talents and resources of the big crime groups into one collaborative council. Cooperation would replace fragmentation; spheres of influence would replace turf wars.

The guest list at this gathering varies depending on who the chronicler happens to be. Definitely present and strong supporters of Luciano's theory of a loose confederacy were Lucky's close friends from New York City, Meyer Lansky, and Frank Costello, and Abner "Longie" Zwillman, top dog in the North Jersey underworld. Zwillman used the alias Abe Long, the derivative of his nickname.

Although a few years younger than his colleagues, Zwillman was more intelligent and insightful than most. A lower level gangster, Joe Stassi, would one day credit members of the Jewish Mafia as the real creators of organized crime. He believed Meyer Lansky, Longy Zwillman, Max Hassel, and a few other top Jewish bootleggers were better organizers and planners than their more violent-prone Italian cousins.

Stassi became a close friend of Hassel's, who befriended him as a young man. Joe said Max paid all his bills and put him up at the Carteret Hotel in Elizabeth, New Jersey, when he was first associated with the North Jersey mob. For a few years, Stassi occupied a seventh-floor apartment just below Max's eighth-floor spread.

When the Seven Group met in Atlantic City, Max Hassel was not yet established in Elizabeth. Had Luciano, Zwillman, and Lansky known Max on a more intimate basis, it is likely he would have been invited. His modus operandi would have appealed to them—up to a point. Other big names at the gathering: Al Capone, Greasy Thumb Guzik, Nig Rosen, Moe Dalitz, Charles "King" Solomon, Arthur Flegenheimer (Dutch Schultz), Frank Erickson, Louis "Lepke" Buchalter, Owney Madden, and the ever-popular Solomon "Cutcher Head Off" Weissman.

The guest list according to some researchers also included Waxey Gordon; on other lists he was not. By 1929, Waxey and Meyer Lansky were sworn enemies. Although this was seen as Luciano's party, it is doubtful he would invite Gordon knowing the animosity between Waxey and Meyer. Lansky had just taken a bride and was on his honeymoon in Atlantic City. This was a classic mixing of business with pleasure.

The host for this league of abominations was Enoch "Nucky" Johnson, an irreverent thug who wasn't intimidated by the star quality of his guests. He controlled Atlantic City and served as his own port authority, expecting a payoff on all incoming shipments. With Jews in the majority, this certainly was no Mafia dominated parley. The two biggest Mafia bosses, Salvatore Maranzano and Joe Masseria, New York's two major old school Mafioso, were not invited. They would never sit down with Jews to discuss the sharing of power.

That Max Hassel wasn't invited, shows he was not yet considered among the bootlegging elite. Possibly his passive reaction to Mickey

Duffy's takeover in Camden weakened his position among the tooth-for-a-tooth rackets heirarchy. For just the opposite reason, Mickey "the Muscler" Duffy was also excluded. Renegade gun slingers were not welcome.

Luciano called the gathering to preach cooperation. His reputation was enhanced by his ability to convince the hard-bitten gangster chiefs to dispense with turf wars and hijackings and work together to improve their profit margins. The Seven Group agreed to divide the East and Midwest into zones of accommodation. Had Luciano been more familiar with Hassel's business flair and attitude for sharing the wealth, he probably would have welcomed Max to this unprecedented peace conference. Surviving tales passed down by close friends of Max do not indicate he worked closely with New York mobsters, other than his well-documented association with Waxey Gordon and Big Maxie Greenberg, and his checkered coexistence with Dutch Schultz.

A single hint came out of the Kefauver hearings in 1951 that Frank Costello had been in Reading during the early 1930s. Costello was New York's slot machine king, and he supposedly visited the horse parlor at the rear of Isaac Marks' cigar store on Court Street during that period. Since Max took phone messages at the cigar store, it seems likely these two major-league racketeers got together at that time. Organized crime historians have never linked Max to Luciano and Lansky. Primarily, that pair was into imported hard liquor, while Hassel dealt almost exclusively in beer after 1923.

It seems logical that Hassel had at least some social contact with Lucky, Meyer, and Bugsy Siegel. Hassel loved the fight game, often attending heavyweight title matches in New York and New Jersey with an entourage. So did Luciano. Waxey financially backed Broadway theater productions and had the means to set up show-girl dates for his mob friends. Hassel displayed an autographed photo of Ethel Merman in his New Jersey Carteret Hotel apartment. He also liked to gamble, another social outlet he possibly explored with Manhattan gangsters who could afford high stakes games. As for Dutch Schultz, it seems likely he and Max might have had face-to-face or telephone negotiations in the 1930s when the Bronx overlord depended so heavily on beer from the Gordon syndicate. At party time, however, it's unlikely the crude, confrontational Dutchman and the restrained, tactful Max would have mixed.

One possibility why Max steered clear of Lansky was the enmity between Meyer and Waxey. Just who screwed whom early in their careers is blurred, but we know they didn't hoist toasts to each other. The day would come when Lansky reportedly leaked information to Internal Revenue about his rival's beer empire. Had Hassel survived Prohibition, Lansky's information might have damaged him, too.

As in most endeavors, ethnic origins mattered when bootleg partnerships were formed. In Philadelphia, it was estimated that 60 percent of the bootleggers were Jewish. That was a WASP guess, but there is sufficient proof that most of those who controlled bootlegging were Jews. Boo Boo Hoff, Waxey Gordon, and Nig Rosen, all were recognized as Philly kingpins at one time or another. The Jewish gangsters gravitated to form a bond of trust that, although lacking the formal Cosa Nostra-type blood oath, was just as effective in pursuit of Prohibition gold. Max Hassel's entree into this Jewish hierarchy was fated from the day he made his first illegal sale of alcohol in the Quaker City.

The two bigtime gangsters who Max would become most closely associated with were Waxey Gordon and Max "Big Maxie" Greenberg. In some circles, Greenberg was known as "Big Head."

Gordon was born Irving Wexler in 1886 in New York City. By 1920 he had served time in reformatories and prison, and was a seasoned criminal from the Lower East Side slums. Like many kids from poor, immigrant families, he scrounged for pennies as a child and was into petty crime by his early teens. In an era of colorful nicknames, Irving became Waxey Gordon, the slick-fingered pickpocket. During the pre-World War I years, Waxey was a member of Dopey Benny's gang specializing in labor battles. Benjamin Fein, a.k.a. Dopey Benny because of a drooping eyelid, hired out his sluggers to either side—sweatshop owners or strikers. Dopey's boys didn't care whose heads they cracked as long as they got paid. Waxey, thickset, powerful, and intrepid, could wield a blackjack with the best of them.

As a teenager, Waxey was a soldier in Dopey Benny's gang as it waged a war with the Five Pointers, an Italian dominated gang and the proving ground for Lucky Luciano and friends. During one fray in 1915 an innocent bystander was killed in the crossfire. Although ten of Dopey Benny's outfit were arrested, only two, Waxey Gordon and Isidore "Jew Murphy" Cohen were tried for murder. Both were acquitted. But before Prohibition began, Waxey was convicted in Philadelphia as a pickpocket, and for robbery in Boston, spending two years in Sing Sing on that charge.

Big Maxie Greenberg, about four years younger than Gordon, was another of the Lower East Siders with a rough and tumble beginning. He and Waxey followed pretty much the same path into adulthood. In the late teens, Greenberg migrated west to join the Egan Rats, a St. Louis strong-arm gang that hired out for all types of violence. Before long, Big Maxie was arrested for grand larceny and sentenced to five years in Leavenworth Prison. Thomas Egan, the Fifth Ward Democratic committeeman had been running his gang of crooks for more than a decade when Greenberg arrived. He had the political connections right up to Woodrow Wilson's White House to win a presidential pardon for Maxie in 1919.

Back in action after serving only six months in Leavenworth, Greenberg was assigned by Egan to haul a $40,000 boatload of booze up the Mississippi River. But the wily Big Maxie had made a deal with the Hogan Gang of St. Louis to buy the whole cargo. When he reported to Egan that the boat sank, with its cargo, the politician didn't believe him. The boat was raised, but the shipment was gone. Egan's Rats did not forget the Rat from Manhattan.

Maxie hightailed it out of St. Louis for Detroit where he began smuggling booze across the Detroit River from Canada. With big ideas, Big Maxie pulled up stakes again, returning to New York to raise money to form his own rum-running outfit in Detroit.

Back on his home turf, he joined forces with Waxey Gordon who one day would form a triumvirate by bringing Max Hassel into the partnership. Like many other Jewish gangsters, Gordon was employed by Arnold Rothstein for special enforcement jobs. Some regarded the millionaire financier and sportsman as the original gardener who nurtured the first sprouts of organized crime. Rothstein, whose family had moved uptown from the Lower East Side, was a gentleman gambler. Respected as a man of high finance, he did not shun the low road to swell his fortune. He was credited with developing a plan to fix the 1919 World Series which was dubbed "The Black Sox Scandal." His money spawned many gambling operations and some of the first systemized bootlegging collaborations. But all this was made possible because of his extraordinary talent for fixing politicians.

In the fall of 1920, Rothstein sat on a bench in Central Park listening to an investment proposition tendered by Max Greenberg. Waxey Gordon had introduced the gambling mogul to Big Maxie, who wanted backing for speedboats to ferry booze from Ontario to Detroit. Including graft money, he needed $175,000 to launch his nautical plan.

Rothstein, called "The Brain" by his disciples, liked the speedboat idea but the geography didn't sit too well. Instead of a Midwest smuggling operation, why not boat liquor into the biggest market in the country—the New York metropolitan area? Rothstein had contacts in England and Canada to buy bonded liquor. Always the gentleman, A. R. insisted that his customers should receive the genuine article, not a moonshine mix. Maxie Greenberg's dream went up in smoke as *The Brain* decided he would become the godfather of seafaring rumrunners. Waxey was offered a junior partnership, but Arnold would run the show. Rothstein agreed to cut Greenberg in on one condition: Maxie had to mortage all his personal property to his benefactor, and buy an expensive life insurance policy from Rothstein's insurance company. Bootlegging was a dangerous business, so Arnie was hedging his bets, as he often did at the racetrack. The befuddled Maxie accepted, and his investment paid off.

Most of the classier Manhattan hotels became Rothstein customers for the bonded whisky and Scotch his minions were soon delivering. Gordon and Greenberg leased motorboats and trucks, found drivers, and developed a rum-running system that was protected by Rothstein bribes to the Coast Guard, local police and politicians at entry points on Long Island and the Jersey shore. Eventually their transportation system included ships of various sizes and shapes.

Rothstein was also backing other young bootleggers. The Bugs and Meyer Gang had replaced Dopey Benny's as the strongest of the Jewish outfits on the Lower East Side. Benny "Bugsy" Siegel was the type of loose cannon Rothstein usually avoided, but he savored Meyer Lansky's intelligence and ingenuity. He invited Meyer to dinner at the Park Central Hotel. Rothstein explained that he would be the CEO of another smuggling venture, with Lansky as his distributor. Luciano, a close friend of Lansky's, was also welcomed aboard by Rothstein, but only with great reluctance did he accept Meyer's plea that Benny Siegel's muscle would be a big asset. A.R. introduced Lansky and Luciano to Sam Bronfman, the Canadian producer of Seagram whisky. With that source, they were off and running.

For a year, Rothstein's rumrunners made huge profits for him and themselves. But these were reckless, ambitious, greedy young men who didn't always follow the rules. Waxey Gordon split his time between New York and Philadelphia, working deals wherever he could. He lacked his mentor's understanding for guaranteeing the customer a quality product. Although he was learning to upgrade his quality of living and how to invest his money, Waxey still had the gangster mentality of "let the buyer beware." Against orders, Waxey began cutting some of his bonded deliveries with cheap moonshine produced in Philadelphia's backroom stills.

A duplicitous scenario boiled over in 1921 when Rothstein realized the antics of his proteges could undermine his organization. Lansky found out about Waxey's deal with Joe "The Boss" Masseria for a big delivery of top-grade Scotch being shipped in through South Jersey. Masseria, with the biggest Mafia family in New York, hated Jews, but, pressed for liquor to supply his customers, through intermediates called on Waxey for help.

The Bugs and Meyer Gang was waiting in ambush, having felled a tree to block a back road northwest of Atlantic City. The Scotch cache had been transferred to a Masseria truck that was now approaching the roadblock after midnight. In the ensuing gun battle, the Jewish gunmen routed the Italians, leaving several of the Masseria gang bloodied and fleeing through the pine barrens. One of The Boss's men recognized Lansky as leader of the hijackers.

Meyer had taken a threefold risk. First, he wanted revenge for an attempted takeover of one of his Brooklyn gambling joints by Masseria gangsters in 1919. He also added fuel to his feud with Waxey Gordon, whom he had never liked. And finally, he had broken ranks with Rothstein by hijacking booze entrusted to Gordon, another of Arnold's hirelings. Waxey, too, was placed in an embarrassing position because the hijacking brought to light his association with Masseria. Rothstein had always kept his distance from The Boss whom he regarded as a clod, uncouth and gluttonous. A.R. felt he had been triple-crossed.

When tipped that one of his tankers was going to be boarded by the Coast Guard, Rothstein had it rerouted to Cuba. Unable to control his burgeoning enterprises, he decided to abandon bootlegging before being exposed. Bad publicity could jeopardize his membership in the prestigious New York Jockey Club. By the end of 1921, he walked away from the hotheads he had fostered to give more attention to his more easily protected gambling operations, and to look after his stable of thoroughbreds.

By default, Waxey Gordon inherited, for a price, the formidable bootlegging operation he had managed for Rothstein. He reinforced his mob with old friends from the neighborhood. No longer the "schlammer" of his Dopey Benny days, he now dealt with Manhattan's plush hotels, even investing in a few. He opened a real estate office in the Knickerbocker Hotel at Broadway and 42nd Street as a front for his bootlegging headquarters. Soon he was making more than $1 million a year, investing heavily in blocks of real estate in New York and Philadelphia, and becoming one of the biggest grafters of his time.

A disgruntled ship captain's wife brought an end to the Gordon smuggling ring, one of the biggest in the country. Hans Fuhrman was captain of the freighter *Natisco* when it was boarded by Prohibition agents off Astoria, Long Island, in September 1925. The seizure was made possible by a tip provided by Fuhrman's wife. She went to authorities because her husband "always came home from voyages drunk and broke." She told of pleading with her husband's bosses to send her part of Hans' pay after each trip, but they said her husband's drinking problem was hers, not theirs. Then she squealed.

In addition to *Natisco's* cargo of timber and building supplies, 4,000 cases of liquor were seized. Records were confiscated from Waxey's Manhattan real estate offices in the Knickerbocker and Longacre buildings on September 23. Maps, radio codes, and lists of customers were found. Gordon, bound for France and Germany with his wife and children aboard the luxury liner *Majestic*, escaped capture. He turned himself in after returning to New York on October 20. A week later, Waxey, Big Maxie Greenberg, and thirteen other members of his gang were indicted and charged with conspiracy to violent prohibition laws.

Fuhrman and his wife, after testifying before the grand jury, were placed under guard at a Manhattan hotel for several months while awaiting the gangs' trial. Despite this around-the-clock protection, Hans was shot and killed in his hotel room. His death was not made public until February 7, 1926, ten days after the shooting. The official cause of death was said to be suicide. The New York prosecutor's office and Mrs. Fuhrman publicly denounced the "suicide" theory.

With the most important witness dead, the case against the smugglers never reached trial. Elimination of witnesses was Waxey's favorite tactic for staying out of jail. This time it worked; seven years later it failed.

Although the smuggling ring was smashed, Gordon's string of gambling joints, whorehouses, and speakeasies, plus his dope dealing, still earned him a very good living. For the next few years he was busy investing in property, his flagship being the Piccadilly Hotel in Manhattan. In his spare time he became a Broadway angel, buying pieces of several successful Broadway shows. Waxey, his wife and children lived in a sumptuous, ten-room apartment at 590 West End Avenue, leased for $6,000 a year. For another $7,000, he brought in an interior decorator who added a well-appointed library that he filled with books costing $4,200. It was rumored he spent more time in the library smoking opium than reading. He also owned what was referred to as a castle, replete with a moat, in South Jersey.

When Rothstein abdicated his bootleg throne, Big Maxie Greenberg took his nest egg and headed back to St. Louis. In March 1921 he was welcomed by the Hogan Gang but not by Egan's Rats. Willie Egan, the politician's son, now ran the gang. One of Willie's drive-by gunman wounded Greenberg and killed John Sweeney, a political lobbyist, as a group of men stood talking on a St. Louis street corner.

These were the early shots of a two-year war that claimed 23 gangster lives. The Hogans, led by Edward "Jellyroll" Hogan, evened the score by killing Willie Egan in the fall of 1921. The Gateway to the West became a shooting gallery as the toll mounted on both sides during 1922. "Big Head" Greenberg was at the core of this feud when he was arrested for questioning about a 1923 murder. While he was giving a statement inside, members of the Egan gang gathered outside a St. Louis police station. Trying to avoid further bloodshed, the police ushered Maxie away through a rear exit. He didn't stop running until he arrived back in Manhattan to again join up with Waxey Gordon.

Avoiding the mounting heat in Manhattan after beating the smuggling rap, Waxey Gordon spent much of his time with the Philadelphia Jewish racketeering crowd for the next few years. Max Hassel was highly regarded in that circle. Max and Waxey evidently compared notes, discussed strategies, and developed a trust and appreciation for each other's talents. Since Gordon's specialty was booze, and Max's was beer, it is likely that the old master got an education about the brewing trade from his younger pal. Was it Max who convinced Waxey that the manufacture and distribution of beer was more profitable and less dangerous than the rumrunning game? Many bootleggers earned piles of money, but only a select few had the smarts and courage to use their capital to full advantage. Hassel and Gordon were among the best.

During 1928, a period of trial and tribulation for Hassel, his beleaguered beer enterprises in Reading were reduced to zero. He was doing better in New Jersey where his Camden County Cereal Company was covering his losses at home. Gordon, too, was looking to expand his operations.

About this same time, Dutch Schultz, after years of small-time thievery, almost overnight became a major player in the distribution of beer in the Bronx. In 1928, Schultz and a friend, Johnny Noe, established a speakeasy, the Hub Social Club. When the money began rolling in, Dutch and Noe opened more watering places in the Bronx. Soon they got into the distribution business, forcing many other clubs to buy their beer or else. Dutch sometimes personally led his enforcers with clubs or guns. To meet the demand of his new customers, Dutch began buying beer from North Jersey breweries. It was these same plants that would soon be under the control of Waxey Gordon.

By 1929, the shifting forces of bootlegging drew Max Hassel, Waxey Gordon, Big Maxie Greenberg, and Dutch Schultz into a collaborative web. Of the four, only one would survive.

11

Max Hassel Up Close and Personal

Everybody has three selves, it's been said: the public, the private, and the secret.

At times, beyond his control, Max Hassel became a very public figure. It was not of his own liking, but he took the risks and paid the price of notoriety.

His private life was far less publicized, the way he wanted it. He did not draw attention to himself, but he seldom sought seclusion.

The secret self of Max remains just that. Only a few quotes from associates take us behind his closed doors and inner thoughts. No diaries or journals, no in-depth magazine or newspaper profiles. What today is routinely laid bare about noted personalities wasn't, in Hassel's case, committed to print, leaving him somewhat a man of mystery.

Research on the *Millionaire Newsboy* reminds us at every turn that he was not the typical bootlegger of his day. His associates have left behind a hazy portrait of a nonviolent man who did not believe brute force was the best avenue to success in a chosen trade that reeked with murder, savagery, and intimidation. He preached accommodation and conciliation even before some of the top bootleggers arrived at the same conclusion. Unlike them, however, there is no evidence he considered violence as an option when negotiation failed.

An instance of Max's business philosophy is illustrated in a tale told by a colleague in a *Sunday Reading Eagle* series in 1934. The anonymous author of the articles was a staunch disciple, a biased employee who truly believed Hassel was special. The writer said his boss adopted the business theory that the customer was always right—up to a point. This is a passage from the first article:

> *Up in Elizabeth one night comes a telephone call from a guy in Jersey who had been buying beer aplenty from Max. The customer complained:*
>
> *"The last load was mighty poor. About half of it was sour. I wouldn't feed it to a pig."*
>
> *We knew this guy as a first-class chiseler who would steal pennies from a blind man's cup, and one of the boys got kind of hot over the phone about it. Max intervened and grabbed the phone.*
>
> *"How many barrels were bad?" Max asked.*
>
> *I couldn't hear the reply, but later someone told me the guy estimated about twenty-five barrels were on the poor side.*
>
> *"Okay," Max replied, "I'll see that they're replaced tomorrow."*
>
> *Then, about a month later, we got another squawk from the same guy. This time he claims that a dozen or more barrels were shaken up too much in transport and busted open. Complaints like this were mighty rare and we knew it was getting to be a racket with this fellow.*
>
> *But again Max says, "All right, they'll be replaced immediately."*
>
> *I told him frankly that I thought he was getting softhearted, and with a little heat Max replies:*
>
> *"Listen, I know I'm being taken for a ride by this fellow, but why cause any trouble. He thinks he's pulling one over on me, but he's not. People may be able to fool me once, but not a second time. Cross him off the list."*
>
> *"You mean," I asked him, "that you aren't going to sell him any more beer?"*
>
> *"You guessed it." he said. "I'm not going to sell him or anybody like him beer. The beer he claimed was bad was replaced immediately because I don't want hard feelings. Neither do I want his business."*
>
> *Which is just one example of how Max handled all his customers.*

Another illustration of Hassel's ability to see the big picture was evident in 1929 when Mickey Duffy, the Philadelphia gangster, had Max physically removed from the Camden brewery he was operating. Instead of trying to avenge that loss, Max retreated and wrote off that escapade as no more of a business loss than if the government had shut him down. It has never been proven that Duffy's murder two years later was related to the 1929 Camden ouster. And even if it was, Hassel's reaction to that incident proved his generalship by not rushing headlong into a shooting war of revenge. Some in his organization had wanted to react in just such a manner, but the cooler head at the top had the patience to let Duffy's own history of violence catch up with him. Max regained his interest in the Camden brewery by making an accommodation with Duffy. Some might read a lack of courage into his avoidance of confrontation, but Max never would have survived in that occupation if any indication of faintheartedness was detected by his loyal followers.

The same *Eagle* author of the previously mentioned series described "the best boss I ever had" this way:

> *Shrewd, kindhearted, unassuming, easygoing, careful, and yet dictatorial...mix 'em all together and you have Max Hassel. Yet I would have hated to buck him.*

With limited education, Max had the native intelligence to run an interstate business that depended on superior organization. There were no training manuals on how to outmaneuver federal agents, no Wharton School correspondence courses on racketeering administration, no political science books explaining the underside of politics in that era of blatant corruption. Just as pilots of that period learned to fly by the seat of their pants, Max was a quick study whose guile and entrepreneurial instincts moved him into the vanguard of the beer runners.

Just as today's movers and shakers ensure profits through political, financial and business cronyism, Max learned where the soft spots were in enforcement, transportation, politics, commerce, and banking. Bribery is an odious practice that reached new heights during Prohibition. Playing by the illegal rules of the dangerous game, he led the pack right up to the finish line.

In some ways, Max played the role of racketeer to the hilt. He didn't need a role model like Arnold Rothstein to school him in manners and fashions. "The Brain" tutored many of his Manhattan proteges such as Lucky Luciano, Meyer Lansky, and Frank Costello to abandon their thuggish style of dress and work toward respectability. But those products of the Lower East Side never lost their rough edge. Max didn't have a rough edge to lose. Ellis Hassel the tailor passed on his love of clothes to his sons, teaching them the importance of appearance in school and in the work place.

Max's parents were honest, unsophisticated immigrants who Max tried to shield from his dirty work. Before Ellis and Sarah died, the neighbors knew the town's biggest bootlegger was the middle sibling of the Hassel family. But nobody shunned the parents because of it. Neighbors and members of their synagogue always treated the Hassel family with respect. When Kesher Israel was renamed Kesher Zion, Max was on the board of directors and gave unfailing support to Jewish charities. His mother died in 1926 before the notoriety began to mount, but Ellis, in failing health, endured four more years of wondering what would happen to his ambitious son.

As Max luxuriated, the price tag on his apparel rose accordingly. Hats were his passion. He changed them almost daily, often passing fedoras on to friends and employees after a single wearing. His headwear was usually a soft gray felt worn at a rakish angle. The brim was turned up on one side, snapped low on the other. Straw hats were his summer choice.

A complete wardrobe change, whether in Jersey, Philadelphia, or other overnight stops, was always taken along. It was not unusual for him to buy several of the same style suits in a variety of colors and fabrics. The haberdashers in town catered to his every whim. Max was a fashion plate who wore the best custom-made suits, nothing gaudy, but conservatively stylish. In the true fashion of the come-lately rich,

Max sported diamond rings and stickpins, carats galore. Brustar's, the upscale Penn Street menswear store was one of Hassel's frequent stops as he replaced fedoras, ties, suits, and shoes that became hand-me-downs long before they showed signs of wear. He generally dressed in grays and tans, always with the obligatory matching handkerchief peeping from the breast pocket. At his estate in Brecknock Township in the 1930s, his costume was more relaxed: knickers with sweater and stockings to match. In later years he wore gold-rimmed glasses, and in public was usually puffing on an expensive cigar.

Sam Lunine, proprietor of a gents' furnishings and clothing store on Penn Street, was another of Hassel's favored merchants. They were also good friends at Kesher Zion where Lunine was synagogue secretary.

Tales of Max's generosity abound. Shortly before his death in 1933, an Allentown policeman said Max had recently been in town. At Sixth and Hamilton Streets, Max asked permission from the cop to park in a restricted zone for a short time. The lawman gave him the okay and said, "Don't bother locking your car." A half hour later when he returned, Max offered the cop $20 for his service—which, of course, was refused.

Max was always an easy touch, friends remember. But don't try to sucker him. He paid the rent for numerous hangers-on who were on call to make deliveries, work as card dealers, or tend to other legal or illegal chores Max might want performed. A dealer who Max had supported for some time was caught skimming from the pot. That ended that fellow's free lodging at the Daniel Boone Hotel.

Although Max was an inveterate gambler, there's no record of him ever having been arrested for running card games, bookie joints, or owning slot machines. When he owned the Colonial Hotel he often could be found there engaged in poker or pinochle games. Harold "Tiny" Hoffner was apt to be stationed in the card room to keep an eye on the game. Max could usually spot a cheater. If he gave Tiny the nod, a large fist was likely to come down on the suspect's head. If this tale is true, maybe there were lapses in Max's anti-violence persona.

In 1925, Ernest B. Posey, a Berks County Representative in the state House, was the flag bearer of a big push to have Pennsylvania legalize parimutuel betting machines at race tracks. An elected official who introduced such legislation always ran the risk of backlash from the anti-gambling forces. It was a safe wager that money from the gambling community was coming his way. Whether Hassel was Posey's patron is not known, but the way Max spread money around to get what he wanted, he would seem to be a logical contributor to that particular cause. To get in on the ground floor of legalized horse race betting would have appealed to him.

Max's propensity for giving away wearing apparel brought him into contact with Tom Promos, now in his late eighties. At 17, Tom lived at 112 South Eighth Street with his mother and half sister. The backyards of the Hassel family home at 738 Franklin and Tom's home abutted. Tom's sister had a small dog that jumped the fence and was mauled by a large dog owned by the Hassels. Max came out, broke up the uneven match and apologized profusely to Tom about the injuries inflicted on the sister's dog.

"Wait here a minute," Max told the youth, "I'll be right back." He returned, handed Tom an expensive, barely worn pair of shoes. Amazed at the stranger's generosity, Tom had no idea who his benefactor was. The shoes, black patent leather inlaid with gray suede instep, were of special significance. They made quite an impression on Kitty, who Tom was courting at the time. Kitty and Tom welcomed the 21st Century as longtime husband and wife.

Estimates by oldtimers placed Max's height in the 5'-2" to 5'-5" range. Tom Promos gave an educated guess of 5-4, because he wore quite a few of his neighbor's almost new hand-me-downs. After the dog scrap, several times when Max and Tom crossed paths in the neighborhood, it was not uncommon for the town's best dressed bachelor to give the youth practically new shirts, jackets and other wearing apparel. Max's generosity probably resulted in part from his friendship with Tom's brother-in-law, Lee "Woody" Wood, a classmate of Hassel's when they attended grammar school.

Woody became a pickup man for Max, driving one of the boss' Cadillacs all over the area collecting large sums due on beer shipments. Woody sometimes took young Tom along on those wild night rides through Berks, Lancaster and other nearby counties. On the dark, narrow, crowned roads Woody didn't always anticipate curves, once crashing through a corn crib just outside of Shillington on a trip to Lancaster.

"He loved to blow his air horn, probably scaring the daylights out of everybody when we drove through small towns in the middle of the night," Tom laughed, recalling those teenage adventures. Was Lee typical of the young men who gave Prohibition a bad name? More likely, he added to the romance of an era like no other in the nation's history. The few survivors still tell their tales with a certain reverence, war stories so to speak, like those of military veterans. If you're a nonegarian in Reading and knew Max Hassel, and even if you didn't, you probably have one tale you love to repeat.

Among the positive memories about Max was his generosity during holiday seasons. At Easter, Thanksgiving, and Christmas he'd send out trucks loaded with food and gifts. Charlie Marks was in charge of distributing food and goodies as the trucks slowly moved along Penn Street. Needy kids and adults swarmed after the vehicles eager to take home a prize from the folk hero whose good name was resurrected each year when his Santas left a trail of good cheer. There was no religious bias when the Jewish bootlegger helped Christians celebrate their most cherished holidays. Sectarian or nonsectarian, Max was always ready with a handout.

A glowing 1933 endorsement of Max's character was offered by George Pomeroy Jr., the president of Pomeroy's department store:

"During the last ten years on various occasions we have taken care of some charity work for him, always with the request that his name should not be mentioned. He would send orphans to the store, and we would outfit them or give them candy or do things for them, but they never knew who was footing the bill. And sometimes he would have parties for the children at the homes, like the Home for Friendless Children. At his request, we loaned the home our Santa Claus to make a Christmas party a little more complete. I know during that time my mother spoke well of him because of the special charities she was interested in for many years, she had asked Mr. Hassel for help at times, and he never failed to help her on those requests.

"Another friend told me some two or three years ago of some poor boy that required a very delicate eye operation, and Max sent him to a Philadelphia hospital."

Pomeroy was linked with Hassel in another venture that wasn't too well-known when they were principal investors in the *Reading Tribune.* The daily newspaper started publication in 1923, with Pomeroy as president and on the board of directors. He resigned both posts in 1925, claiming he needed to devote more time to his stores in Reading, Harrisburg, Pottsville, and Pottstown. Robert Grey Bushong was named to replace Pomeroy as the paper's president. That same year, Max hired Bushong to represent him in court. Newspaper competition was strong in Reading at the time the *Tribune* folded in 1926.

Jacob Koralski, highly acclaimed during his 20 years as editor of the *Reading Jewish Voice,* a bilingual monthly publication, had a strong influence on Max. Prominent in Jewish affairs, Koralski promoted the idea of providing loans to help young Jews gain better educations. When Hassel's father died in 1930, Max and his family set up the Elias-Sarah Hassel Free Loan Society. Max made an endowment of $15,000 for loans up to $150. For years the society gave interest-free loans to families in need.

The loan society was initiated at an opportune time. The Depression had begun, and families struggled to make ends meet, much less pay for higher education. Herbert Kaplan was in his last year of Jefferson Medical School in Philadelphia when his family felt the pinch in 1931. Bernard Rosenthal, a Reading attorney and one of the society trustees, was approached for assistance. Norman Kaplan, who died at 95, recalled that Rosenthal arranged a $300 loan for his older brother. Herbert graduated the following year, interned at St. Joseph's Hospital in Reading, then set up a medical practice in Collegeville.

Thirty years after the loan society was formed, Max's brothers and sisters started the Hassel Foundation. Morris had achieved considerable wealth in the real estate business in Philadelphia and Atlantic City. The other siblings invested well. Since 1961 the foundation has grown steadily. It currently has assets exceeding $7 million. Each year the Philadelphia-based foundation supports education, research, health and human services, arts and culture, with emphasis on Jewish organizations. Last year's grants totaled close to $400,000. Among Berks County beneficiaries of the Hassel Foundation in the last two decades: Reading Hospital, Albright College, Exeter High School, Reading High School, Reading Rotary Club (Rainbow Project), Caron Foundation, and Pro Kids of Berks County.

The charitable legacy of Max Hassel lives on. The heirs of Max's sister, Lena, have been very active in the foundation since the deaths of Morris (1969) and Calvin (1973). Dr. Sarle Cohen, Lena's son, other relatives, and Michael H. Krekstein, esq. are the foundation trustees.

Evidence of the Hassel family's spiritual and financial support to Kesher Zion Synagogue are prominent. The ark and menorah were donated by the Hassels. A commemoration for the Sidney Barrer family and an elevator in the synagogue were made possible by the Hassel Foundation. Morris Hassel was the benefactor when the KZ religious school was added. He also financed the construction of the Morris Hassel Religious School across the street from the Chelsea Hebrew Congregation in Atlantic City where he owned property.

None of Max's acquaintances who survived him by six or more decades could recall when or where he bought his first car. But they do remember that he always traveled first class and loved to tinker with the engines. Albert Golden was always happy to see Max or one of his emissaries walk into his Cadillac agency at 318 Bingaman Street. A

Caddy Custom Imperial sold for $4,485 in 1925, and Max usually bought the best. Later when he was spending most of his time in North Jersey he had a fleet of Lincolns, most of them purchased and serviced at Windsor Motors on North Fourth Street near Washington.

On one occasion, Jake Kozloff accompanied Max when he went shopping at Windsor Motors. Max took a liking to a top-of-the-line Lincoln. Instead of asking the price, he began stripping one hundred dollar bills from an impressive roll, piling them on the hood of the car. When the stack reached a substantial height he said, "That's what I'll pay for it." The salesman counted the money but wasn't pleased. "I won't break even for that amount," he complained. A true car salesman was he. Max gave him a take-it-or-leave-it look. The salesman took it.

In the early 1930's Paul Webber, who had an Oldsmobile and Buick dealership in Rehrersburg, became a good friend of Hassel's. Webber and his wife occasionally came to Reading on a Saturday to shop and have dinner. Like others on a weekend, they would visit some of the many stores on Penn Street. Then it was off to the Berkshire Hotel to dine. If Max was in town, he would sit at their table and talk cars. On occasions when Webber had a shipment of new automobiles coming in and needed possibly $20,000 to pay for them, Max would offer to loan him the money. No written agreement was necessary if Max trusted the borrower; a handshake did the trick.

Ed Engle of Denver, who, as a young man knew Webber, remembers Paul telling about Max ordering six new trucks from him just before he died.

Max's generous nature didn't usually extend to autos. He either traded in his cars or sold them to subordinates. One such exchange was negotiated by Hassel and Max Dunsky who worked for him. Dunsky bought a used Dusenbury from Hassel, then hired Tony Verdone as his driver. Tony was the father of Jere Verdone, a former Reading policeman and head of the vice squad. Jere tells us that his dad was no master mechanic but he knew enough about engines to impress Dunsky. Tony's career as a wheelman was not uneventful. First a load of beer was hijacked from the car, then he lost his job after a traffic accident, causing extensive damage to the Duse.

Another story told by the late Shandy Hill, sports editor of the *Reading Times,* and managing editor of the *Pottstown Mercury*:

"Max often walked through the *Times* newsroom to chat with his good friend, Managing Editor Abe Hurwitz. On one occasion just after Max left the office there was what sounded like an explosion outside our building at Sixth and Walnut streets. We all rushed out to see what happened. People were running for cover or lying flat on the ground. They recognized Max and the yellow Moon roadster he was driving. Lots of us thought he was the target of a bomber. The explosion turned out to be the loudest backfire I ever heard. Max, still seated in his classy sports model, was ready to move on, but the car's engine wasn't. I was sports editor then and the assignment Hurwitz gave me wasn't about a ball game: 'Get your tin lizzie and give Max a push.' I did amid a cheering crowd of Hassel fans."

One aspect of his secret life wasn't much of a secret. Max had a long-running affair with an attractive married woman. In the neighborhood the residents were well aware that Max was romancing a lady just up the street from his family home at 738 Franklin. "Oh, yes, they were more than just friends," a neighbor recalled. His mistress was seven years older than Max.

Mrs. Mary DeAngelo was 82 when she revealed a fond memory of Max Hassel. Often as a child she attended hoedowns at the Walnutown Hotel. Like many parents in the Fleetwood area, hers took the kids along when they went to the weekly dances.

"I was attending dance school at that time, probably about 1928 or 1929," Mary recalled. "After I was doing the Charleston, this man came up to me and said, 'I'm going to take you to Hollywood.'"

A few years later when Max Hassel's picture was in the paper, Mary said she remembered he was the man who praised her dancing. "I know he was just kidding about taking me to Hollywood, but it made me feel good and I never forgot what he looked like."

Another oldtimer recalled that Max "paid top dollar for his cars, clothes and women." Although he never married, Max certainly was not a one-woman man. The girls he was usually seen with at the better night spots in Reading were often hired for the night. In his own circle it was known that his generosity extended to the fair sex—a $100 "gift" was not uncommon. As the owner of two hotels he certainly did not lack private accommodations. If he dated a "nice" girl he didn't usually show her off in Reading, where he was too well-known. This was to protect her reputation. He didn't worry about enhancing his.

It was this same attitude that he adopted in regard to his public relationship with reputable men who came under his influence. If he would meet a prominent businessman, judge, or political figure on Penn Street, the best they could expect from Max was a slight nod of recognition. It didn't matter that they had spent the previous day in his swimming pool at The Farm; he refused to incite gossip by stopping to chat with them. Max would give this explanation for seemingly snubbing well-placed friends:

"Everyone knows I'm in the racket. To be sure, they're friends of mine. I make it a practice of never to stop and talk in any public place. If they want to talk to me, they know where they can find me."

Max openly mingled with the racketeering element that gathered daily on the northwest corner of Sixth and Penn streets in front of the Crystal. The restaurant was always a popular eating place where regular guests could dine and occasionally observe a few characters playing the role or conversing in hushed voices. Max certainly turned heads when he joined a few of the boys for dinner or a snack.

Wilson Austin, the attorney who served as a Berks County judge, county solicitor, and city solicitor, was beginning his career in law during the Hassel era. Over the years, Wils knew the ins and outs of Reading politics like few others. It was his contention that none of Reading's racketeers was more generous to politicians at election time than was Max Hassel. It was not uncommon for him to pump $20,000 into an election campaign, Austin claimed.

Clerks and waitresses were always happy to see Max drop by. Emily Lebo served tables in a tavern operated by her father, Harry Lebo, at Sixth and Walnut streets. When she waited on a particularly handsome customer one day he left her with an unforgettable memory and a $50 tip. Maybe Max wasn't always so generous, but it didn't hurt to be young and pretty to please him.

Max was always very protective of his family. Because of Calvin's inadequacies, he was kept out of any bootlegging activities. The youngest of the siblings, Morris, was right in the thick of things with Max for several years. In 1927 he was held up at North Tenth and Elm streets at 2 a.m. He told police the robbers made off with $1,000 in cash. As Morris matured, he took to investing in real estate that served him very well over the years. After Max died, Morris accumulated considerable wealth, procuring property in Philadelphia, Atlantic City and Miami, Florida.

Lena Hassel was active in the Junior Hadassah and the Kyrath Club. The latter and the Migdals, a men's Jewish organization, performed minstrel shows and musical comedies as Jewish fund-raisers. Max attended and supported these performances when he wasn't too busy with business matters.

As his reputation for giving grew, requests for donations kept pace. The Jewish community could always count on Max for a sizable contribution for any charitable cause. As a character witness with considerable flair, Sigmund S. Schweriner, a local retail furniture dealer, once offered this flowery testimonial:

"Well, it is a very pleasurable thing to narrate and to speak. There wasn't a time that I seen Mr. Hassel and I asked for a mild or rather substantial thing for charities, there were no questions. He didn't say a thing who was going to get it, but he had no thought I would keep it, that I would just put it at a place it was greatly needed for hunger, for starvation, for the kiddies for their shoes or dresses or for Dad and Mother. He was always ready and limitless."

It is easy to give money away if you have enough of it, and Max certainly had plenty. But giving time and support to school and playground development was a side of Hassel that few heard about. He became friendly with Thomas J. Evans, a Carpenter Steel foreman who was also president of the Reading Board of Education. From about 1927 until he died, Max took great interest in child development. Evans was convinced of Max's sincerity, not just from the financial support he offered, but because he attended school pageants and lectures. Evans saw a side of Max that few others did. As he matured, Max became more introspective and interested in social issues. While he quietly was serving humanity, his life was juxtaposed with the inhumanity of his peers.

Altruism was not the hallmark of big city racketeers. They spread money around but generally for the purpose of financial gain or trying to camouflage their true motives. There's considerable evidence to indicate Max Hassel had real concern for the less fortunate in his hometown. Of the big name gangsters, only Al Capone was noted for providing for the indigent.

During the Depression, Reading's jobless formed the Taxpayers Protective League. Max befriended the league by supplying funds for an investigation of unfair labor practices against employers. He also bought gasoline for league members in car parades to promote their cause. When Max died, Harry Alexander, organizer of the TPL, said, "Hassel always gave where it was needed. Last Thanksgiving he handed out 1,500 baskets for the needy." The league sent a large floral arrangement to 738 Franklin Street the day of his funeral.

Another characteristic he shared with very few of his beer-moving cohorts was his capacity for exercise. Maybe vanity played a role in his passion for staying fit, but he always retained a trim figure among men who dissipated, gorging on food and drink, paying little attention to physical fitness. In his suite at the Elizabeth Cartaret Hotel in the 1930s Max outfitted one room as a gymnasium. He tried to get other members in his outfit to take advantage of the weights and exercise machines he made available, but few ever did. It was his practice to rise early for a strenuous workout before his high-living friends were out of bed. He even threatened to fire his subordinates if they didn't stay in better shape, but he never did.

As a youth he found time to play baseball, but his business ventures as a teenager kept him too busy to spend much time practicing. It's no surprise that he played shortstop, the position associated with good hands, quick thinking, and leadership. It is possible he took up golf when the Berkleigh Country Club was built in 1926. Prejudice kept Jews from joining most local private clubs so they built their own. When the Riverside Golf Club was opened by William Luden in 1930 along River Road in Muhlenberg Township, Max was a regular hacker whenever he was in town. He always picked up the tab for his four-some: green fees were $1 apiece plus $1 for the caddy.

In the same neighborhood, Max and friends were regulars at Henry Witman's Riverview Inn. This was a roadhouse about a mile north of the golf club for those who could afford the prices of entertainment imported from New York or Philadelphia. The best way to offend Max was to try to pick up the tab at the Riverview or any other night spot he visited. He was THE MAN, and in his circle, he paid. Maybe he'd run into William Luden at the Riverview Inn, where the patrons could gape as the two millionaires talked golf. The cough drop king owned a summer home a mile north of the fashionable drinking spot, where a nickel Coke cost ninety cents at showtime.

Sandy Heron, the Scotsman brought over to be the Riverside club professional, gave Max lessons, but progress was slow. One of Hassel's cronies once wrote about his boss' efforts to emulate Bobby Jones, America's golfing idol of the '20s:

> Once in a while I used to play golf with him. He played in Reading and at various courses in Jersey. Max liked the game…in fact, I guess it was his favorite hobby. but honest, he was a lousy golfer. His other hobby was pinochle. He was the best two-handed pinochle player in the state. I'd a matched him against anybody.

Seeking privacy and a place to relax and entertain, Max began scouring the countryside for a site where he could escape the limelight. As usual when he acquired property, he used straw buyers after he decided to purchase a farm tract in Robeson Township near Beckersville. In November 1928, John Breen of Reading purchased six tracts of land from Irwin and Bertha Frees and relatives. Breen paid just $2,500 for 108 acres. The following July, Breen turned the title over to Calvin Hassel who became the owner of record for the next forty years.

"The Farm" became Max's hideaway from the daily pressures of staying one step ahead of tax collectors, Prohibition agents, conniving customers, and dangerous competitors. He spent thousands of dollars renovating the stone, two-and-a-half story farmhouse on the property, and added a swimming pool and tennis court.

A defective flue caused a fire in the house on December 8, 1930, gutting its interior. Max was away at the time it was discovered at 6:30 a.m. by neighbors, the Edwin Baldwin family. Water pumped from the swimming pool by volunteer firemen prevented destruction of the house. During the following winter and spring, the place was refurbished a second time with all the latest conveniences, including a hot water system.

Mrs. Jules Bookbinder recalls trips to The Farm as a teenager with the Deborah Club, a Jewish organization for girls. The club had a standing invitation to swim and frolic at The Farm. Mrs. Bookbinder said the girls had to find their own rides, often in an open "flivver" with a rumble seat and running boards. Max had a special dressing room for the girls. Mrs. Bookbinder's days at the farm were among the happiest of her childhood memories. The girls would mingle with the likes of Reading Detective Charlie Dentith, Judge H. Robert Mays, former Reading cop Freddie Marks, and Isaac Eberly, the wealthy knitting mill magnate. The Farm became a melting pot of Prohibition's worst and best, including a host of innocents there for a good time.

Tessie Knoblauch was the Deborah Club chaperone who saw to it that the girls heeded Max's firm rule that young people did not indulge in alcoholic beverages, which were in ample supply. Despite his bent for fitness, Max seldom took to the tennis court. He usually had his morning swim before the crowd arrived.

It was a sign of social distinction to be invited to The Farm, something many respectable families accepted because the gatherings were away from prying eyes of the temperance people. Max would often stay up past midnight with the revelers. Unlike some of his best friends, he was always under control, never overindulging, absolutely never making a fool of himself.

And what did the neighboring farmers think when Max and his entourage transposed the rolling hills of Robeson Township into a playground? Shirley Shirey tells about those days in the early 1930s when she was a young girl living on an adjacent farm. Her grandparents, Andrew and Mary Keller, owned the property. These were people of the land for generations, unaccustomed to the lively activities of their new neighbors

"I'll always remember the women who were so well-dressed, so stylish" Shirley said. "Carloads of them would arrive, big and expensive cars. It was a dirt road leading to our land from Beckersville before they bought the place next to ours. Right after that it was paved. The paving went as far as their property, then stopped." Shirley, who still resides on the farm, said she wasn't sure if the Hassels paid to have Golf Course Road improved, but it seems more than coincidental that the city slickers and the macadam made their appearance about the same time.

Max was a Gatsby-like figure, well aware of his notoriety but also currying respectabilty. Some literary historians believe F. Scott Fitzgerald's fictional hero was fashioned after Arnold Rothstein. In many ways, a comparison can be drawn between Rothstein and Hassel. Their beginnings, however, were nothing alike: A.R. came from a modestly well-to-do family; Max derived from poor immigrants. A.R. was established in gambling and other illicit activities before Prohibition; Max ventured into bootlegging but tried to avoid the accompanying violence. Both were well-mannered, stylish, ambitious, had complex personalities and were gifted with high intelligence. If Rothstein inspired the Gatsby character, his weekend parties at his Long Island estate were a cut above Max's outings at The Farm. To his credit, Max did not have the criminal vision of Rothstein. Both were cautious but Max took greater personal risks. Both had organizational skills. While Max had close control over subordinates, Rothstein operated more like a CEO who used subcontractors. Arnold liked playing the role of respectable financier at the same time he was bankrolling bootleggers who would become infamous as the country's foremost gangsters. There was no mystery about who Max was, but he seemed to have a mystical hold over his loyal followers.

Quite likely Max had golf in mind when he bought The Farm. By 1931 he decided he needed more land to build a golf course. This time James and Viella Hill fronted the purchase of forty-two acres adjacent to The Farm. Joseph and Ruth Meier had paid $5,000 for the land seven years earlier but sold it to the Hills for $1 plus "other valuable considerations" in November 1931. In the usual progression of such matters, Calvin Hassel then relieved the Hills of the deed a year later for another dollar and other valuable considerations. Max now owned about 150 acres.

Robert White was a famed golf architect from St. Andrews, Scotland. He designed Berkleigh Country Club's first nine-hole course in 1926. In 1932, Max hired White to lay out a private nine-holer on The Farm property. After Max's death, the Hassel family retained it as a private course. Calvin employed architect Elmer Adams to design a clubhouse, with living quarters on the second floor. Adams remembers his first apprehensive encounter with Calvin and friends who retained the dapper attire reminiscent of the racketeer cult. In 1940, local entrepreneur Jack Shapiro leased the golf course, opening it to the public and called it Green Hills Golf Course. Since then, several individuals and groups have operated the course, including the late Andy Shapiro, son of the first lessee. Six decades after Max was preparing to add another nine holes to the course, Andy Shapiro and Sarle Cohen, nephew of Max, were shaping plans to do just that. In March 2002 Andy died unexpectedly, so the expansion was stalled again.

As 1930 dawned, with most of his legal problems behind him for the time being, Max settled in at the Carteret Hotel in Elizabeth. He was now firmly established as a partner with Waxey Gordon and Maxie Greenberg. But it was also a time of personal loss. Max's father had been in poor health for years, even before his wife died in 1926. A stroke further disabled Ellis late in 1929. In January 1930, Max moved him to Miami hoping the warm weather would help speed recovery. But the 67-year-old Ellis passed away seven weeks later on February 25.

12

Moving Into the Big Leagues

Harassed on all sides by government agencies in 1928 and early 1929, Max Hassel figured the bootlegging environment in North Jersey had to be an improvement over what he was enduring in his hometown. He had survived grand jury investigations and indictments in much better shape than the Philadelphia racketeers. He had wiped his tax slate clean, for the moment at least, and Waxey Gordon was coaxing him to join his combine. Max weighed the opportunity to make loads of money against the dangers inherent in doing business with the New York-New Jersey gangsters. His local confidants were telling him to stay put in Reading, but his own vision of becoming a major player was irresistible. Max opted for the ultimate.

In July 1929 he signed his first lease at the Carteret Hotel, a new high-rise in Elizabeth, New Jersey. Among the few from Reading who went along with Max were Harry Rhode, his driver, and Louis Cohn, one of his top assistants.

Shortly after he arrived, Max took a liking to another newcomer from New York. Joe Stassi was at the Carteret to attend an underworld meeting that summer. When the session was extended to the next day, Max ordered a room for Joe that night. Years later "Hoboken Joe" recalled, "I went there for an afternoon and stayed fourteen years." Soon after his arrival, Stassi rented an apartment on the seventh floor, directly below Hassel's suite on the top floor.

Stassi was an independent, not officially connected to any one Manhattan or Jersey family, but available to do all types of jobs for the bosses. Hassel employed him occasionally, but he wasn't on the payroll as were other regulars. Joe and Max were alike in that they preferred to stay out of the lime light rather than coming across as swaggering toughs. Joe survived because he was efficient, unobtrusive, and kept his mouth shut. He admired Max's straightforward way of doing business—a standup guy in gangster parlance. By his own admission, however, Stassi would take contracts to murder if certain people gave the orders.

In the history of Prohibition, 1929 was a watershed year. The formation of the Seven Group in Atlantic City curbed the mob's disruptive violence to some degree. Profits improved and a modicum of order was brought to the liquor business. At the same time, however, the illegal beer trade was undergoing a drastic realignment of power.

When Hassel settled in Elizabeth that summer, Gordon already had made furtive inroads into the Irish-run breweries in Union, Hudson, Essex, and Passaic counties. He didn't use a frontal attack in his takeover, but rather became an adviser and financial backer until he was ready to grab the whole pie.

Jay Culhane was reputed to be the main power broker among the Irish beer bootleggers in the four-county area. Two others prominent in the trade were Frankie Dunn and James "Bugs" Donovan. During the early years of Prohibition, Dunn led a feared gang of hijackers. Donovan's trucks were frequent targets until he offered Dunn a partnership in his Union City Brewery. After a couple of years they had a falling out. Donovan joined up with Frenchy Dillon, another prominent beerman. During this power struggle, Dunn gave up his share in the Union City Brewery to Donovan, while retaining control of the Eureka Cereal Company in Paterson.

In the fall of 1929, two major developments were quite probably related to Waxey Gordon's takeover of the North Jersey market. Within a period of days, Bugs Donovan was killed and Frankie Dunn announced his retirement as a bootlegger.

Donovan, in September 1929, was making his regular Saturday night visit to his girlfriend on Twenty-first Street in Manhattan. He parked a few doors from the building where Grace McDonald had an apartment. Before he could step from his sedan he was cut down by a fusillade of shots fired from a car that had just pulled up next to his. Grace rushed outside to find her boyfriend dead.

The following night on First Avenue, two of Donovan's cronies were shot in separate murder attempts. They survived, but the ranks of the Irish bootleggers were beginning to thin. Frankie Dunn prolonged his life by a few months by spreading the word he was quitting the rackets to try his hand at investment and financial ventures.

Waxey Gordon had first made his presence felt in 1928 by getting chummy with Jay Culhane, who had partial interest in the Union City and Paterson breweries. Gordon provided money to improve the Eureka Cereal and Union City beer plants. He also developed better techniques for moving real beer undetected past federal inspectors. Although no formal announcement was made, Gordon was gradually usurping Culhane's primacy.

With Hassel's arrival in mid-1929, followed by the elimination of Donovan a few months later, Dunn decided to step aside to make room for the new regime. It became obvious to Max that the real peril of the business was not the government but the treacherous leadership of the organization he had joined. Although his reputation had preceded him, the Jersey racketeers viewed Max with some suspicion. But not for long.

Under Gordon's stewardship, a new piping system that was becoming all too familiar was installed at the Eureka Cereal Company in Paterson. Fire hoses were inserted through the city sewer lines from the brewery to a nearby garage on Main Street. Real beer was pumped through the hose, but special care had to be taken to control the flow rate to protect the quality of the beer. At the filling station, the beer was barreled and loaded onto delivery trucks. The federal guards at the Eureka plant tabulated only near beer that was being produced, while thousands of gallons of real beer were released daily from other vats.

Rather than believe the feds were fooled, it stands to reason the guards were being well paid by the racketeers not to get too nosy. The average number of inspectors on the federal payroll at any one time during Prohibition was 2,500. That small contingent was responsible for preventing violations of the Volstead Act across the nation against a far bigger army of bootleggers. The Prohibition agency acquired a terrible reputation because of its inability to retain honest brewery watchers who could resist the lure of gangster bribes. Inspectors' annual salaries ranged from $1,000 to $2,500 a year, a fraction of what the racketeers were paying.

To further gain a firm grip on the beer industry, it is likely the Gordon crowd entered an alliance with Abe Zwillman and Willie Moretti, two New Yorkers who were the mob's New Jersey bosses. Waxey very probably nuzzled up to Jersey City's Mayor Frank "I am the law" Hague, a state-of-the-art political crook. The Hague machine tentacles extended well beyond his city's limits for more than three decades. To make money as a racketeer, you had to pay those who controlled law enforcement. Hague wanted a cut of all illegal activity being operated in his domain.

Added to the explosive mix of personalities that destabilized the beer business in 1929 was Dutch Schultz. His sudden rise to prominence in bootlegging circles did not make life easier for the North Jersey group as it consolidated its holdings.

Schultz, a low-level crook during the early years of Prohibition, began spreading his wings in 1928. Within a year after opening his first speakeasy he was anointed beer baron of the Bronx. Through threat and force he attracted a large speakeasy clientele. Soon his truckers were distributing most of the beer in his borough. Then he began moving into midtown Manhattan, for years the fiefdom of Owney "the Killer" Madden. Owney operated the Phenix Cereal Beverage Company, the biggest brewery in New York City. Like many of the top racketeers, Owney was leery of doing business with Schultz, so the

Dutchman began buying his beer in North Jersey. This would eventually bring him into conflict with Gordon and Hassel.

Running parallel to what was known as "The War of the Jews," was Gordon's ongoing campaign that could have been called "The Irish Wipeout." After Donovan's murder, Harry "the Giant Killer" Veasey was the next to go on January 30, 1930. Veasey and Joe Stassi were longtime pals. They had been hired by Hoboken distributor, Bill Simms, to follow his beer trucks and pay cops and state policemen to assure his barrel-laden vehicles weren't stopped.

"We'd slip them $5—that was enough," Stassi claimed.

While serving time together as teenagers in Brooklyn's Raymond Street jail, Stassi was smitten by Veasey's macho image. Young Joe said he reported to the guards that he had gonorrhea just so he could be transferred to Harry's tier and listen to his idol's stories. (Joe shrugged off further explanation when telling this tale in his old age.)

Stassi told about Frankie Dunn giving him and Harry a car and $250 apiece each week to grease the route over which his beer was delivered. Although Joe looked up to Harry as a role model, he said he wasn't surprised his friend was killed. Veasey was small, well-mannered, dressed stylish, and wore glasses. "He looked like a clerk," recalled Joe. But being a class act was no help when his number was up. Although he gave his attackers quite a fight, Harry was battered and knifed before being shot three times. Honoring his reputation as a dude, Harry's killers laid his bloodied and muddied head on his carefully folded overcoat in the back seat of his car which was found on a Hoboken street. Two others in Harry's small gang also were slain in the previous two months. Stassi, known to the police as Hoboken Joe, said he knew that Frankie Dunn ordered Veasey's murder.

The reality of trying to quit the mob was brought home in dramatic fashion to Dunn on March 7, 1930. The good-looking, flamboyant Frankie, a husky six-footer, had turned to other pursuits after his "retirement." He bought a barrel-making business as a front, but police learned he was emulating Arnold Rothstein by becoming a financial backer of illegal ventures. He also bought a seven-story office building in Hoboken that became the scene of his murder.

As Dunn entered the building one afternoon, two men followed him through the revolving door and knocked him down. From the other direction in the long, narrow lobby came his assassin with a Thompson sub-machine gun. Although a full clip of ammunition was emptied, only two of twenty-four slugs pierced Frankie's prone body. Dunn managed to stagger out to the sidewalk but died several hours later in a hospital.

It was a four-man team that carried out the execution. Three of them escaped, but Frank Dugan, the not-so-deadeyed shooter, got caught up in a gun battle with Hoboken police. After fleeing the building, Dugan backed through the doorway of a nearby home where he let loose with his Tommy gun in every direction—hitting nobody. Inside the house he found himself on the third floor unable to open a hallway skylight. Trapped, he put the machine gun to his head and managed to kill himself with a single shot. That ended a shootout that the neighborhood talked about for years.

Dugan had been a member of Dunn's crew until a short time before the murder. Police claimed that some of Frankie's old buddies were not pleased with their share of the wealth when he abandoned them. Also, reports that Dunn was responsible for the Veasey murder did not sit well with Harry's friends. In gangland rub outs, there usually was an abundance of motive pointing in several directions.

In the next two weeks, Henry Engel, another discard of Dunn's gang, and Milton Green, a young beer hijacker of promise, were gunned down in Bayonne and Paterson respectively. North Jersey was beginning to look like Flanders Field. By keeping his head down and carrying out his assignments with no fanfare, Joe Stassi escaped the slaughter to become possibly the oldest surviving gangster of that gory war.

As the news of the North Jersey blood bath filtered back to Reading, the boys at Sixth and Penn swapped "I told you so" boasts about Max's new environs. If he was worried, he made no move to desert the Cart-eret. Possibly he ordered more locks for his eighth floor headquarters. By now he knew nobody was untouchable on the North Jersey battle-field.

Jay Culhane and Frenchy Dillon, two of the area's big-timers before Waxey took over, saved their necks by joining Gordon's gang, being rewarded with very limited responsibility.

After Donovan was killed, George Bissell was concerned about the $101,000 owed to him by Eureka Cereal Company. Bissell was the brewery's chief supplier of malts, hops, and syrup. When he went to the brewery to talk about the outstanding bill, he met a gentleman who introduced himself, "I'm Waxey Gordon, the new owner."

To celebrate his takeover, Waxey held a banquet at a popular restau-rant, the Singac Gardens near Paterson. He invited about one hundred guests: police chiefs, mayors, and speakeasy operators, all of them on his payroll. The dinner was a symbolic show of defiance to the law by Waxey and his cronies. He proudly introduced his new brewmaster, 48-year-old Oscar Brocker, who was lured away from a Meriden, Conn., plant. Brocker had worked in breweries since he was ten years old. Now he was earning $10,000 a year plus five cents extra for every barrel of real beer made by Eureka. Whether Max Hassel attended is not known, but reason tells us he probably was invited.

It's easy to understand why the government claimed Waxey made more than a million dollars in 1930. Brocker would testify at Gordon's trial in 1933 that it cost $2.05 cents to produce a half barrel of beer that wholesaled for $8 to $11. He said plant overhead was about $4,500 a month. Brocker's bonus that year was more than his salary.

The Prohibition Bureau was at a loss to stop the consolidation of Gordon's power throughout the area. His organization was spreading money in all directions, as witnessed at the Singac Gardens bash. Spies inside and outside of North Jersey law enforcement made it very diffi-cult to spring surprise raids. But the syndicate's early-warning system broke down on March 21, 1930, when a raiding party was formed at an unlikely base far from the target, Newark, New Jersey.

A federal flying squad left Albany, New York, early that morning. It arrived well before noon, entering the Hensler Brewery while a full crew of workers was in the building. Thirty-six men and women employees were arrested and 7,000 barrels of beer were seized.

A crowd of rough-looking characters soon arrived outside the Hensler plant. Lawmen and news photographers taking pictures were threatened by Waxey Gordon's henchmen. Rumors of a counterattack had everybody on edge, but no further attempt was made to hinder the raiders.

The unidentified operators of the brewery used the same type of piping system that worked so well in Paterson. A 500-foot pipeline running from the brewery to a nearby garage where the beer was confiscated had all the earmarks of a Gordon operation.

If Waxey could be described as the syndicate's chairman of the board, it was Big Maxie Greenberg who was the CEO, overseeing Gordon's expansive real estate and hotel holdings, and gambling enterprises. Max Hassel was brought into the North Jersey circle because of his long experience in the beer business, plus his special talent for wooing politicians. Max was the outfit's main man in Washington, D.C.

Just how many breweries the trio eventually controlled is vague, but the government placed the number at sixteen or seventeen by 1933. The Gordon/Hassel/Greenberg combine was easily the biggest producer of real beer in the heavily populated New York to Philadelphia corridor, and then some. Its interests in breweries stretched, from Buffalo, Elmira and Syracuse down through eastern Pennsylvania and New Jersey, even into Delaware and Maryland. In addition to the partner's breweries that were licensed to produce near beer, they also controlled quite a few smaller, unlicensed plants, sometimes called "cold water" or "wildcat" operations.

Although Hassel had no stomach for gunplay, he ventured into the big time well aware of how Gordon had gained control so quickly.

Since many of Waxey's inner circle were survivors of the Lower East Side slum wars, to them Max Hassel was something of an anomaly: a small city dude with a strong business resume, but short on the type of war stories they liked telling. The New York gangsters had earned their stripes the hard way, not by making an honest buck peddling cigars door to door or selling newspapers on a street corner. He soon earned their respect, however, by being a straight shooter, not only with them but with his customers, too. The longer they knew him, the troops began viewing Hassel as the real brains of the outfit. Waxey and Big Maxie handled the rough stuff, while Max became more important as the diplomatic link to the centers of power.

Despite their very different backgrounds, Max and Waxey shared several mutual interests: golf, gambling, and expensive clothing. Both were hoteliers. In other ways they were opposites. Waxey, a convicted dope dealer, reportedly liked to retire to his home library, and stuff all air escapes with towels to saturate the room with opium smoke. Cigar smoke was the only kind Max was inhaling.

When the dust had cleared after the violent overthrow of the Irish beermen, Max was in charge of the organization's Harrison plant about ten miles north of Elizabeth. Hassel was rarely seen at the brewery. Much more visible was Louis Cohn who many of the workers assumed was the owner. Known as Louis "Blackie" Black, Cohn frequently went to Gordon's Piccadilly Hotel in Manhattan on matters other than beer production. His aliases appeared on numerous bank transactions.

Since leaving Reading, Hassel used the name Jimmy Feldman. Most of the Jersey mobsters called him that. When he signed his name it was usually James Feldman or M.H. Feldman, or any of several other names to hide his identity. The few Reading loyalists he brought with him to Elizabeth continued to call him Max or Boss. Joe Stassi said he always referred to him as Max. Unlike Gordon, who reveled in being a public figure, Max preferred anonymity. He didn't care to make himself familiar to the citizens of Harrison or Elizabeth, a port city at the southwest tip of Newark Bay.

Among the chain of breweries Gordon and company had collected, was the Rising Sun Brewery in Elizabeth. Although Mickey Duffy's later activities pointed to him as the Rising Sun operator, Gordon and Hassel also had their fingers in that pie. Duffy and Max had patched up their differences and became relatively close associates. Although Duffy's media name was Mickey, Hassel and Stassi always referred to him as Mike.

Vincent Liotta, the president of Oneida Manufacturing Company, was listed as the nominal owner of the old Rising Sun property who leased it to the combine. Most of the brewery workers were members of Duffy's Philadelphia gang. For that reason, beer shipments from that plant were being tracked by both the Newark and Philadelphia offices of the Bureau of Prohibition. Colonel Sam Wynne was especially anxious to corral Duffy because of the Philadelphian's unabashed defiance and penchant for violence in and around the Quaker City.

When the agency padlocked Camden Cereal early in 1930, it is believed Duffy swore revenge on John Finiello, the Philadelphia agent responsible for closing the plant. Finiello, a naturalized immigrant from Italy, was a decorated World War I veteran known as the "Fighting Sergeant" of Company D, 111th Infantry Regiment, 28th National Guard Division. His reputation as an honest and courageous dry was preeminent throughout the underworld. Finiello was also on Duffy's hit list for having taken a $10,000 bribe to avert a raid on an Egg Harbor, N.J., distillery. Finiello turned the money over to Colonel Wynne. The raid proceeded as scheduled and Duffy lost his ten grand.

Nick Delmore, a nightclub operator in nearby Berkley Heights, was pay master at the Rising Sun Brewery in Elizabeth. The plant was equipped with a warning system from a lookout post in an apartment across the street. It also had an elaborate 400-foot-long escape tunnel. Gun-toting guards noticed a dry agent snooping near the brewery early in September 1930. The agent, John Smith, heeded the guards' order to "get out and don't come back." Smith returned to his hotel room in Newark, but within hours a messenger knocked on the door and left an even stronger warning. "Stay away from Rising Sun. You won't get away with it. They will kill you."

Smith and Finiello were members of a raiding party that left Philadelphia the morning of September 16. Robert Young, the bureau's special supervisor of breweries in Pennsylvania and New Jersey, was in the team's lead car when it was sideswiped and damaged by another sedan that sped away. This staged accident just outside Philadelphia indicated the Elizabeth mob had been warned about Young's flying squad. A replacement sedan soon arrived and the convoy continued to Elizabeth. Entrance to the brewery was gained without resistance. As one group of agents lined up workers in the boiler room, a dozen armed thugs in hiding suddenly got the drop on them. Nine workers were told to flee by the gunmen. As agents were being disarmed, John Finiello arrived on the scene from another section of the building. "There's Finiello," Nick Delmore yelled, "get him!"

Several gangster guns turned on the fearless agent who drew his service pistol. It jammed as eight bullets took him down. Two of the shooters were identified by workers as Delmore, the man who paid them each week, and Sammy Grossman, a known Duffy gunman.

Grossman was the prime suspect the previous year in the murder of Hughie McLoon, a former mascot for the Philadelphia Athletics baseball team. Grossman beat that rap. Delmore took off for Florida, returned to Jersey a few years later and was never prosecuted.

Another of the five men eventually charged in the agent's slaying was William Weisman. Through an anonymous tip, police in Newark checked out a garage on the property of Weisman's brother-in-law. Tests on a loaded handgun found under the back seat of a car proved to be one of the murder weapons. But like so many gangland shootings, witnesses disappeared, refused to testify, or were killed—end of case.

Max Hassel, identified as a "former brewer," was on the Prohibition Bureau's list of people the feds questioned. The proximity of his headquarters in the Elizabeth Carteret made him a reasonable suspect.

Duffy, too, underwent interrogation. Since nobody saw either Max or Mickey in the brewery, and alibis about their whereabouts held up, questioning was just a formality.

As a result of the Finiello murder, Duffy became an emotional target of the feds. Also, the reckless defiance of Mickey's underlings destroyed any hopes he might have had of becoming a true partner in the Gordon/Hassel/Greenberg combine. Duffy was never accepted by the inner circle of mob chieftains. They wanted him out of the business as much as the government did. It was rumored that Duffy was paying blackmailers to withhold information about Finiello's murder. The fact that his own peers would use extortion against him shows just where Mickey stood with the mob.

Despite his many enemies, Duffy managed to survive almost a year after the Finiello slaying. Then he was shot three times in the head as he lay drugged in his suite in Atlantic City's Ambassador Hotel on August 29, 1931. At first, police believed members of his own gang had doped him before administering the coup de grace. The early suspects were his chauffeur, Joe Beatty, and top lieutenants, Sammy Grossman and Albert Silverman. After questioning, the trio was released.

Another suspect and Duffy crony, Herbert Green, was held in the Atlantic City jail. Police reported that somebody tried to kill Green with poisoned coffee delivered to his jail cell. A messenger said the pot of coffee was sent by Green's sister. Green, who had no sister, told guards he wasn't thirsty. The turnkey and patrolman who drank the coffee lapsed into unconsciousness. They survived, but tests showed a quantity of morphine in the java.

Also suspected of being in Atlantic City the afternoon Duffy was killed was Paul "Dago" Corbo. Better known as Frankie Carbo, years later he became czar of the boxing game. Carbo and a teenage night-club dancer, Ophelia Malfatto, were seized in a West Sixty-Seventh Street hotel room by New York City police. Carbo claimed he was in a Manhattan hospital being treated for a nose ailment when Duffy was shot. That alibi was proved false but he was never charged with the slaying. Carbo had already served fourteen months in Sing Sing for killing a Bronx butcher, and in his long criminal career was a suspect in four other murders.

Max Hassel again moved about with caution after Duffy got his. He feared retribution from Mickey's gang. If Carbo was the shooter, and many in the underworld thought he was, it's highly possible that Gordon's North Jersey syndicate felt it had good reason to hire him.

Philadelphia's Ritz-Carlton Hotel catered to not only the rich and famous, but also to the rich and notorious. Mickey Duffy and Max Hassel were regular patrons at the popular downtown hotel. Investigators found many incriminating letters and documents in Duffy's hotel suite after he was killed. A letter describing Duffy's power play at the Camden brewery when Hassel was ousted, proved more damaging to Max's former contact man, Yates Fetterman, than it did to him. The ex-dry administrator was soon the target of a grand jury probe. Duffy had inherited Fetterman's services when he took over the brewery in 1929. Of course there was no bill of sale to link Hassel to the exchange of management, when the brewery was padlocked in 1930. Other documents Duffy left behind indicated he was implicated in Finiello's murder.

The day before Duffy was buried in Philadelphia, his top lieutenants assessed their numbers writers an 8 percent levy on the daily take to buy flowers for their fallen chief's funeral. The grounds of Duffy's $65,000 estate on City Line Avenue were overrun by curiosity seekers when his body was returned from Atlantic City.

The final chapter of the Mickey Duffy era was written a few months after his death. Sammy Grossman, twice a suspect in the Finiello and Duffy murders, was free on $25,000 bail as a material witness but still on the wanted list by various parties. He was seen in his usual Philadelphia haunts just before Christmas 1931, but time was running out. Three days after the holiday the police received word that survivors of the Duffy mob were about to rub out the 27-year-old hood in the Jewish Social Club at Broad Street and Girard Avenue.

Hoping to capture the would-be assassins, the police began setting up machine guns on buildings overlooking the club. But neighbors complained that somebody might get shot in the crossfire. While this debate boiled, a five-man team carried out its mission in a second-floor room over the club. Too bad for Albert Skale, 25, because he was in the room, too, and went down with Grossman. Herman Cohen, who reportedly drove Frankie Carbo out of Atlantic City on the day of Duffy's murder, was leader of the Grossman execution squad. Herman was also manager of the Jewish Social Club. He and four others were arrested later in Jersey. The purpose and nuances of mob hits often were beyond common sense reasoning.

Although Hassel was regarded primarily as a beerman, another incident described by Joe Stassi indicates Max's far-flung interests included an illegal still being operated in a vacant Bethlehem Steel building in Allentown. His role in the deal was to influence a local judge to issue a restraining order against the Prohibition Bureau to prevent dismantling of the place. The big still had been operating at capacity for several weeks before it was shut down. When the agency got wind of the restraining order, it appealed to the federal court to have the local judge's order rescinded. Max dispatched Joe Stassi to Allentown to try to block the feds in the event they tried to start the dismantling process.

"I had the local judge's order in my hand when they came knocking," Joe said, "but they shoved me aside and began breaking up the place." He laughed at the recollection of his futile attempt to stop the federal government by waving a document from a crooked judge.

While the Duffy gang was decimated by internal strife, Max Hassel and his partners continued to consolidate their power. Waxey Gordon had just come off a very good year in 1930. The government later tabulated his income at $1.4 million, but Waxey saw it differently. He sent Internal Revenue a $10.76 income tax payment that year. Shortly after that, the U.S. attorney in New York reported Gordon was Public Enemy No. 1.

After Hassel's original two-year lease at the Carteret ran out, as H.C. Jameison he signed a new lease on July 1, 1931. This time, instead of just paying for his six-room suite, he rented the entire eighth floor of one wing of the hotel for $150 a week. By 1933 the rent had expanded to $600 a week, paid faithfully every Monday by various flunkies Max dispatched with the cash. While there were several individual rooms in the leasing agreement, the only entrance to Hassel's suite was identified as Room 824.

The syndicate chief was a bit more extravagant regarding his own comfort. Whenever Waxey Gordon visited his Eureka brewery in Paterson, he stayed in the Alexander Hamilton Hotel. One eight-week visit in a small suite cost him more than $1,900. For his gang he rented an eight-room house for $125 a week. Waxey didn't mind doing business right at his brewery and became a popular figure in Paterson. Few in Elizabeth knew anything about Max Hassel.

As the outfit's business increased, telephone traffic became so heavy that a third Carteret operator was hired. Hoping to gain the operators' trust not to discuss his phone calls, Max arranged to pay them an extra $65 a month. A number the girls were often asked to dial was Nutley 3244. That was Henry Fred Dihlmann's number. The Harrison plant's brewmaster rarely saw Max but talked with him by phone several times a week. Room 824 was the syndicate's control central. From his suite, Max administered much of the combine's widespread affairs. He called Reading almost daily to keep abreast of family and business matters.

Just before real beer became legal, during a 21-day period in March/ April 1933, there were 3,000 toll calls made from Hassel's hotel office. His weekly phone bills were running from $250 to $275. Is it any wonder he had to hire another Bernadine? One of the perks for the Carteret was free beer for its coffee shop and restaurant.

Max had accounts in Elizabethport Bank just two doors from the Carteret. He also had dealings at the New Jersey National Bank and Trust Company in Newark where he became friendly with John Stamler, a lawyer and president of the bank. New Jersey National was among the many banks that collapsed in 1932.

Max didn't neglect his Pennsylvania holdings while in Jersey. His Reiker Brewery in Lancaster had been a good moneymaker for years. Although it had been padlocked from time to time in the 1920s, it gained a new life in 1930 after hoses were run through the city sewers to another building at a lower elevation several blocks away. A tale that survived the decades: midgets were used to drag the hose lines through the conduits. The filling station at the end of the line was not discovered until early in 1933. Government checkers stationed in the brewery could honestly say the only beer leaving the Reiker loading docks was near beer. Down below, a flood of high-powered amber was flowing out to area speakeasies. After the 1933 raid, a grand jury inquiry resulted in the ousting of the Lancaster police chief, and jail time for a few bootleggers.

Despite the big profits rolling into the syndicate's coffers, all of its breweries didn't always finish in the black. Beginning in October 1932 and for the next five months, Briggs Brewery in Elmira was a losing operation. The reason for the deficit was the high cost of "ice" to keep police and politicians cool in the New York city. Although the plant turned out 123,935 gallons of real beer for a profit of $56,849 during that period, the biggest expenditure was the $33,305 paid in bribes. The plant had experienced two raids but beat both liquor violations on court rulings of improper prosecution by the government. It was during those probes the feds discovered that the method of secreting real beer through sewer lines was also used in Elmira.

According to the underworld's business logic, extortion was a marketing tool used not only to bring clients into line, but also utilized by one gang against another. As Dutch Schultz expanded his distribution services in the Bronx, he wanted an even greater share of the production profits. He had been buying beer from Gordon and Hassel for some time when he demanded a partnership in the Jersey combine. The Triple X partners, Waxey, Maxie, and Max, voted not to bring the Dutchman aboard without him advancing a considerable sum up front. Schultz, never one to accept rejection quietly, turned loose crews of hijackers. Trucks leaving Paterson, Harrison, and Newark breweries needed armed guards. It was nightly combat, the Dutchman's marauders waylaying syndicate trucks and funneling the loot into speakeasies in the Bronx and Manhattan. It seems likely it was Hassel who argued that it would be better to make a deal with Schultz than to try to outgun him. That appears to be what happened. Federal authorities would learn that Max alone was paying $8,000 tribute a month to free his Harrison drivers from the risk of road raids.

Another hijack annoyance came from the leftover elements of the old Irish mobs. Those who refused to join Waxey's gang mounted periodic raids on the monopoly's vehicles, trying to avenge their bosses' murders. But they lacked the fire power to retake what was originally theirs.

During the summer of 1932, Waxey Gordon spent quite a bit of time in Asbury Park, the North Jersey shore resort. Because of his differences with Schultz, Waxey decided to obtain handgun permits for himself, Big Maxie, and Max Hassel. Using local businessmen and a former Monmouth County jury commissioner as character references, Waxey had no trouble convincing the Asbury police chief to issue his trio licenses. Whether Hassel ever felt the need to carry a gun after that is problematic, but no evidence has been found that a gun was ever registered in his name.

After a period of relative calm, Dutch Schultz received word from Nig Rosen that Hassel was selling a better grade of brew to favored distributors in the Philadelphia area than the beer being shipped to Nig's distributors. The prohibition on real beer was about to end when this dispute cropped up, so Max ignored the Dutchman's ultimatum to give Rosen associates equal treatment. This defiance to one of Prohibition's most feared characters was not typical of Hassel's style, but by this time he envisioned becoming a legitimate, tax-paying brewer with the government on his side.

13

Sinister Plans for the Future

Prohibition was tottering as Herbert Hoover and Franklin Delano Roosevelt campaigned for the presidency during the summer of 1932. FDR made no bones about it—he supported repeal of the 18th Amendment with no reservations. Hoover, trying to appease the conservatives in his Republican Party, also called for repeal with a stipulation that the old saloon system would not be reinstituted. He admitted the well-intentioned ban on booze and beer had backfired, causing an unrelenting rise in crime that was even worse than the tragic results of alcoholism.

That same summer, Max Hassel had his own agenda that started at home. Things had quieted down for him back in Reading. Except for occasional weekend visits, he was totally committed to expanding his business in North Jersey. With both parents now deceased, he decided it was time to help his family rise above their Franklin Street environs.

Before Prohibition, a migration of wealth began its move from the Centre Avenue district to Reading's fast developing Hampden Heights in the northeast at the foot of Mt. Penn. Max Hassel became part of that movement when he bought a parcel of land from George D. Horst, one of the town's most influencial industrialists. The $13,100 plot on the southeast corner of Bern Street and Alsace Road was deeded to Fannie and Max Abramson. Although Max gained great prominence in the community, within the Hassel family itself his sister Fannie was recognized as the matriarch. She was a strong, energetic woman who invested wisely and gained considerable wealth. Construction on a large stone house was started on the new property late in 1932.

By the end of 1931, Lucky Luciano and his crowd had engineered the murders of Joe Masseria and Salvatore Maranzano, the rival Mafia leaders. This had taken care of the Italian leadership that Luciano and Meyer Lansky felt were detrimental to the philosophy of cooperation promoted at the Seven Group convention in 1929. Now it became Lansky's responsibility to rid the mob's Jewish faction that didn't always toe the line.

Waxey Gordon was at the top of Meyer's hit list. But Gordon's gang was so loyal to its leader, no hitmen could breach his cordon of guards. This underworld struggle became known as "The War of the Jews." Unable to bring down Waxey with bullets, Meyer used a more devious method to eliminate his foe. Through his brother Jake, Lansky began feeding the government information about Waxey's beer empire.

Luciano assumed leadership of Unione Siciliano and formed what became known as The Commission with the godfathers of Mafia families having equal votes on vital issues. Jewish mobsters were not admitted to this exclusive club but Meyer Lansky and Longy Zwillman had considerable input when crucial organized crime matters were debated. They helped set policy through their longtime alliance with Frank Costello and Luciano. Dutch Schultz and Waxey Gordon, both Jews, were not completely excluded because of their gangs' fire power. When The Commission laid out its plans for the post-Prohibition era it had to take them into consideration. Of more concern was Max Hassel who had set his own post-Prohibition agenda.

As Franklin Roosevelt entered the White House in 1933, a peaceful revolution was about to sweep the country. The voters hoped and prayed he could lead them out of the Great Depression. Prohibition was in shambles as state after state passed laws to repeal the 18th Amendment. The public was demanding a revival of the past when you could stop at the corner bar, enter through the front door and order a beer without feeling uneasy about it. As a forerunner to the repeal of the 18th, the legalization of 3.2 beer in April 1933 allowed bar owners to regain their status as respectable businessmen.

Weeks before that momentous occasion, Luciano invited Unione Siciliano representatives from all over the East to his suite in the Waldorf Towers for an important strategy sitdown. The main topic was how to retain control of the beer and liquor industries. Most of these crooks already had a big stake in hard liquor and wine, but now they also wanted a share of the beer business that was controlled in the New York metropolitan area by Gordon, Hassel, Greenberg, and Dutch Schultz. Owney Madden was now out of the picture. After serving a short term in prison in 1932 for parole violation, he moved to Hot Springs, Arkansas, where he established a gambling resort often frequented by mobsters on the run.

The Commission approved a plan to notify future operators of licensed distilleries and breweries they could expect to pay a duty on every case of liquor and every barrel of beer shipped out of their plants. Owners who refused to ante up would be advised that bombings and truck hijackings might convince them to toe the line. Another tool the mob could use was rigged union elections which placed crooked union officials in a position to call work stoppages. Coastal bootlegging was expected to continue with the rate of tribute set at $2 a case on all liquor smuggled into the country on the eastern seaboard. Brewers were given a choice: sell untaxed beer to the mob at bargain prices, or sell them taxed beer at less than wholesale prices. Either way, legitimate beermen, or carryover wildcat brewers, would have to pay a mob levy.

The Commission's grand plan envisioned control of the beer trade in sixteen eastern and southern states. To make sure brewers did not attempt to shortchange them, the racketeers were prepared to hire 2,500 men of dubious character to serve as "checkers" at the breweries. Unlike government checkers during Prohibition, these guys, if lax on the job, could lose more than their jobs.

Despite The Commission's de facto joint chiefs role, the mob was still fragmented, with each gang leader concerned about what the legalization of alcoholic beverages meant to him. Mob-controlled speakeasies would be replaced by licensed taverns if the barmen were willing to stand up to threats of extortion. The racketeers were confident that wouldn't happen. Coastal liquor smuggling would be minimized, but the racketeers still expected kickbacks from those who continued the practice.

As the end of the prohibition on beer approached, brewery operators scrambled to obtain government permits. Licensing procedures were murky at best with plenty of confusion about whether federal or state licenses held precedence. By courting the right politicians and bureaucrats who held sway over the issuing of licenses, Max Hassel gained an edge on the competition.

High in the ranks of those who thrived on using his political clout was William J. Egan, a member of the New Jersey Beer Control Commission. Egan was also an elected member of the Newark Board of Commissioners. He and Hassel were well-acquainted, and became more so as the rush began to corner the beer market.

To attend the presidential inauguration in early March was a status symbol among the bureaucracy. Many state administrators had their travel and lodging paid by influence peddlers. Egan was among the freeloaders who was in the audience when FDR was sworn into office, thanks to Max Hassel.

On March 2, James Feldman registered at the Carlton Hotel in Washington D.C. The following day, Egan, his wife, and two children arrived from Newark to stay in the suite registered under Hassel's alias. The purpose of Max's generosity was to pave the way for federal licenses for the North Jersey gang's numerous breweries authorizing them to manufacture 3.2 beer the following month. By law, brewery officials with criminal records were excluded. Despite his federal and state bribery arrests, Max was never convicted. Although he pleaded guilty to tax evasion, it was his understanding that when he made settlement with the government, his criminal record was cleared. *Sounds good to us,* licensing officials reasoned. While Waxey, Big Maxie, and

Dutch knew they could not wash themselves that clean, Max Hassel pulled off a coup by getting a single federal permit covering several breweries the syndicate controlled.

Egan had been Newark's director of safety before being named to Jersey's beer commission. He was in the position of offering protection to Gordon and Hassel as they gained a monopoly of the North Jersey beer business in 1929. Max had cultivated other Washington movers and shakers over the years, so that when Prohibition was in its last gasp, he knew where to spread the money to assure a smooth transition into legalized beer. Two of his lawyers, Robert Grey Bushong and John Scott, had been congressmen. Another Republican power broker, Joseph R. Grundy, Philadelphia knitting mill tycoon, was also no stranger to Max. His longtime association with Tommy Seidel, the Berks County Republican Party chairman during much of the Prohibition era, was Fred Marks' close friend. Many avenues leading to licensing authorities were open to him.

Unlike most of his peers, Max anxiously awaited the passage of the 21st Amendment ending the ban on alcoholic beverages. For years he hoped for the day he could operate his breweries without fear of raids, without the pressure of the IRS hounding him, without the constant threat of violence among competitors. Unlike many of his hardscrabble associates, Max remembered the emotional rewards of a hard-earned legal dollar. He had the confidence they lacked of adapting to a world of free enterprise. The mobsters knew their long criminal records excluded them from joining the legal business world. They were too seeped in every type of criminal activity to even consider going straight. The mobsters had fought and bled to make their fortunes. It was fuzzy thinking to believe that just because Prohibition had created organized crime, another constitutional amendment would make it go away. Relatively speaking, Max wanted to return to the straight and narrow.

Just how the transition scenario played out has always been murky. Some authorities believed the New York mob was more interested in controlling distilleries and off-shore bootlegging, leaving Schultz free to take care of any rebellious forces in the beer sector. It wasn't until many years later that a lone surviving mobster claimed The Commission was issuing all the orders concerning booze and beer.

Hassel made a dangerous choice. He was determined to pay the government tax, not his mob dues. This was not a spontaneous decision. For years he had talked about becoming a legitimate brewer when Prohibition ended. He envisioned becoming a brewer mogul, not a gangster. He could argue that, with a broad interpretation of his tax settlement, he had no criminal record. A racketeer, yes; a gangster, a mobster, no. He had tried for thirteen years to separate himself from the violence, successfully navigating through the rough waters, for the most part, avoiding the in-your-face aspects of bootlegging. He could rationalize that he balanced the morality books by using the proceeds of Prohibition's money machine to oil his philanthropic enterprises. He could hope that a new-found adherence to the law would secure his dream of citizenship.

A side plot during the death throes of Prohibition was the dramatic disappearance of Schultz after a federal grand jury indicted him on income tax evasion charges in January 1933. For the next 22 months he remained a fugitive, although he never ran very far. He remained in New York City, was often seen in familiar haunts, expanded his profitable numbers racket in Harlem, and conducted other business as usual until November the following year.

The murder of Al Lillien, a close friend of Hassel's, must have caused him great concern as well as some grief. In their trade, every business move, every personal choice was a life or death decision. Lillien had made his share of crucial decisions that cultivated friends, but just as many enemies. Some years earlier he ran a traffic control center for rumrunners from his palatial home at Atlantic Highlands. He had purchased the homestead of the late Gay Nineties show business entrepreneur, Oscar Hammerstein. From his elevated site overlooking the Jersey side of the entrance to New York's Lower Bay, with state of the art radio equipment, he kept nautical bootleggers informed about the locations of Coast Guard cutters.

After Max moved to Elizabeth he had dealings with Lillien and they became close social friends. On March 23, 1933, Al's body was found, shot in the head three times in his spacious home. There were plenty of suspects because it was generally known that Lillien had more than once tipped the Coast Guard at the expense of bootleggers not on his early-warning system. One clue to the murder was a pair of pallbearers gloves and an ace of spades left behind by the killer. Police believed the face card might have had some symbolic connection to the murder of Boston's top mobster, Charles "King" Soloman, two months earlier. From the gloves, police determined that the killer had only one thumb. Years earlier, Big Maxie Greenberg had lost a thumb. He was an unlikely suspect, but before police could link "Big Head" to the murder, Max Hassel's partner was history.

Max for years had taken a non-violent stance in his business dealings, but after his confrontations with Mickey Duffy he was convinced negotiation skills were not enough. He began bringing along bodyguards whenever he was dealing with metropolitan gangsters. Louis Parkowitz, a New York thug, became his protector. Parkowitz often accompanied him on weekends to The Farm, not so much to watch over him but to get away from the big city cauldron.

The Gordon-Hassel breweries were swamped with orders weeks before the prohibition was lifted on 3.2 beer. Louis Cohn, also known as Lefler and Blackie, handled a flood of calls from distributors up and down the East Coast. Cohn was a vital cog in the Gordon-Hassel organization, constantly working the phones in Room 824 at the Carteret. In addition to dealing with distributors anxious to buy the Harrison Brewery's Old Heidelberg beer, Cohn played a central role in the Hassel gang by contracting for brewery equipment for the organization's scattered plants in New Jersey and Pennsylvania. A bonding company agent recalled visiting Room 824 to arrange a $100,000 permit bond for Harrison Brewery. He said Cohn was besieged with phone calls that day as they tried to complete their business.

As the legalization of strong beer drew closer, beermen in New York, Jersey, and Pennsylvania were scrambling to obtain licenses. Gordon and Hassel were one giant step ahead of them. Although the federal officials in charge of industrial alcohol licensing often revoked licenses of suspected criminals, federal or state courts regularly reinstated them. This suggests that top officials of the regulatory agencies were more honest than many of the courts. Certainly Max Hassel was on the books as a repeat offender of dealing in illegal beer. But that did not prevent him from being the first out of the gate when real beer became legal. He certainly intended to continue his interest in the Harrison Brewery, but more important he wanted to put the Reading Brewery back on its feet.

Health Brewing Company of Reading—that was the name Max used on the license application when he applied for a federal license. Also included on the application were the Harrison Brewery and other plants he controlled with Gordon and Greenberg.

Health Brewing Company certainly had an aura of respectability about it. Max was pulling out all the marketing stops available at that time. On the license application, Samuel Lunine was listed as president of Health Brewing. Lunine, still a haberdasher and an official at Kesher Zion, had loaned his name to Max in 1931 as the straw buyer and president of Reading Brewing Company.

After the brewery was dismantled in 1928 there doesn't appear to have been much activity there for a few years. Some near beer continued to be produced, but merely a dribble compared with the real beer gusher of the mid-twenties. By late 1932, Hassel was busy placing orders for new kettles, hoses, racking machines, and other equipment for the South Ninth Street plant. His supplier was Shock, Gusner and Company, a New York firm that worked with George J. Meyer Manufacturing Company to redesign and refurbish the idle brewery. These two companies were hired by Hassel to also refit Hensler Brewery,

Newark, N.J.; Union City Brewery, Union City; and Seitz Brewery, Easton, Pa.

In Pennsylvania, seven of the state's twenty-eight breweries were licensed when beer became legal. Reading Brewery was one of the seven. Huge copper vats with five hundred barrel capacities were installed. Each vat could brew three batches of 3.2 beer in twenty-four hours. In preparation for the grand opening on April 7, Sam Lunine was spokesman for the brewery, with the public still unaware that it was now operated under the name Health Brewing Company.

An interesting sidelight: When the ban on real beer ended on April 6, there was a race for distributor licenses. Hyman Liever still had his Berks Bottling Works on South Sixth Street in Reading. He received the first county distributor's license in May 1933.

In New Jersey, the Harrison Brewery was primed to deliver its first barrels of 3.2 Old Heidelberg beer when the ban was lifted. Every barrel that left the place contained a federal tax stamp. Schultz, Luciano, Lansky, and the other mobsters did not look kindly on renegades. Since Max Hassel had made known his intention of running legitimate breweries, it is not clear whether his partners thoroughly agreed with him. They were career criminals, so who could tell what they were up to?

The quality of Hassel's beer immediately attracted many new legitimate distributors. Companies that had obtained beer through Schultz were now dealing directly with Hassel. The Hassel-Gordon breweries were so blitzed with orders, they could barely fill them. Even smaller breweries, unable to supply their own distributors, were calling. Dutch Schultz wanted a discount on the wholesale rate but the syndicate turned him down.

Even though Schultz's fearsome career was dotted with murderous resolutions, the boys, as Max referred to his soldiers, were proud of their leaders for rejecting the New York mob's demands for a piece of the Jersey breweries. All too often it had proved a fatal mistake to defy the Dutchman but Max felt this time the law was in his corner. The boys recognized Waxey as the big boss, but respected Jimmy Feldman as equally important to the outfit. They knew it was Feldman who had maneuvered their gang into a very favorable post-Prohibition position.

Waxey must have known he would lose a lot of power if Hassel succeeded in making a peaceful transition. With his criminal record, he would have to become a very silent partner. It's possible Gordon hoped to continue his operation of breweries behind a screen of dummy owners. We don't know what arrangements the partners made to resolve a peaceful split. Or did they ever resolve it?

One of Hassel's close associates recalled sitting in the office of a Reading lawyer early in April 1933. Other attorneys in Hassel's legal stable were also present. The debate between Max and most of the others was about which way to go. As the boss, as the master of adjusting to the situation and the times, he would not be shunted from the mode of action he had set for himself. It was indeed a perilous course and his aides were not shy about reminding him of it. Max was aware of the Dewey tax investigation, but he must have felt he could weather another tax case with no more than a fine.

Max had a more immediate problem to resolve, one that he felt could reinforce his ascent into the legal business community, or further block his way. Back in Reading, three Berks County judges acting as agents for the federal government, were setting the stage for a fateful decision that could make or break the man they knew all too well.

14

Final Pursuit of his Dream

Max Hassel rang up a remarkable record in his battles with the U.S. government. His early mischief as a licensed buyer of industrial alcohol from the government ended with a warning and a citation, but each time the $20,000 bond he had entered to obtain a permit was returned to him. Three times he was arrested and charged with bribery. Three times he avoided conviction or fines. Over and over federal and state Prohibition agents raided breweries in which he had an interest, but seldom was he charged and never was he personally found guilty of liquor violations. In 1929 he pleaded guilty to income tax evasion. By agreeing to pay $150,000, far less than he allegedly owed, he again dodged jail time.

Always resourceful, he left fuzzy paper trails that stymied federal investigators and prosecutors. He used his wealth to hire top lawyers with political connections. Sometimes when he was charged with bribery or tax evasion, government officials would make public announcements that they had airtight evidence to convict their most wanted bootlegger. Through guile, payoffs, and diplomacy, he never spent an hour behind bars. Although Hassel and his attorneys managed to outmaneuver the government for a dozen years, there was one federal bureau he could not manipulate. The Immigration and Naturalization Service never granted him citizenship.

At the age of 20, as part owner of the Schuylkill Extract Company, he had to surrender his license to withdraw alcohol from government warehouses because he was an alien. Until that time he probably was too busy to worry about naturalization. But, deprived of his profitable bootlegging operation, he realized how important citizenship could be. In April 1922, about the time he was starting up Berks Products Company under an assumed name, he went to the Berks County Courthouse to declare his intention to apply for citizenship. This was the first step of the somewhat extended process.

In October 1924 he was granted a citizenship hearing. The INS proceeding was in Reading's Baer Building. Four days before the hearing, the applicant had petitioned the county court to have his name legally changed from Mendel Gassel to Max Hassel. The petition languished in the court for years, but there's no record it was ever acted upon. But this didn't deter Max from using the name he chose for the rest of his life.

Max had no trouble meeting two of the principal criteria for obtaining citizenship: he could speak English and he was more than willing to renounce all allegiances to his former country, by now under Bolshevic rule. But his early run-ins with the Prohibition Agency and his publicized connection with illegal breweries left him with a record that, if not criminal, was at best, dubious. The INS had turned down aliens with slates far less cluttered with such a variety of suspected violations. His character witnesses at the hearing were Charlie Marks and P. A. Breen. Although a former Prohibition officer, Marks' record was about as bad as Hassel's. Breen was another young fellow employed by Max. Enough of his activities as a bootlegger was exposed that the INS denied him citizenship on this first try, but left his case open for appeal.

In subsequent naturalization documents, Max's family name was listed as Gassel, with Hassel in parenthesis, indicating the name-change application was still under consideration. However, many court and recorder of deeds records throughout his career almost always referred to him as Max Hassel without the a.k.a.

Charlie Matten, representing Max throughout his long naturalization ordeal, filed the first of many appeals after the initial petition was rejected. Appeal arguments were scheduled for February 1925, but three times the government postponed the hearing to await further investigation. Hassel's name kept popping up in the newspaper as either lessee or owner of local breweries that had been charged with liquor violations. These delays hurt Max's chances of getting his papers because the longer he had to wait, the more damaging his reputation as a bootlegger became.

Then in 1926 it was Matten's turn to request a postponement because Max was tied up with the bribery case involving two state police employees. Also in 1926, the government was pressing Max for unpaid income taxes. In December of that year, Max appeared at the office of the district director of Naturalization in Philadelphia with an affidavit applying for a certified copy of his declaration of intention then on file in Berks County Court. He stated under oath that he intended to file for citizenship in Philadelphia because his permanent address was now in the Sylvania Hotel, Locust and Juniper streets. He hired Max Aron, a Philadelphia lawyer and Pennsylvania state senator to work with Matten.

For the next couple of years Max and Matten decided the legal climate was too hot to push for citizenship. Not until 1929, after Max had made temporary peace with Internal Revenue and beaten the last of three bribery charges, did he resume his quest to shed his alien status. Although Max now presumed his case was being handled by INS' Philadelphia office, the Reading court felt it had not relinquished jurisdiction.

Berks President Judge Paul Schaeffer set a November hearing date, but Max failed to appear on the advice of Matten. A civil suit had been filed against him in his failed attempt to buy a Norristown brewery. Finally, Judge Schaeffer lost patience and dismissed Hassel's original 1924 petition of appeal, now declaring the case closed. During the early '30s as Max spent more and more time in North Jersey, thoughts of becoming a citizen never left his mind. His post-Prohibition plans included trips to Europe to hire brewmasters. He needed his papers to obtain a passport which would ensure he could return from abroad.

A determined effort to press Hassel's citizenship campaign was launched by Matten in June 1932. Berks County Court was petitioned to set aside Judge Schaeffer's 1929 dismissal decree. Judge Schaeffer, who had declared Hassel's case closed, was still a member of the county court. In October, attorney Adrien Bonnelly represented Max at a hearing before the three Berks judges, Schaeffer, May, and Shanaman. He claimed his client had never received proper notice about closure of his case. For the next four months court documents flew back and forth as the INS tried to shoot down appeals by Matten and Bonnelly. Finally in February 1933, Matten won arguments for a new hearing.

Max's life as a bootlegger was now reviewed as never before at a day-long session before the same three Berks judges on March 27. Seventy pages of testimony were taken as Max's record of arrests and tax problems were thoroughly explored by Henry L. Mulle, senior naturalization examiner.

Max was cooperative but not overly helpful. He often asked that questions be repeated, a well-practiced ploy to take some of the steam out of Mulle's aggressive examination. Hassel's answers usually were direct with little embellishment. He did not provide information that was not asked of him. He corrected Mulle's assumptions occasionally, sometimes denying accusations. Frequently, he claimed not to remember, then feigned delayed-recall when Mulle presented incriminating documents such as one on which Max admitted forging Stanley Miller's signature. Miller was the ghost owner of Berks Products Company, Max's second venture into the government alcohol market. It was Mulle's goal to drag out as much of Hassel's shady record as he could, but the judges occasionally harnessed his repetitive questioning.

The very early years of Max's racketeering hadn't previously been exposed to the public. His partnerships in the Schuylkill Extract and Berks Products companies to cover his illegal sales of alcohol had not been uncovered by the press. At the citizenship hearing, Max claimed he knew very little about Stanley Miller but insisted he was an actual person who personally dealt with dry agents. Mulle never succeeded in flustering the witness. Max was always low-key, testifying without emotion. No restless body language or facial tics exposed any nervousness he might have felt. His life in the rackets, where he faced tough and dangerous decisions every day, had prepared him to stand his ground before the tenacious prosecutor.

Despite his highly publicized arrests and court cases, Max continued the subterfuge that his interest in breweries was only as an investor in real estate. As for what went on behind the closed doors of the beer plants he rented or leased, he claimed to have no knowledge. Of course he was the lessee of record when Lauer Brewery was raided several times, but he still insisted the illegal beer that was seized belonged to somebody else, not him.

Some obvious areas that Mulle failed to probe raise the question—was the hearing something of a sham, a cover for clearing the path leading to naturalization? Mulle asked about the size of Max's alcohol allotment when he ran Schuylkill Extract.

"Would you say it was a few gallons a month, or 1,500 gallons a month, or 200 gallons a month?"

Max said he had posted a $20,000 bond, as the government required, then continued, "I think the allotment was…"

Before he could finish, Mulle broke in with another question, "How long did you retain that permit?"

"Until I was told I had no right to it, and I surrendered it," Max answered.

Mulle did not return to the amount of alcohol Max bought from the government, nor did he provide figures from the division that distributed the alcohol. Hassel claimed his company "made all kinds of extract." Mulle did not ask him to be more specific, nor did he introduce any searching questions about the customers to whom Hassel sold extracts. Although Max claimed Berks Products was a chemical company, he could not remember the name of his chemist or what the formulas for making extracts were. He did remember the formulas were kept in a safe.

Mulle seemed intent on finding out where Hassel had earned his income, other than in his hometown. Max said he lived in the Sylvania Hotel in Philadelphia three or four days a week in 1927. Except for his later residence in the Elizabeth Carteret Hotel, Max denied ever having established residence outside of Reading. It is known that he rented a suite in the Ritz Carlton Hotel in Philadelphia, but that did not come out at the hearing. Max always claimed his activities in the Quaker City centered on real estate and financial business.

Mulle asked Max, "Ever been outside of the United States?"

"I don't think so," Max replied. This was a safe answer from a man who wasn't sure how much the government knew.

"Ever been to Canada?" Mulle pressed.

"I don't think so," Max hedged.

This line of questioning stopped there, leaving another dead end that dangled a reasonable question: When somebody goes to Canada or any other place outside the U.S., wouldn't he remember it? If Max did visit Canada, it's quite probable it was a working trip focusing on beer or alcohol.

When Mulle asked about Hassel's brewery connections, Max claimed his only interest was as a stockholder in various companies. He admitted the stock wasn't always in his name. His only involvement with Fisher Brewery, he testified, was through his holdings in Union Realty and Hyde Park Development companies. At another point in the hearing he admitted owning two thirds of the stock in the Fisher Brewery buildings. Mulle ask Hassel about two judgments for unpaid beer taxes entered by the government against Fisher Brewing Company, one for $79,300 and another for $99,840 in 1927.

"Do you recall addressing a petition to the judges at the Federal Court in Philadelphia in which you stated that you have never been connected in any way, directly or indirectly, with the Fisher Brewing Company?" Mulle asked.

"I do." Max said.

"You signed that petition?"

"That is right, sir."

"And swore to it?"

"I swore to it. I had nothing to do with the Fisher Brewing Company, and the Fisher Brewing Company was never engaged in illegal stock. I just simply owned the building."

Max said he bought the property from the Union Realty Company. Although his name never appeared on the deed he admitted owning 75 percent of the stock in a holding company, Hyde Park Development Company, owner of the building. Then in 1925 or 1926, Max said, he bought the rest of the Hyde Park stock. He admitted he sometimes used straw buyers when he purchased property.

When asked how much money he made in 1920, Max said he didn't know.

He probably didn't. With his widespread business interests even then it is doubtful he had bothered declaring income from all of them. He said he didn't remember whether he filed an income tax return. Mulle produced a tax form, with Max's signature, showing he admitted to $10,000 income from the sale of stocks and bonds, etc. "Now is that the sole item of income? Just how did you make that profit?" Mulle asked.

"I'm sorry but I haven't accounts of 1920," Max said. That very likely was true. Long ago he had dumped records he had kept of his cigar business and other enterprises. Profits and losses were filed away in his head. He had an accountant in later years, but not when he first started to climb the ladder. For the year 1920 the government placed Max's income at $15,000, stating he owed taxes on the $5,000 he hadn't declared.

Charlie Matten objected when Mulle started to review Hassel's income tax troubles in the mid-1920s that were settled with the government in 1929. Max admitted paying $150,000 to get out from under the original government claim that he owed $1.24 million in unpaid taxes on his income covering the years 1920 through 1924. "Did you plead guilty to those charges" in 1928, the prosecutor asked.

"I did," Max replied. "I went to Philadelphia and arranged with John R. K. Scott to represent me. During the later part of 1926 to 1928 there were constant negotiations with the government. We couldn't agree on any terms. So the final was that they just indicted me to come to some definite conclusion. Mr. Scott advised me to plead guilty. I objected to it. Mr. Scott told me there was an arrangement with the court, with the federal attorney, with the IRS commissioner in Washington that this thing would not be used against me, that it was a matter of form to get this thing out of the way. Naturally I pleaded guilty."

Edmund J. Wrigley, a special Internal Revenue agent, testified about a $102,000 loss claim Hassel declared on his 1930 return. This pertained to the final padlocking of the Fisher Brewery. Wrigley said that during his investigation he had Max backtrack the money trail from the time he bought stock in the brewery in 1921 to its closing in 1929. Wrigley recited a confusion of payments on mortgages and loans from Izzy Liever's Union Realty Company, plus transactions with Maurice Muchnick, Bill Moehler, and Wallace C. Fritz, sometimes straw owners. Wrigley said his agency did not agree with Hassel's calculations that the government, by closing the Fisher plant, had cost Max more than $100,000 in stock losses in 1929.

And so it went. Max stood fast on his claim that he was not a bootlegger, merely an investor. He named a Michael Levin as the last lessee of Fisher's, and he remembered visiting the brewery only once. That was at the request of two federal agents, he said:

"They told my brother they wanted to do business with me, wanted to deal with me with reference to the Fisher company. I told them I had nothing to do with the company, and didn't want to do business with them." He said he presumed the agents were interested in "merchandise going out of the plant."

He named Meredith B. Kerstatter and Paul C. Hurley as the Prohibition agents. The pair had appeared against Max in a 1927 bribery case which was thrown out by a federal judge for lack of evidence. Kerstatter was a government witness at the naturalization hearing. Charlie Matten's cross-examination exposed the agent's poor memory, and that certainly didn't help Mulle's case.

Several extended periods of testimony dealt with the Reading Brewing Company, Max again insisting he was merely a disinterested stockholder who had no influence in the manufacture of beer. He admitted having "a 50 percent interest in ownership of the brewery buildings, but not in the Reading Brewing Company." This was just so much double talk that frustrated Mulle as he tried to link Hassel directly to the production of illegal beer.

When Reading Brewery was known as the August Manufacturing Company it was operated by Prudent Products Company which leased the plant. The only lease Max admitted holding was the two-year, $2,500-a-month lease held by Frank Lauer. Hassel said he paid the rent at the Lauer Brewery from 1923 to 1925. But, he claimed, after only a month or six weeks of acquiring the lease, he sublet the brewery to Stephen Gierot who operated the Gierot Manufacturing Company. But because he was responsible for the original lease, Max said, he continued to pay Lauer the $2,500 rent each month. So, once again Max shielded himself with another layer of phony paper as the feds tried to trace who profitted from the manufacture of illegal beer.

After questioning Max about his connections with each of the three breweries, Mulle entered documents showing liquor violations against owners of each plant. Hassel was listed on government warrants as an official, if not an owner, of the Fisher, Lauer, and Reading breweries. Although some of these violations were eventually dismissed, Mulle managed to get them on the record "merely for the consideration of the court." He also questioned Max about his involvement with a Coal Region brewery. Again Max denied knowing the reported owner of the brewery or having anything to do with the application for a federal license. Mulle led Max through a series of questions until Matten finally heated up the courtroom with an objection: "It seems to me it is not fair to merely place on the record a lot of rumors."

Mulle retaliated by introducing a document showing Max Hassel and Waxey Gordon were involved in a bid to obtain a federal license for a brewery in Pittston, Pennsylvania. The straw owner, James J. Barrett, was refused a permit because Hassel and Gordon were believed to be the real operators of the brewery, the federal supervisor of licenses had testified at a hearing in Scranton. Such questionable evidence probably would not have been admissible in criminal court. But when licenses were at stake, personalities, suspicions, bribery, and politics were all factors in determining who passed the test and who didn't.

When Mulle completed his case, Charlie Matten recalled Max to testify about his more recent occupation. The client said for the past five years he was in the financial business. He said he was president of Berkshire Security Company in Philadelphia, a substantial firm that was currently prospering.

"I just simply finance people that are interested in various things such as hotels, possibly breweries, and other mercantile business," he stated. "I can mention quite a few of them in Reading."

He also told about his early career in the wholesale cigar business when he had a chain of cigar stores. As for his well-established credit with banks, Max claimed it was "to the extent of $30,000" when he was still a teenager.

"Are you interested in any charitable associations? If so, name some of them," Matten said. "Is there a loan company run for charity?"

"I would rather have somebody else answer that instead of me," Max replied.

And that opened the door for Matten to introduce a cast of respected Reading professionals as character witnesses. Matten hoped to engender the image of a Roarin' Twenties Robin Hood. Unabashed, these men of prominence polished the other side of the apple to show that Max was certainly much more than the tax-dodging scoundrel Mulle made him out to be. One after another they paraded before the three-judge panel extolling Hassel's generosity. They supported the rationale that if justice was to be served, Max's philanthropies must be weighed against his alleged crimes. To the man, these businessmen, merchants, lawyers, and educators denied any personal knowledge of Hassel's bootlegging activities, other than what they read in the newspapers.

Wellington M. Bertolet was the first character witness. As a member of the bar, Bertolet said he met Hassel on numerous occasions in the past six or seven years, only once involving a business matter. On all other occasions it was to solicit funds from Max for charitable causes. William Bitting, a manufacturer of hosiery and machinery, and a director at Reading National Bank, said from what he observed in their banking dealings, he believed Max would be a very good citizen of the United States.

George Pomeroy Jr., president of Reading's largest department store, re-viewed his long acquaintanceship with Max. Among the numerous cash boys his company employed, Pomeroy testified, his father, the founder of the business, chose Max to be his personal messenger. As for the adult Hassel, Pomeroy recalled numerous occasions when Max was billed for merchandise consigned to needy individuals or charities. He reiterated Hassel's interest in contributing unsolicited donations to be used for the education of many Reading teenagers of all faiths.

"Honest and dependable," was the merchant's assessment of the man who badly wanted to become a U.S. citizen. Pomeroy, too, cast a "yes" when asked by Matten if Max deserved to be allowed to realize his dream.

Even more supportive of Max's attitude toward education was Thomas Evans, a Carpenter Steel foreman and president of the Reading Board of Education. He stated:

"Well, my connection with Max Hassel was this: I met him and I know he was very much interested in the welfare of children of our schools. I met him at different recreational centers, especially at our public lectures at Southern Junior High School and at pageants at the

Senior High School. I know he has paid tuition fees for quite a number of young men and women to take up college courses."

And like other witnesses before and after, Evans regarded Max as a strong candidate for citizenship.

When Mulle cross-examined William Jenner, a local general contractor, what he knew about Max's reputation as a manufacturer of beer, the witness replied:

"I wouldn't answer that question personally. We hear a lot of fairy stories about a man. I only speak of what I know."

Other character witness said they knew Max only through dealings in the financial or hotel business, but none came forth to connect him with beer. Max had a loyal following. In their statements, his charity far outweighed the illegal beer he made and distributed. If it meant stretching the truth to help their generous friend, then so be it.

Probably those who gave him the strongest personal endorsements were the men who knew him best—a pair of local lawyers, Manny Weiss and Barney Hoffman. Weiss, who was appointed assistant district attorney in 1928, stated there had been no criminal complaints or charges against Hassel in the past six years. In his testimonial, Weiss stated:

"I have known the man for the past ten years. I know what the average citizen does for himself and for his community. I know of my own personal knowledge what Max Hassel has done, not only for the Jewish community but for the gentile community. I know that any man who is as well disposed as that certainly must make a good citizen of the United States. I have no personal knowledge of any violations of the law that he has ever committed, and I believe he will make an excellent citizen if this court gives him the opportunity to have his papers."

Weiss then gave a brief history of the Hassel Free Loan Society operated through the Kesher Zion Synagogue.

Barney Hoffman was an equally magnanimous advocate of the man he had represented on occasion. When Mulle asked Hoffman whether Max had been engaged in any Reading brewing operations in the past six or seven years, the criminal attorney said: "I know he has not, and I think I would be in the position to know."

Mulle asked, "How would you know that?"

"I have practiced around here, and know people who were engaged in that business. It would not take me very long to find out. I represent nine-tenths of them in the business."

There were no prosecution witnesses to testify about Max's presence in North Jersey for the past several years. Although Tom Dewey was certainly investigating Max as a subordinate to Waxey Gordon, Mulle did not choose to bring Hassel's more current activities to the judges' attention.

A week after the hearing, Mulle filed a petition opposing the admission of Mendel Gassel for citizenship. The government attorney declared in his brief:

"Although he (Hassel) was not violating the laws of the United States in such a way as to make him amenable to punishment, the Court states that the Prohibition law was a principle of our Constitution and the policy of laws, and that even though the petitioner professed sympathy with the national Prohibition Act, his conduct indicated a lack of such attachment."

At the hearing, Mulle had tried to paint a dark picture of Hassel's business dealings, but the evidence he submitted was at best, questionable. The judges, all well acquainted with Hassel's background, certainly knew how Max built his fortune. Robert Mays, of the three-judge tribunal, was often a weekend visitor at "The Farm." With his strong Pennsylvania Dutch accent, Mays was a regular customer at the Colonial Cigar Store on Court Street, buying his daily numbers slips. The cigar store was Max's message center. Max would snub the judge if they crossed paths on Penn Street, but he was a welcomed guest around the pool on the Hassel estate near Beckersville. For Mays, if not for Judge Schaeffer, it would have been easy to find plenty of flaws in Mulle's presentation of evidence.

The naturalization hearing was Max Hassel's final court appearance. It was also his last visit to Reading. Following the hearing, Hassel returned to Elizabeth. Safely ensconced in the Carteret Hotel, Max rarely, if ever, left the place again. The war was on. He knew he was on somebody's hit list, whether it be Dutch Schultz's, or The Commission's. Extra security measures were taken at the Carteret. Nobody could enter Hassel's suite without being recognized by the guard assigned to screen visitors to Room 824. But even the strongest castle is not impregnable.

15

You Can't Quit the Mob

Max Hassel lived under the sword of Damocles. He walked through the valley of death the last years of his life.

Wednesday, April 12, 1933

Harry Rhode was ready that morning to drive Max Hassel to Reading from Elizabeth. Work on his nine-hole golf course was progressing at The Farm, as was the building of his home for his family in Hampden Heights. And Max had other business matters to attend to at the Reading Brewery which was up and running again. But shortly before they were to leave the Carteret Hotel the boss changed his mind. "No, you go," Max told his driver, "I'll call you when I want to go home."

Rhode, an excellent wheelman, drove the boss' Lincoln at high speed over the New Jersey and Pennsylvania roads that were mostly two-lane and in need of repair after a harsh winter. Harry said Max postponed his return to Reading that day because he wanted to play cards with the boys. That's what he told Rhode. But he had other things on his mind more important than poker or gin rummy. He possibly thought better of leaving his headquarters, given the turbulence permeating his sphere of associates and competitors. The prohibition on real beer had been lifted but the transition was not going smoothly behind the scenes.

During the early hours of that spring afternoon, Hassel, Waxey Gordon, and Big Maxie Greenberg talked business in Room 824, the entrance to Max's six-room suite on the top floor of the Carteret's rear wing. There was serious discussion all week about threats made by

Dutch Schultz through his lieutenants. Schultz was in hiding in Brooklyn, dodging a subpoena issued by U.S. Assistant Attorney Thomas Dewey for unpaid income taxes. Other members of the Gordon syndicate were in and out of the apartment during the afternoon. Lou Parkowitz was stationed at the door, screening everybody who came in.

Even more worrisome than the Schultz problem, was information Max had received that other Jewish and Italian elements of the mob in Manhattan were planning a takeover of the entire beer and liquor industry along the East Coast as Prohibition wound down. Hassel had made it known that he would not become a partner in this ambitious enterprise. He had decided to go it alone, if necessary. He rejected any plan that would not allow him to become a legitimate brewer. Whether Greenberg and Gordon were of the same mind was questionable. They had more to lose than gain by joining the Luciano/Lansky clique since Gordon and Hassel breweries were licensed to make 3.2 beer, so why share their profits with the New York crowd? But the idea of going straight was contrary to the code by which they lived.

One of the mysteries of that afternoon was Big Maxie's movements from 2:30 to sometime after 4 o'clock. A taxi driver told police he drove Greenberg and two other men from the hotel to the Harrison brewery. About 4 o'clock, the same cabbie transported them back to the Carteret, he said. The taxi driver, George Hickman, claimed to know Greenberg by sight. He said Big Maxie went directly into the hotel on his return from Harrison. The other two lingered outside for a few minutes then entered the building, he said. There was some conjecture that they were bodyguards making sure nobody followed Greenberg up to the eighth floor. The Carteret barber said Big Maxie waved to him on entering the hotel about 4:10 o'clock. But another version developed by investigators was that Big Maxie never left the hotel. His bullet-proof sedan was not taken from the hotel garage that afternoon, employees told police. Doubts were raised that Greenberg would risk taking a taxi without his bodyguard when rival racketeers were believed to be gunning for him. The two strangers with Big

Maxie were said to be beer salesmen in some reports. Waxey Gordon would later admit to police that sometime during the afternoon he retired to Room 804 down the hall from Hassel's suite. Supposedly, Waxey was attending a more private meeting. Nancy Presser was a young but well-travelled mob prostitute. This day, allegedly, it was Waxey's turn to enjoy the 22-year-old Nancy's favors. Waxey later denied the matinee had been scheduled as an excuse to get out of the line of fire. Although he claimed he left the room to talk to some other people, investigators did not reveal who they were.

Max Hassel and Maxie Greenberg were shot and killed in the suite at approximately 4:30 p.m. Police said there were two gunmen. A positive reenactment of the murder scene was never established by investigators.

Lou Parkowitz told police he was in Room 821 at the time of the shooting. He claimed he was asked to leave the suite when Max and several others in the room began serious discussions. Parkowitz, on hearing gunfire, said he ran back to the apartment and found the dead bodies of Hassel and Greenberg. He said he passed several men running toward him in the hall as they fled the murder scene.

The lone door to the suite opened into a living room. Next was a room that had been converted into Hassel's office. Farther back were bedrooms, a bathroom and another room where Max had installed exercise equipment. Parkowitz told police he found Hassel's body face down on the floor near the office doorway leading to the living room. There were three bullet holes in the back of his head. Slumped over a closed rolltop desk in the office was Greenberg, shot five times in the chest and head. Parkowitz said he immediately phoned the hotel's front desk.

John F. Robertson, the hotel's assistant manager, took the call, then notified the Elizabeth police. Robertson said he awakened his napping boss, Pierre Kuneyl, who ordered Robertson not to go upstairs to the scene of the murders. Robertson ignored those orders when a hotel employee reported finding a pistol on a rear staircase.

Parkowitz was considered to be the major domo of Hassel's head-quarters. He was a seasoned veteran of the North Jersey subworld with important contacts. Among the several hats he wore were bodyguard, secretary, and middleman in dealings with Hassel's associates and competitors. Although a New Yorker, he became a familiar face at Hassel's country home near Beckersville on summer weekends. On this spring afternoon, however, even though *the heat* was on because of dire warnings from various factions, Parkowitz insisted he left Room 824 about ten minutes after 4 o'clock. Because Parkowitz was considered Hassel's security chief, his absence during the shooting that followed, made him a prime suspect in the plot.

Parkowitz identified the victims as Max Greenberg and Jimmy Feldman. Early rumors that a sub-machine gun was used in the murder were quashed when the Union County coroner's office said bullets from a .38 caliber blue-black "police special" had killed the pair.

After talking with hotel personnel, the police revealed the shooters evidently escaped down a flight of winding stairs around the service elevator shaft used to take trash and other things down to a rear entrance that opened into an alley. It was on these stairs that the pistol, still warm, was found between the fifth and sixth floors by the hotel worker. Police didn't learn about this gun till a week later.

Police said only $25 was found in Hassel's pocket. The small amount recovered, led many to wonder whether the killers, or others, robbed Max of a roll of thousands that he usually carried. In addition to the handgun in Greenberg's coat pocket, investigators found $1,734 in cash, plus a $2,500 check. When Maxie's clothing was examined, agents found a deputy sheriff's badge from Rensselaer County, New York. In one of the bedrooms there were several bottles of liquor, a barrel of beer, and ten sets of golf clubs. The costly pigskin golf bags might have carried more than golf clubs if the occasion merited it. Weapons of various sizes and firepower were sometimes stashed next to putters and drivers if a bodyguard was expected to do his job. As for important evidence found by the investigators, two filing cabinets and a small safe in Max's office proved to be the big prizes.

It was quite apparent the murderers caught Hassel and the boys with their defenses down. Police said eight half-filled glasses containing whisky and a couple of whisky bottles were on a round table in the office. It would appear there were plenty of witnesses to the shootings. Something that baffled police was a piece of cement, about the size of a brick, on the floor near Hassel's body. The solid, jagged object was certainly out of place in the well-furnished suite.

An autographed picture of Broadway star Ethel Merman was packed up with other evidence, but proved of no significance. Gordon, and his penchant for backing stage shows, might have given it to Max, although Ethel had signed it "To Mike, the best trombone player who has played for me."

In 1933, there was no television to bring viewers the latest spot news, and radio coverage was cursory at best. By 6 p.m. the first vague telephone reports about Hassel's murder had filtered back to Reading. In City Hall, Detectives John St. Clair and Jake Rapp received the first phone call from Elizabeth police. Not until 9 p.m. was his death verified to the general public when the early edition of the *Philadelphia Inquirer* reached Reading. The hometown residents found it hard to believe that their folk hero was dead. The *New York Times* carried the story in its early Wednesday evening edition, mistaking the real names of both victims: James Feldman, 33, and Joseph Greenberg, about 30. The Gotham newspaper had Hassel's age about right. Max would have turned 33 in twelve days, but Big Maxie was 41.

Even before Hassel was officially identified as one of the victims, a carload of relatives and henchmen was speeding toward Elizabeth from Reading. When Max's longtime friends, Charlie Dentith, Freddie Marks, and Harry Rhode heard Jimmy Feldman was dead, they notified Morris and Calvin Hassel. The five of them set out for Elizabeth immediately. With Rhode trying to set a speed record, his passengers questioned their own mortality. The Lincoln, chauffeured by a less than sober Harry, careened and jolted over narrow highways. Arriving in Elizabeth before midnight, the brothers and friends had a sleepless night trying to convince local authorities to release Max's body so he could be buried according to Hebrew tradition: before sundown of the first day after death. That was arranged Thursday morning but it wasn't until the afternoon that the body was entrained to Reading.

Claims may be true that never in the history of Reading was there a greater spontaneous outpouring of curiosity, and for many the feeling of great loss, than on that Thursday when the entire city awoke to the news that Max Hassel had been murdered. Few really knew Max intimately but gossip about his public persona was deeply etched in the city's psyche.

Imperfect heroes often possess a mystique that transcends that of the truly great in the minds of the masses. *Max is dead* washed like a tidal wave through the neighborhoods. Reading civic leaders far more deserving were memorialized, but with Max's death, it seemed a great era had ended. Fantasy, romance, hero worship were never more evident than when a Sinatra-like mob was drawn together to pay homage to the little man who defied the law but gave so much to the community. His passing left some feeling cheated that they would never know how the final chapters of his colorful life might have played out had he survived Prohibition.

When reports filtered out that Hassel's body would be taken to the Henninger Funeral Home, 229 North Fifth Street, the rush was on about 6 p.m. The corpse in a pine box was brought from the Franklin Street Station with police opening a path through the dense crowd. Inside the funeral home the corpse was hurriedly prepared for viewing.

At 7:30 p.m. the line forming outside began to move past Max's $2,000 brass casket. The crowd on Fifth Street continued to grow. The sidewalks on both sides of the street in the two blocks from Washington to Elm were clogged with mourners. Then the crush of eager viewers overflowed into Fifth Street, bringing traffic to a halt. Police

Commissioner Stanley Giles estimated the throng at 15,000. Giles assigned thirty policemen to keep a path open for vehicles.

Through an iron gate police admitted groups of twenty-five to thirty persons into the funeral home. Police estimated about 8,000 viewers passed by the gold appointed casket. The procession was halted at 11 p.m. Another 1,500 still hoping for a last look at the city's foremost celebrity of an unforgettable generation were turned away.

The next morning another large crowd gathered outside the Hassel home at 738 Franklin Street. Fred Marks was the doorman, admitting only close relatives and intimate friends. A steady stream of flowers and other gifts were delivered to the house. The body was removed from 738 at 1 p.m. and taken to Kesher Zion Synagogue for services. A gridlock of people quickly gathered at North Eighth and Court Streets.

Rabbi Max J. Routtenberg had the difficult task of keeping a shine on the public image of the wealthy bootlegger. The holy man was far better acquainted with the charitable Max than with the beerman Max striving for legitimacy in a world of deception and violence. A wonderful person, yes, but…Rationalization could not hide the manner of life that led to ill-gotten, if well-spent, wealth.

"There were really two Max Hassels," said the rabbi, "Each was the product of different environments."

After giving numerous illustrations of Hassel's generosity, Rabbi Routtenberg continued:

"There was one jewel in the Hassel diadem that shone brighter than the rest, and that was the commandment, Honor Thy Father and Thy Mother. There was never a more devoted son than Max Hassel. He not only worked for them in boyhood, but cared for them in later life, and has now left behind the Hassel Free Loan Society that will carry on his work. His family was the cornerstone of his life. He was not only a brother to his brothers and sisters, he was also a father."

Then speaking directly to Max's kin:

"You should keep in mind that Reading loved your brother. No greater tribute could have been paid him than that which was expressed by the thousands who passed by his body last evening and the crowd gathered outside the synagogue this afternoon. His was always the desire to help his fellow man. He did not want his wealth to be buried with him. He wanted his generosity to continue after his death. Max Hassel the glamorous figure is dead, shot by the bullets of an assassin. But Max Hassel the benefactor is not dead. His philanthropies will be carried on."

The funeral procession to what was then called the Green Tree area just east of Grill was made up of more than a hundred cars. If not the largest funeral in Reading's history, some oldtimers still claim those bragging rights to this day. The state police were out in force to handle the major traffic problem caused by the long line of cars in the funeral procession. Vehicles of the uninvited added to the congestion.

Max was buried in the old portion of the Kesher Zion Congregation Memorial Grounds next to the graves of his mother and father, Sarah and Elias. This area along Route 724 was known as Green Tree Hill. Paul Kantner who still lives with his wife Shirley, in Grill, recalls he was 6 years old that Friday when Max was buried:

"We were returning from market and the state police wouldn't let us up the hill even when we told them where we lived. The people and cars—never saw anything like it." Paul's father finally managed to get his family back to their farm after lengthy negotiations with the troopers.

It was Paul's father, Charles Kantner, who sold three acres of land to Kesher Zion in the 1940's. His farm was adjacent to the cemetery. A second section of Kesher Zion cemetery was dedicated in 1961 on the tract purchased from Charles Kantner. The remains of Max and his parents were relocated to a 40-foot square Hassel family plot just inside the entrance to the new KZ cemetery. Hassel's brothers, sisters and their husbands, are also interred there. A large Hassel memorial stone identifies the plot. Max was dead and buried but his remains did not rest in peace.

More than a thousand curiosity seekers roamed the cemetery the next day. One woman was caught trying to steal a marker from Hassel's grave. Others reached through a fence to grab dirt or grass at the burial site. Still another swiped leaves from one of the funeral wreaths. A New Jersey Protestant minister who said he was a close friend of Max's in Elizabeth, made the trip on Friday to pay his last respects.

A rumor that Waxey Gordon had slipped into town to attend his buddy's funeral was not verified.

Another piece of gossip whispered over the weekend spread the misinformation that Max's body was dug up and moved. Each telling of the tale seemed to add authenticity. So on Sunday, Rabbi Routtenberg issued a statement:

"In behalf of the Hassel family, I wish to state that rumors that Max Hassel's body has been removed from his grave to another location while a crypt will be built are without foundation."

16

The Aftershocks

E lizabeth and Union County police swarmed all over the Carteret Hotel the evening of April 12, 1933. They rounded up plenty of witnesses, but nobody would admit being present when Max Hassel and Big Maxie Greenberg were killed. A variety of reasons for leaving the murder scene were given by several gang members who admitted being there before the shooting started. If human sources were of little help, a small locked safe and two filing cabinets certainly provided the government with plenty of leads.

Early investigators tentatively explored the files, but after Union County Prosecutor Abe David arrived at the scene late Wednesday afternoon the cabinets were sealed, with orders forbidding anyone to browse until the next day. At the moment, David was more interested in finding somebody who could open the safe. Whisky glasses on the round office table were dusted for fingerprints. Before leaving for the night, David secured the suite with a police guard.

Federal investigators converged en masse on the Carteret the next morning. The U.S. Attorney's office, the IRS, and the Prohibition Agency each sent four representatives. The FBI sent two. Abe David, as the senior county law officer, gave the feds permission to examine the contents of the safe—if they could get it open. Since none of the early suspects, including Parkowitz, admitted knowing the combination, the safe was taken to the city police headquarters. A locksmith used a drill to open it.

The wealth of written material in the safe surprised and elated the investigators. Seized documents were said to contain names, places, and dates about Hassel's operation. The prize catch was a detailed report on the New York mob's plan to infiltrate all the distilleries and breweries on the East Coast. With all this data, U.S. Attorney General Cummings vowed that the government could keep the legal beer and liquor industries "free from corruption and graft."

On the down side, the probers found that full pages in a small red book had been ripped out. There were suspicions that the guarded safe had been entered during the night. The G-men believed the missing pages contained the names of local politicians and police who were on Hassel's payroll.

However, a list with the names of thirty federal agents was left untouched. Beside twenty of the names was written *OK*, indicating these were drys who could be bribed. Next to the other ten names were notations, *Do not deal.* The Prohibition enforcers interpreted this as further evidence that the locals were protecting their own, but only too happy to embarrass the feds. One of the "untouchable" names was that of Edward P. Mulrooney, former New York City police commissioner, and currently head of the New York State Beer Commission.

Ten days after the murder, the police list of thirty-seven thrity-seven dry agents found in Greenberg's pocket after he was shot. There was a notation that the Xs behind the names of seven agents meant they were "no good." Major Andrew W. McCampbell, New York Prohibition administrator, said most big bootleggers kept lists of agents, just as the agents kept files of them.

Another document showed that Hassel had raised $125,000 from wildcat brewery operators to bribe state and federal officials in an effort to oust John D. Pennington, Prohibition administrator for Pennsylvania, New Jersey and Delaware. The syndicate's breweries had permits to make near beer, but the unlicensed wildcats were regularly raided by the drys.

When Pennington learned of this he revealed that a United States senator from Jersey and two state legislators had tried to get him fired before and after the November 1932 elections. Some of the $125,000 was used by the mob to support friendly candidates. U.S. Senator Hamilton K. Kean of New Jersey claimed his reason for wanting Pennington discharged was because dry agents had unnecessarily ransacked a South Jersey Lions Club during a liquor raid.

Federal Judge William Clark, who seemed the most determined to bring the mob down, wanted the names of all those on the suspected bribery lists publicized. He also supported arguments to let the press publish the names of the racketeers who were revealed in Hassel's notes as leaders of the conspiracy to gain control of the beer and liquor industries. Justice Department prosecutors, however, thwarted his demands by arguing that potential cases against suspects would be jeopardized.

Gossip leaked to the press put the finger on Frankie Carbo as having been seen in the Carteret that afternoon. If this were true, nothing came of it at that time. But a few years later, Carbo was arrested outside the old Madison Square Garden in Manhattan and charged with the murders of Hassel and Greenberg. He was held in jail for almost six months but the charges were dropped "for lack of evidence." Carbo's history of beating murder charges continued for another ten years when he was a suspect in Bugsy Siegal's murder, but never charged. Shortly thereafter he became recognized as the czar of boxing. In 1961 he received a 25-year sentence for conspiracy and extortion. He tried to force a boxer to pay him part of a fight purse.

Theories abounded about Carbo as one of the Hassel-Greenberg hitmen. He was known to be a contract killer for Murder Inc., the mob's hired-gun wing. Carbo was a likely candidate to carry out the elimination of Gordon and his two principal associates as roadblocks to the Commission's grandiose scheme to take over their many beer assets. Several questions begged askance: How did Carbo get into Room 824? Was Carbo working both sides of the street? Was he there on the pretense of laboring for Gordon's gang? Did Waxey pay him to thwart Hassel's determination to sell beer the legal way? Possibly Gordon agreed with Luciano and company that it was more profitable to stay on the wrong side of the law. Many scenarios were suggested by investigators, but they never could bolt down a solid case.

Another supposition was that Greenberg was the real target because he was fond of chiseling his customers, then bragging about it. Hassel just happened to witness "Big Head's" murder, so he got it, too, was the thinking.

Although the murders sent shock waves throughout the underworld, no time was wasted on celebration or mourning. Within hours after Max and Maxie died, fleets of mob trucks converged on the Gordon-Hassel-Greenberg plants in Paterson, Harrison, Union City and Newark. Before sunrise the vats were drained dry. The trucks carried away 228 loads. Each load averaged 126 halves. Although the authorities did not identify the movers, it stands to reason the Gordon organization wanted to clean house before the police came snooping. However, reports circulated that the Schultz mob had emptied the breweries as Waxey and his followers went into hiding. A third possibility was advanced: the New York mob, having executed two of the big three beer barons, sent their trucks to pick up the spoils of war. Whoever the thieves were, metropolitan guzzlers hoisted more than a few Old Heidelbergs for the next several weeks.

Documents found in the safe revealed that a federal license had been issued to Hassel's Harrison Cereal Company less than a week before 3.2 beer became legal on April 7. That permit was also used to legitimize beer production in several other breweries under the syndicate's control, including the Reading Brewery which was operating under the name, the Health Beverage Company. Named as a middleman in the licensing process was Aaron Sapiro, a New York lawyer who had personal contact with A. V. Dalrymple, the national Prohibition director. Dalrymple admitted as much but denied being informed about the background of the Harrison Cereal Company's real owner, Max Hassel. As big names were being tossed about, there were news reports that President Roosevelt was vitally interested in the case. Indeed he was, but the growing scandal never implicated the White House.

Hassel was touted as the *shtadlan* who engineered the license trans-action with the government. In English, he was the fixer. Federal Judge Clark did his best to unravel the tangled mess that the murders had exposed. A lengthy legal battle now ensued as lawyers for the straw owners of the breweries appealed injunctions by the government to close down their profitable plants. After the vats were drained follow-ing the murders, the breweries started up again. Production continued while Judge Clark held hearings to decide what the disposition of the breweries would be. Even before Max was buried, the family coverup began. As soon as Morris learned that Max was dead he notified Manny Weiss, one of Hassel's local lawyers. Wilson Austin, a young Reading attorney in 1933, said many years later that Weiss and Morris immediately went to Reading Bank and Trust Company the next morning to unload as much cash as possible from Max's safe-deposit boxes. How much they took was never revealed, but when Internal Revenue agents arrived with a court order two weeks later, only a small amount of cash was found. Austin, who became a power in the Demo-cratic party, was always a fount of inside information.

But the feds didn't dally when they began the hunt for Max's hid-den cache in North Jersey. A safe-deposit box key was found in Max's hotel safe. But the bank where the box was located—nobody knew that. After trips to numerous area banks, the hidden treasure was dis-covered in the most obvious place: the Elizabethport Banking Com-pany only a few steps from the Carteret.

Two and a half weeks after the murders, representatives from Eliza-beth, Union County, and state and federal law enforcement were present for the grand opening. Edmund Wrigley, special agent for the U.S. Attorney's office, headed the dignitaries as they gathered around the largest safe-deposit box the Elizabethport Bank rented. Even in death, Hassel left the impression he always traveled first class. Wrigley refused to release to the press what or how much was found, but with more than a dozen men in attendance, newspapers announced that unofficial sources revealed $213,500 in cash, mostly in $1,000 bills, was recovered. In addition to money, another $50,000 in negotiable bonds was found. Manny Weiss represented the Hassel family at the much publicized opening.

Among the documents found in the box was a note for $50,000 Max had loaned to the brothers John J. and Charles J. Stamler, both attorneys. John was the former president of the New Jersey Bank and Trust Company of Newark. A victim of shady accounting practices and the Depression, the bank was closed in 1932 by New Jersey authorities. The brothers denied ever having borrowed money from Hassel amd claimed the signatures on the note were not theirs.

The guessing game about the size of Hassel's estate became popular at Reading gatherings. Published estimates ranged between $5 million to $15 million. Sources of these unverified ball-park figures that were guesstimates based on other unreliable sources claimed Max had had interest in fourteen to seventeen breweries in New Jersey and Pennsylvania. The bootleggers' bookkeeping systems were not set up to make it easy for prosecutors and tax investigators to learn much about their business. They kept track of how much was owed to them, and bank records gave some indication how they moved money around, but the trail was never easy to follow. Hassel was particularly careful to shield his hidden interests.

Supplier records were also falsified to minimize their dealings with the likes of Waxey, Boo Boo, The Muscler, Jimmy Feldman, and all the racketeers with a.ka.'s a yard long. Just how the Gordon-Hassel-Greenberg cartel shared profits was known only to them. They didn't answer to a board of directors, only to each other and to whomever owned a piece in these different breweries. Since ghost owners were listed on the titles of many of Hassel's real estate holdings, no realistic figure of his total estate was ever compiled for public consumption. But we can surmise that when he died he was in far better financial condition than most of those whose lives ended at the point of a gun. Since many racketeers were big spenders and died broke, there were those in

Reading who believed Max, too, spent as much as he made. There is plenty of evidence to prove that didn't happen.

The U.S. Attorney General's office placed a $21,000 tax lien against Hassel's estate. This action concerned Max's 1930 tax return when he listed a questionable $102,000 in real estate losses.

Max did not leave a will. The day before the Elizabethport box was opened, Morris Hassel made application for letters of administration. According to the laws of Pennsylvania, since Max died intestate, his two brothers and two sisters were his sole heirs. As the administrator of the will, Morris compiled a record of his brother's assets. Initially, he placed the value of Max's personal property at $10,000.

Several months later when the letters of administration were published, the total figure was just over $200,000, including ownership of an $11,000 property at 11 North Ninth Street. That left each sibling an inheritance of about $50,000. The letters of administration did not mention the Beckersville farm and golf course, a house at 1715 Alsace Road that was being built in 1933 for the Hassel family, or his hotel properties. Hassel's widespread interest in breweries and other real estate, titled under fictitious names, also were not included in his estate. Of course Morris knew the status of these investments, some of which eventually went into the Hassel Foundation.

In 1946, Morris and Calvin sold their interest in Old Reading Brewery, Inc., for $1.3 million to Reading Brewing Company controlled by the Fishman family. The brewing building was demolished in 1976, but other structures in the large complex are still in use at South Ninth and Laurel streets.

The Berkshire Hotel continued in business after Max was killed, but during an equity proceeding initiated by Farmers National Bank and Trust Company in December 1933, Judge H. Robert Mays named a receiver to take over its operation. The new home at 1715 Alsace Road, completed after Max died, was occupied by Fannie and Max Abramson, and Lena and Jules Cohen and their son Sarle. Calvin also moved in for a time. Max's heirs still own the Robeson Township property which includes the old stone farm house and pool and Green Hills Golf Course.

With Hassel and Greenberg gone, Tom Dewey concentrated his tax case on Waxey Gordon, who disappeared after his partners were murdered. A couple of weeks later, Dewey subpoenaed him to appear in court to face income tax evasion charges. Dewey's investigation was headed by Internal Revenue's Hugh Whittier, leader of the government team that sent Al Capone to prison. Dewey claimed Waxey owed $382,974 on more than $1.5 million in earnings during 1930 and 1931.

After the Elizabeth murders, Waxey holed up in the penthouse he leased in a Central Park West apartment house. Protected by a squad of gunmen, he dared not move beyond his terraced balcony above Central Park. The beer baron was paying the price for rejecting the mob's post-Prohibition strategy. Three weeks after the Carteret murders, the *Manhattan Evening Journal* exposed Waxey's hideout. The paper said Internal Revenue agents were tailing a Broadway showgirl, known to be one of Waxey's favorites, but the woman failed to rendezvous with the gangster.

Over the years, the penthouse had been a favorite gathering place for many of the actors and dancers in Broadway shows Waxey helped finance. Max Hassel was an occasional guest. But it was not party time in April 1933 when the country's biggest brewer was hiding behind locked doors in fear of his life. Revenue agents trying to serve a warrant couldn't get through Gordon's cordon of guards. The hotel elevator didn't even run to the penthouse.

Right after the *Journal* story appeared, Gordon was smuggled out, taken to the Catskill Mountains where his minions rented a hunting lodge at White Lake, N.Y. Two federal agents and five state policemen, acting on a tip, captured Waxey and two bodyguards in the lodge on Sunday, May 21. The dark-jowled gangster with a two-day growth was still snoring in bed, wearing white pajamas at 10:30 a.m. when taken into custody. The great man who had made and spent millions was less than a heroic figure as he sat up grumbling, "What's it all about?" then reached for a cigar and chewed on it. A large roll of bills "in the thousands" was confiscated.

Local residents had suspicions about the tough-looking, very private trio with the big new automobile who paid $1,500 to rent the eight-room lodge. They were happy to see the strangers carted away. Waxey's only complaint was about being fingerprinted and photographed at a state police barracks. "If I knew you was gonna take my picture, I'd have taken a shave," he groused.

When he was returned to New York City, the 46-year-old celebrity gangster claimed he had paid his income taxes the previous two years. And as for his disappearance in White Lake, that was just a normal vacation trip. He admitted being in the Carteret at the time of the murders:

"I heard a noise around 4:15 that afternoon." he stated. "It sounded like breaking glass or someone dropping dishes." He said he rushed out of the bedroom and joined the stampede of gangsters fleeing down the hall on hearing reports that his partners were shot. His interrogators weren't buying that story. He insisted he was NOT in the room when Max and Maxie were killed. "If I was in that room I'd have got the same thing," he insisted. "I'd have got the works, same as they did. They was both good friends of mine."

He denied being with a woman in another room of the suite. Big shot gangsters did not like being publicly linked to the likes of Nancy Presser. Three years later she was a principal witness in Lucky Luciano's prostitution trial. Lucky told the court it was laughable to think he would have anything to do with a druggie like Nancy. But it was her testimony that helped send him to prison.

Waxey's arraignment after being brought back to Manhattan was marked by a court aide's humorous slip. When the clerk handed Waxey a copy of an indictment, a scowl crossed the gangster's face.

"Here take this back," Gordon whispered. "You've got the wrong indictment. This one's for Dutch Schultz."

Indeed, the document was meant for Arthur Flegenheimer. The Dutchman, who was a fugitive at the time, would elude Tom Dewey's subpoena servers until November 1934 when he surrendered in Albany N.Y. He had been indicted three months before Waxey was, accounting for the mixup.

While in custody, Waxey tried to sell the Eureka Cereal Company. He negotiated with George Bissell, supplier of brewing ingredients whom he met in 1929 when he first took over the brewery in Paterson. Bissell, acting as a real estate broker, met with Gordon a few months before the gangster's trial. Bissell said he had a buyer willing to pay $600,000. Gordon turned down the offer.

Had Hassel and Greenberg not been killed, it is possible the mob could have made the transition into the post-Prohibition era with far less attention focused on it. Instead, a flurry of investigations were opened to find out who was issuing federal licenses to breweries that were controlled by criminals.

The government reported that more than forty high-level gangsters had taken cover as a result of the ledgers and papers found in Hassel's safe. Many were lying low to stay out of the line of fire between the Gordon and Schultz gangs. Several Prohibition agency officials would have liked to disappear for a while, too, as they passed the buck from one department to another in the licensing probe.

Starting in May, hearings were held in Newark federal court to determine ownership of the newly licensed breweries operated by the syndicate. The Harrison Beverage Company was selected by federal prosecutor Norman Morrison as the first target in his quest to prove numerous breweries were controlled by racketeers. Dozens of witnesses were called to testify over a period of several weeks. Like the ghosts they were, those who claimed ownership were easy to see through.

Reginald C. Samson testified that he was secretary-treasurer and general manager of the Harrison plant. He said he lived in Drexel Hill near Philadelphia, therefore he wasn't too familiar with day-to-day operations. Samson claimed Hassel was merely a beer distributor, not owner of the plant. Joseph Oschwald, a beer salesman who claimed to have been on the Harrison board of directors since 1930, testified he wasn't sure who was in charge, how many employees there were, or the size of the payroll. The alleged company president and vice president were never located.

Prosecutor Morrison introduced telephone records showing that Frederick Dihlman, the burly Harrison brewmaster, had received many calls from the Carteret headquarters of Hassel in the weeks preceding the murders. Dihlman claimed the calls were not about the beer business—they were from Lou Parkowitz who wanted racing bets placed with a bookie Dihlman knew. In an affidavit, Parkowitz offered the same flimsy alibi—anything to prove Hassel was not the big boss the government claimed he was.

When company attorneys filed for an injunction to bar the government from shutting down the brewery, a federal judge in Philadelphia rejected the petition because he agreed that Samson, Oschwald, and other claimants were mere "blinds," not the real owners or board members.

The Harrison Brewery's license was revoked and the company was given until the end of July to halt production. But the remnants of Gordon's mob wouldn't quit. Final revocation of the Harrison license was again delayed on the last day of the month when counsel for the brewery presented an affidavit from Lou Cohn. He did not appear in court. Although under indictment for tax evasion, as a fugitive he had dodged subpoena servers for almost three months. Now believed to have a financial interest in the Harrison plant, Cohn claimed in his affidavit that he was in Cleveland the day government witnesses said he was seen in the brewery. That was the day his bosses were murdered. Brewery workers had told government investigators that they thought "Blackie" (Cohn) was the owner, judging from the way he gave orders to everybody. Cohn also denied he had any interest on the Harrison Brewery.

In the final session of the long revocation hearing, James Doran, U.S. commissioner of industrial alcohol, accepted the recommendation of the board of review he had appointed that the Harrison permit be revoked and closure of the brewery was ordered.

Running parallel to the Harrison hearing was another court review of ownership of the Reading Brewery. This lengthy proceeding was held intermittently in Philadelphia from late June to August.

When Hassel filed for a federal beer license in March 1933, the Health Beverage Company was on the list of breweries that would be covered by the permit. Health Beverage was in reality, the Reading Brewery. At that time Sam Lunine was the latest in a long line of straw-men who had been listed as owners of the brewery. When the license covering Health Beverage was approved, the brewery was under Lunine's name. Since the government was quite sure the Hassel family still owned the brewery, revocation of the permit was initiated.

Affidavits were taken and witnesses were subpoenaed to appear in federal court. Again telephone slips were introduced to show the heavy flow of calls between Hassel's headquarters in the Carteret Hotel and the Health Beverage Company in Reading.

One of the first affidavits mentioned in court was supposedly taken from Reading Fire Chief Harry Brown. After the government released a report that Brown claimed to have seen members of the Hassel family during a visit to inspect the Reading Brewery, the chief denied he ever made such a statement. He admitted inspecting the brewery but the only official he saw there was Sam Lunine. A few days later he was summoned to Philly to testify in court. He again denied telling Prohibition agents that he saw Morris and Calvin Hassel, and Max's brother-in-law, Max Abramson, in the brewery. According to Chief Brown, he felt Max Hassel's public image was "50-50 good and 50-50 bad." Asked to explain, he said:

"Max's charitable side was the good but he was a general sport." Max was a known gambler, he said.

John H. Missimer, engineer of the brewery's ice plant, further tested the credibility of the Prohibition investigators by denying he told them he saw Max's car parked outside the brewery. L. J. Miller, president of Miller Printing Company, testified it was Lunine who had given him a contract for beer barrel labels. Sam White and Warren Heddens, the government investigators, either submitted forged statements, or underestimated the loyalty Readingites felt toward Max Hassel.

Lunine was on the witness stand for three days trying to convince government prosecutor Randolph Shaw that he, not Hassel or Max's friends and family, controlled Health Beverage Company. When Shaw asked him, "Isn't it a fact that five telephone calls were made that afternoon from your brewery to the Elizabeth Carteret Hotel?" (The day of Hassel's murder.)

"Not that I know of," Lunine replied.

Sam offered some telling statistics. He said since he took ownership of the brewery in 1931, gross receipts from near beer produced at the plant totaled only $900. Since April 1933 when 3.2 beer became legal, he said, his profit was approximately 15 percent of the gross receipts, or roughly $105,000. Taxes consumed nearly half of his gross receipts. He paid nearly $300,000 in taxes to the federal government and $50,000 to the state out of receipts of $740,000.

David Brodstein testified that his brother-in-law, Louis Cohn, financed his interest in the brewery's bottling works. He said Cohn paid for the machinery in the bottling plant and persuaded him to obtain a bottling concession from Lunine. Throughout the revocation hearings for several Hassel breweries, Cohn's name frequently was mentioned as a top lieutenant of Hassel.

As the case dragged on, the defense continually presented witnesses who backed Lunine's claim that he was indeed sole owner of Health Beverage Company. Eight employees and a neighborhood coal dealer swore by Lunine. The prosecution accused the defense of stalling. But the big guns were yet to come. Near the end, Berks County District

Attorney John P. Wanner took the stand and offered what could be considered a eulogy for Max Hassel:

"He was a public benefactor. He had helped the poor and oppressed and was a champion of the needy. In his later days he bore the title of 'beer baron.' But we of Berks County are wet, and don't hold anything like that against him."

Wanner's assessment of Berks Countians' attitude about illegal beer was mirrored almost twenty-five years later by Ralph Kreitz when he appeared before the Kefauver Committee that was investigating organized crime. Ralph claimed candidates couldn't get elected to public office in Reading if they opposed illegal gambling.

Others who appeared to offer ringing testimonials were Harry D. Lebo, clerk of Berks County Criminal Court; the Rev. A. O. Eshelman; Major Joseph B. Eisenbrown of the Pennsylvania National Guard; Oliver Focht, Berks County deputy sheriff; and 29 others who signed laudatory affidavits. These plaudits did little to resolve ownership of Health Beverage, but the government certainly got an earful about the home folks' opinion of the late Max Hassel.

It appears that the findings of the federal review board were turned over to the Pennsylvania Alcohol Permit Board. At a closed hearing on August 15, the permit board announced the revocation of the Health Beverage permit would be held in abeyance. It was stipulated that the company could continue to make 3.2 point beer, but if the board obtained proof that the Hassel family or its agents were connected with the plant, Lunine would voluntarily surrender the permit or waive his right to oppose revocation.

After his arrest in May, Waxey Gordon felt he was safer in Manhattan's Federal Detention Center than on the street, so he declined to pay the $100,000 bail charge. Gordon's gang suffered along with the boss. They were a faithful crew, but since the Carteret murders, they knew Dutch Schultz and other Manhattan gangsters wanted to finish the job of destroying the New Jersey beer cartel. These antagonists did not believe in halfway measures. Lopping off the head of a rackets gang did not kill the body. Since Gordon was no close friend of Luciano and associates, some believe Lucky, Louis "Lepke" Buchalter, Abe Zwillman and Meyer Lansky all might have had a hand in wiping out the Jersey mob. The Lansky-Gordon feud went back more than ten years.

One spinoff of Max Hassel's murder was a Manhattan chase scene worthy of a Jimmy Cagney gangster movie. The Gordon gang initiated this round of the war three days after Waxey's capture Crowds were pouring out of Broadway movie theaters south of Seventy-Ninth Street on a warm spring evening. A window-shopper was viewing a shoe display when a bullet grazed his head, knocking him to the ground. The roar of speeding cars and gunfire turned heads. An expensive sedan was racing north on the Great White Way. A second light-colored car pulled abreast, its occupants directing tommy gun fire into the larger car. A nurse on the sidewalk went down, shot through both hips and the stomach. For two blocks the gangster drivers fought for position until the big sedan pulled ahead. Another woman pedestrian was wounded, a slug in her back at Eighty-First Street.

The car from which the firefight started ended the chase by turning east into one-way west traffic on Eighty-Second Street, forcing oncoming cars onto the sidewalk. The target car, now riddled with bullet holes, continued to 84th Street where the driver lost control, crashing against a traffic island railing. Its two bleeding occupants fled, leaving a pearl gray fedora behind. The car, decorated with eleven bullet holes, was equipped with inch and a half thick bullet proof windows, padded sides, and a steel roof. Steel jacketed bullets had been fired into the chase car that was abandoned not far from the shooting.

Backfires from a truck on Eighty-First Street that crossed Broadway just after the mobsters' cars passed by, further heightened fears that the vehicle was somehow involved in the shootout. Police seized three men on the truck for questioning before releasing them. Ironically, the vehicle was hauling a load of toy pistols.

The three wounded victims were rushed to the hospital. The nurse, 45-year-old Mrs. Sadie Fortine, was hospitalized for two months. Injuries to the other two were not serious. Police theorized that the would-be assassins were Gordon men trying to pick off Schultz near a bar he frequented. A police official was quoted:

"If Dutch Schultz were to try on the gray fedora hat, we are willing to bet it would fit him. It stands to reason that no gang is going to take a chance and try to put some punk on the spot in that congested place. They would be crazy to take the risk."

The outbreak of mob killings, starting with Al Lillien's on March 23, continued for the next three months. Thirty-four gangsters met violent deaths during that period, with Gordon's organization practically decimated. It is interesting to note that Dutch Schultz was hiding from the tax agents and Waxey Gordon was in jail, but that didn't diminish their soldiers' taste for battle. Schultz usually could be found at his favorite pleasure spots, often visiting Polly Adler's bordello. But for some curious reason, the Manhattan cops and Tom Dewey's investigators never managed to locate him.

Famous names linked to Max Hassel kept popping up as various investigations continued after the twin murders. The most bizarre story to hit the headlines was not mob-related. The tale was told during a criminal trial in Washington, D.C., for Gaston Means, labeled "the greatest liar since Baron Munchhausen," a German legendary hunter/soldier noted for stretching tales of exploits beyond belief.

Gaston Means was an infamous con man, a rotund and voluble former Justice Department agent who got caught trying to parlay the Lindbergh kidnapping into a big score. His pigeon was Mrs. Evelyn Walsh McLean, a close friend of Charles Lindbergh and his wife. The wealthy socialite offered a large reward for information leading to the recovery of Lindbergh's little boy who had been snatched from his New Jersey home in 1932. Means told Mrs. McLean that he had a contact who knew the kidnappers and where the toddler was being held. For $100,000 he could obtain that information and recover the child, he told the gullible society lady. Actually, he walked off with $104,000. The body of the victim was eventually found. Means was tried and convicted of defrauding Mrs. McLean and received a fifteen-year prison sentence.

In May 1933 he went to trial a second time for conspiring with Norman "The Fox" Whitaker for trying to inveigle an additional $35,000 from Mrs. McLean. This time Means outdid himself, surpassing even the wild tales he fabricated the first time around. At this second trial the secret operative extraordinaire, Communist hunter, and convicted swindler shocked the nation by claiming the small body Lindbergh had identified as his son, was really a *plant,* and the real child was still alive. The next bomb he dropped was that he would name the kidnappers. This cunning fellow obviously kept up with the news because he selected a pair of dead men as the alleged villains.

With a round, straight face, Means stated Max Hassel and Big Maxie Greenberg pulled off the evil deed when they were delivering three bottles of beer to Lindbergh's home. They saw the 20-month-old Charles Lindbergh Jr. unattended, so they grabbed him and fled. And the cash found by the government in Hassel's Elizabethport Bank safety deposit box was actually Mrs. McLean's money. That fairy tale fooled nobody.

Prosecutors introduced evidence that the money found in Hassel's safe deposit box was in dominations of $50 and $1,000. The McLean money was paid in $10 and $100 bills.

The roly-poly liar then feigned surprise when the prosecutor said Hassel and Greenberg had been killed two months earlier. That's why, Means reasoned, there had been no answer to a letter he sent just ten days ago urging Hassel to come to Washington and testify in his defense. For being the most creative liar in recent court history, Gaston was awarded with another two years in prison.

An affidavit signed by Henry Mulle, the IRS examiner, was introduced during the Harrison Brewery license revocation hearings. Mulle's affidavit reviewed testimony taken at the IRS hearing in March. Norman Morrison, assistant attorney general, perusing the affidavit said Hassel was a "tax dodger, a man who had defrauded the government of large amounts of taxes and not to be trusted with a permit."

At this hearing the name of Jack Dempsey was introduced. From a telegram found in Hassel's safe the day after he was killed, the trail led back to the former heavyweight boxing champ when a former partner of Dempsey's wanted to get a concession to distribute Old Heidelberg beer in the south. Dempsey told the ex-partner, Walter Kirsh, to see Abe Lyman, a popular New York bandleader. Lyman told Kirsh to call Mr. Sherman at Harrison Brewery. A meeting was arranged at Waxey Gordon's Hotel Picadilly in Manhattan where Kirsh and Maxie Greenberg met. Big Maxie agreed to put Kirsh's name on the waiting list which was rapidly growing as 3.2 beer was about to become legal. Actually, Hassel had no role in this nonbinding oral agreement, and Dempsey was merely a twice-removed middleman. But when the story broke, the local headline read, *DEMPSEY NAMED IN MAX HASSEL BEER PURCHASE.*

When Waxey Gordon was indicted for income tax evasion on April 27, 1933, it seems reasonable to believe that Max Hassel and Big Maxie Greenberg also would have faced charges had they lived. Thomas Dewey had been compiling a case against Gordon for more than two years, so how could he not have caught Max and Maxie when he cast his net? Since lesser lights were also indicted, it seems certain the 31-year-old chief assistant U.S. attorney would have gone after Gordon's partners. Louis Cohn was indicted, along with Sam Gurock, another of Waxey's top assistants.

Cohn and Gurack had access to numerous bank accounts under various ghost names: James Henderson, J.B. Cowen, J. Alexander, and Murry Luxemberg. And the feds believed Gordon's money was hidden in those accounts. Like Gordon, who ran when initially indicted, Cohn and Gurack also fled, and were still fugitives when Waxey went to trial in November of that year.

Four months before the trial, Waxey's attorney petitioned the court for a bill of particulars showing why Dewey claimed Waxey had been earning $1 million a year. Was he selling whisky, beer, or tea—what business was he in? It didn't matter, Dewey argued, "I do not care to think whether he sold whisky or tea. What I know is that he had an income and that no tax was paid on it."

Shortly before the trial, Dewey mentioned that four witnesses he had been counting on to help prove his case against Gordon had been killed. He refused to reveal names, but the *New York Times* reported the casualty list included Maxie Greenberg; William Oppenheimer, a Gordon beer salesman, killed the day before he was to appear before the federal grand jury; Abe Durst, a Gordon beer salesman killed with a "squealer" slash on each cheek the day before he was to be served a subpoena, and Murray Marks, another Gordon henchman killed the previous Thursday in the Bronx.

If Dewey actually planned to use Greenberg as a prosecution witness, this certainly would offer a motive for Big Maxie's murder. However, nobody ever enlarged on the *Times'* report that came from an unnamed source. The theory that the Hassel-Greenberg rubout was an inside job gains credibility if Waxey believed that one of his closest associates had been turned. No such scenario was developed when Dewey laid out his case against Gordon in court.

Dewey, as Gordon's trial began on November 11, told the jury he would call 150 of the 200 names on his witness list. He talked about many of Gordon's records being destroyed and replaced by phony documents, about witnesses whose veracity was questionable because they had been intimidated and threatened, and about Gordon's lavish spending over the years. Federal Judge Frank J. Coleman said Waxey would be locked up each night during the trial and the jury would be secured in a nearby hotel.

As the trial progressed, Dewey had bank managers twisting in the witness chair trying to justify their indifference to letting racketeers deposit dirty money in their banks. Brewmasters testified to the huge profits being made by Gordon, and merchants and salesmen told tales about dealing with Waxey and his cohorts. The defendant's life was laid bare, from his arrests as a teenage pickpocket to his rise to emi-nence in New York's underworld.

A few days into the trial, Dewey was promoted to U.S. attorney of New York's Southern District.

Robert Dalzell, a member of an established Paterson trucking firm that hauled malt and hops for Gordon's brewery there, testified that he was ordered by "Blackie" (Lou Cohn), to destroy his company's books after Waxey was indicted. Dalzell said he then prepared a phony set of ledgers that Internal Revenue seized. Dalzell said Blackie was autho-rized to make bank deposits under phony names, and withdrawals.

Only when Gordon took the stand in his own defense was Max Hassel's name prominently mentioned. After listening for more than a week how he operated his multimillion dollar bootlegging empire for several years, Waxey claimed he was just a hireling. He testified that Jimmy Feldman (Hassel) and Maxie Greenberg were the real beer bar-ons; he merely took orders from them. His pay was only $300 a week, he stated. He already had admitted leasing a Manhattan apartment for $6,000 a year, buying $3,000 automobiles, and spending thousands of dollars on clothes and adornments for his apartment. To protect against golfing accidents he had taken out a $30,000 insurance policy. His wife, Leah, liked nice things, he claimed, which accounted for his extravagant spending.

He said he mourned the deaths of his two close friends, Max and Maxie, but denied knowing who killed them. But they, not him, ran the organization, he insisted. If the jury was to believe him, Waxey was just a 47-year-old married man with children who wanted the best for his family. By taking the witness stand, he had to expose his long crim-inal record. But he denied being responsible for the deaths of rival brewery owners who were killed during the early 1930s when he was earning millions of dollars a year, according to the government's inves-tigators.

The jury believed Tom Dewey when he said the evidence proved it was Waxey Gordon, not Hassel and Greenberg, who headed the biggest beer organization in the country. Testimony appeared to point to Hassel as an operations and contact man, with Greenberg closely linked to gang enforcement. Hassel had the polish and smarts to deal with politicians and suppliers, while Greenberg was more experienced in extortion and keeping friends and foe in line.

Gordon was sentenced to ten years in a federal prison and fined $80,000. A few days after the trial, Gordon's teenage son was killed in a traffic accident while returning to a military school. No foul play was suspected.

As for Louis Cohn and Sam Gurock, the co-defendants in Gordon's tax case, they were on the run at the time of Waxey's trial. A document from the National Archives obtained sixty-eight years later indicated prosecution of that pair ended with Gordon's conviction. It also showed that Louis Cohn was as creative as Max Hassel in the mob tradition of using phony names. He later returned to Reading.

Many former bootleggers and gamblers explained away their illegal pasts by insisting they were just trying to make a living. They admitted to being racketeers but denied they were gangsters. Their definition of *gangster* was a violent criminal who didn't care who got hurt as long as he got his share.

Some of Max Hassel's staunchest defenders were respected community leaders who offered veiled assessment of only half the man. But even those who grudgingly admitted he was a racketeer never pegged him as a gangster. Like so many contemporaries, Max violated the Volstead Act on a daily basis for more than thirteen years. He made millions, probably bribed hundreds on the government payroll, and was associated with crooks of the worst stripe. In future decades when Reading's notoriety as a corrupt city gained it national prominence, who could judge to what extent Prohibition's pollution continued to clog the political system? Max certainly must be included among the foremost polluters. But he shouldn't be omitted from its list of do-gooders.

When Waxey Gordon chanced to take the witness stand, Tom Dewey skinned him alive. If Hassel had survived and chose to testify, his past performances seem to indicate he wouldn't have rubbed his thumbs, squirmed on the witness stand, or barely could be heard as was the case with Waxey. The jury might have weighed his record as a racketeer against the esteem he was accorded as a humanitarian. To this day, the Hassel Foundation donates hundreds of thousands of dollars to charities annually. If the word *criminal* applies, Max Hassel was an uncommon one.

In books about Prohibition, Max Hassel has been little more than a footnote. Although the Internal Revenue ranked him among the nation's top tax dodgers, he managed to keep a low-key, nonviolent profile all through that ruthless era. Only in his hometown could he be considered well-known. Though often a shadowy figure, he was revered. It's too bad he got caught in the crossfire of warring mobsters. Had he lived, he might have faded into genteel prosperity as just one of the many wealthy survivors of the nation's "Great Experiment."

17

Almost Seven Decades Later

I t never ends. I thought I had obtained just about all the information I could about Max Hassel after nine years of looking in every direction. Although I knew there were holes in the story that I had been unable to fill, I felt I wasn't going to uncover further important facts.

In early fall of 2001, I received an e-mail from a friend in New Jersey. "Run out and buy the September issue of *Gentlemen's Quarterly,*" Fred Tamarri wrote "there's a story about Max Hassel." *Gentlemen's Quarterly?* Was this men's fashion magazine doing an article on fashion plates of the past? No, Fred indicated, there's a guy in Florida who claims he killed Max Hassel.

My math skills are limited but I immediately figured the guy would have to be close to a 100 years old. Before I bought the magazine I was very skeptical about what I would find. But there it was on Page 330 with a full-page photo of the man who admitted, guardingly, to killing Max Hassel. His name—Joe Stassi.

At 94, Stassi was still getting around on a walker. He was lucid and willing to talk about his long career as a gangster. It will be remembered that Joe leased an apartment on the seventh floor of the Carteret Hotel, just below Hassel's suite. He and Max had become fast friends, often chatting about life in general during the exciting and dangerous fading days of Prohibition. Joe was among the many gangsters questioned after Hassel was killed, but he never appeared to be a strong suspect.

About the time of Max's murder, Stassi was establishing himself as the first dog track operator in New Jersey. He claimed he ran the track at Linden a few years without a license because he paid off local and state police. Then the state closed him down because a new law limited parimutuel betting to horse racing.

Also in the early 1930s he married Frances Paxton, a beautiful former Miss California. They met in a New York nightclub where Frances was performing with a dancing trio. Stassi steadily moved up in the mob until he became a casino partner with Santo Trafficante in Havana. Trafficante was head of the Florida Mafia. When Fidel Castro ousted General Fulgencio Batista at the end of 1958, Joe soon headed back to the mainland, minus his casino investment. As U.S. Attorney General Bobby Kennedy launched his anti-Mafia crusade, Joe went into hiding for a few years.

When he turned himself in to face drug charges, he was sentenced to forty years in a federal prison in 1966. While in prison, Joe became friendly with Richard Stratton, also serving eight years on drug related charges. They remained friends, having breakfast with a known organized crime figure. Although his wife of almost 65 years was ill with cancer, he was ordered back to the Metropolitan Detention Center to serve another year. Frances died while Stassi completed his sentence.

Free again, Joe sold his Brooklyn house and resettled in Florida. In his Miami home he told Stratton, now a writer, of his early life in New York and the disappointment of his Sicilian immigrant parents when he got caught up in the street life of the Lower East Side gangs.

"My ambition was always to be a gangster, a gunman, whatever you want to call it," Joe admitted.

He certainly was not a well-known name to organized crime historians. By his own account he was an independent who was not a member of any Mafia family but a friend of and worker for several. In the 1960s he was convicted on narcotic charges, but he claimed the government framed him. Arnold Stone, a government attorney with the Justice Department's Organized Crime Section of the Criminal Division, told Stratton there was no vendetta by Bobby Kennedy.

As Stassi tells it, he and Joe Kennedy had once shared the same mistress in the same Manhattan hotel. When Kennedy found out, he ordered the hotel management to evict Stassi. Joe left. The Kennedys eventually evened the score by sending him to prison on a trumped up charge, according to Joe. It was Stone's opinion that Stassi now admitted being responsible for headline murders because he would rather leave a legacy of hitman than dope peddler.

Stassi had served most of his sentence in federal prisons by the time he met Stratton. When his new acquaintance uncovered information that helped Joe gain an early release, he was forever grateful. And out of this friendship, Joe told the writer about his association with Max Hassel.

Stratton learned that despite the lack of any published accounts of Joe's life of crime, he was well known to the FBI. He was too well acquainted with all the notorious New York gangsters for government sleuths not to have been familiar with some of his adventures.

During the first interview he had with Stratton, Joe disclosed inside revelations about organized crime from its inception up into the 1960s. His personal contact with all the major gangsters read like a Mafia Who's Who. But he held back some of his own murderous activities.

Some months after Stratton returned to New York to organize the material Joe had given him, he received an urgent call from Florida. Joe was in the hospital being treated for a suspected heart attack. He wanted Richard to rush down so he could complete the story.

Stratton was very much surprised on his arrival at the hospital to find Joe waiting to be escorted home. The tough old guy didn't have a heart problem. He had fallen, bruising his ribs. But his resolve to unburden himself of past sins was still strong.

At home, with a cameraman recording his confessions, Joe laid a shocker on Stratton when he admitted engineering the assassination of Dutch Schultz.

As stated in the GQ article, "The Man Who Killed Dutch Schultz," Joe said Abner "Abe" Zwillman and Meyer Lansky gave him the contract to kill Schultz because they were afraid the uncontrollable Dutchman would carry out his threat to have Tom Dewey killed. Stassi said he subcontracted the job to Charlie "The Bug" Workman and Emmanuel "Mendy" Weiss. They carried out the assassination in Newark's Palace Chophouse on October 23, 1935. Workman, who eventually served twenty-three years in prison for the murder, died without revealing who paid him to knock off the Dutchman. Weiss was never indicted for killing Dutch Schultz but he was convicted in another murder and died in the electric chair.

As Stassi continued his interview with Stratton, he became more emotional when he said he was ordered by Mafia bosses to kill his best friend. He wouldn't admit the best friend was Max Hassel, but it was events leading to Hassel's murder that he wanted to talked about. Tears welled in old Joe's eyes as he recalled a scene that occurred a few years before the Dutch Schultz hit. Now bent with osteoporosis, he was a pitiful shell of the once hardened killer. He spoke distractedly about the shock and torment he experienced when ordered to kill a close pal. He paused, rubbing his eyes as he explained what it meant to be a Mafia hitman: you subjugated your personal feelings or risked losing your own life.

It was early April 1933 when he was summoned to a Manhattan meeting with the mob's hierarchy. Whatever the assignment, he expected it to be big, befitting the rank of his hosts. Joe was aware that the New York mob was at odds with the Gordon/Hassel/Greenberg gang as the prohibition on beer was about to end. But he had no inkling of what was about to be laid on him by Meyer Lansky, Joe Adonis, and Abe Zwillman. These were three of the most powerful men in the mob. Joe knew whatever they told him to do, he better do it.

The orders were short and direct: kill Max Hassel and Maxie Greenberg.

This blockbuster, following the five-star bulletin about the Schultz rubout, left Stratton wondering where all this was going. He sputtered, "I thought you were close to Max."

"You don't listen!" Joe spouted in his raspy voice. "That's what I'm trying to tell you."

Joe's anger spilled over. For decades the mob's indifference to fellowship, its cold approach to business regardless of personal relationships, festered in his mind. His voice was barely audible as he talked about that day almost seven decades ago when he faced up to three of gangland's most formidable characters.

Joe should have known better than question his orders, but the shock of hearing that he must kill his best friend was so unsettling that he blurted:

"Kill Max Hassel? Why? Max is no more of a threat to you than a cockroach."

Implanted in Joe's memory was the angry response from Adonis:

"Yeah, well. That's all he is, a cockroach, so kill him." These quotes were recorded by Stratton on video.

Joe, fighting back tears, paused to settle himself, then continued his tale:

"Max had been talking to me. 'If there's a war, who do you think would win?' he asked me. I used to tell him, 'Max, as far as you're concerned, nobody's gonna bother you.' And I meant it because everyone knew Max Hassel never cheated anyone, never hit or beat no one. Greenberg was the one. I could understand (him being targeted). I heard him bragging, 'I fucked them with a pencil.' That was one of his famous sayings. Greenberg was taking everything, bullying everybody. They all had reason to kill him. But not Max Hassel."

Stassi and Adonis were not on good terms. Earlier in his career, a dispute arose from the way Joe had carried out an assignment. Adonis wanted him eliminated, but the Lansky-Luciano faction voted no, and Joe lived to regret the day he was given the Hassel contract.

He told Stratton that the mob had been having trouble with Green-berg for several months but was unable to settle on a plan to have him eliminated.

"They knew I was the only one who could arrange it," Stassi said.

When he questioned why Hassel had to go and was put down by Adonis, Joe knew better than to extend the argument. "They were all looking at me. What did I have to say? I started laughing.

"'Why are you laughing?' they asked.

I told them, 'It's the easiest thing in the world.'"

No doubt about it, Joe was possibly the only person, except for the closest members of Hassel's coterie, who could have entered Room 824 without being frisked. Max would not have admitted anybody who was even slightly suspicious at that ominous period when control of the beer business was at stake.

Having already told Stratton he hired two gunmen to kill Dutch Schultz, it appeared he might be leading up to another such arrange-ment. So Stratton pressed him:

"Who did it?"

Joe would only say, "It's not important. What I'm trying to say—anybody who wants to be a gangster, a wiseguy, a made Mafia soldier, or whatever you want to call it, is going to have to face what I went through. I loved the guy."

There was a lengthy pause as he worked his tongue and licked his lips before continuing:

"I killed my best friend on orders from Abe and Meyer."

Stratton asked, "Max Hassel?"

"No. Another party."

"Who?"

Silence. There was a thin shroud that resisted Joe's will to unburden his conscience. He could not quite break the vow of omerta. Although he never officially took the pledge, it was ingrained in his psyche. Con-fession was a weakness. The complete truth must wait no matter how much he wants to turn it loose.

Who could this "best friend" be? if not Max Hassel. Richard Stratton believes there was no better friend to Joe than Max.

A week before Christmas 2001, I flew to Florida. Joe was now living with a friend near Kissimee, an Orlando suburb. I had called ahead and he willingly agreed to talk with me. It was rather a surreal experience dealing with Joe. He readily answered questions about Hassel, always punctuating his answers with praise about the man who, "never bragged, never cheated anybody, never talked bad about anyone."

Seated at a small desk, a walker at his side, Joe repeated almost word for word some of the tales he told Stratton. But the big story, the one he always leaves open-ended, he becomes the matador waving his red cape to misdirect the bull. *Quick on his feet* might apply if only Joe didn't move about slower than Tim Conway's little old man. But his mind is alert and suspicious when dealing with the secrets he's harbored so long.

"About the Dutch Schultz contract in Richard's article?" I ask, trying to lead up to the first confession, rather than asking the tough questions about Max right away. It's as if I stuck him with a needle. He rages about Richard Stratton and the *GQ* story being "100 percent bullshit." It is hard to follow what is happening. Something about a contract he signed with the writer, and "you can tell him I said so," as he roasts his friend.

Later, while discussing my visit to Florida with Stratton, I learned that Joe wanted a clause added to their contract in which his heirs will receive whatever financial remuneration he's been promised for sharing his life story, in the event he dies. Stratton is producing a video documentary about Stassi, possibly followed by a book. Joe's confession, lacking an actual "I killed Max Hassel," cannot be refuted with his "bullshit" outburst. It's on videotape. He can't blame Stratton for being misquoted.

I waited until the following day to broach his connection to the Hassel murder. By now I decided to go right to the heart of the matter: *"Joe, I came down here on the belief that you killed Max."*

All he offers is one of his well practiced pauses—the lips and tongue working overtime, but no words of anger, denial, or agreement.

"Did you or didn't you kill him?"

"No."

"Do you know who did?"

Another show of closed eyes and lip-smacking as he seems ready to doze off.

"Do you know the names of the shooters?"

"Silver. I heard one of them was called Silver."

"Was that a last name or a nickname?"

"I don't know."

"How many of them were there, how many shooters?"

"I would have to say two."

Then I asked him where he was at the time Max and Maxie were killed.

"At Brown's Tavern. Lots of cops hung out there. At Court and Main streets. Yeah, in Elizabeth, about two miles from the Carteret. Some guy came in about 5 o'clock and told us what happened to Max."

"Did the cops question you?"

"I didn't go back to the hotel. A day or two later I ran into a detective and he told me the district attorney was looking for me. I called him and said I'd come in the next morning. An assistant DA questioned me for a couple of hours. That was the only time I was questioned."

He now seemed more accessible, more willing to open up. I tried again:

"Did you shoot Max?"

"Anytime something happened, the chief of police blamed it on Hoboken Joe. You might have thought I was a one-man crime wave." Joe is very good at diverting interrogation. He continued on about the chief whom he met at a New Year's Eve party in the Carteret. After that they were good friends. But he warded off or ignored any further discussion of Hassel's murder. So I took a new tack. Frankie Carbo had been mentioned as a suspect at the time of Hassel's murder. I asked:

Did you know Frankie Carbo?

Joe seemed suddenly energized. I had plucked a familiar name out of the past.

"Sure I knew him. I got him out of jail."

"How did that happen?"

"They locked him up a couple of years later, but I helped prove he wasn't there. (This was about Carbo's arrest in 1935) I talked to him in jail, then I went to the hotel and got a desk clerk to show me the work schedule for that day. It showed the bellboy wasn't even working that day."

The day he was referring to was April 12, 1933, the day of the murders. A bellhop had told police he saw Carbo in the hotel shortly before the shooting. Carbo knew he was wanted for questioning after the murders but he eluded the police for more than two years before he was arrested outside the old Madison Square Garden during the summer of 1935.

Joe said he passed the new information about the bellhop to Carbo's lawyer. After checking the hotel records, the prosecutor decided to drop charges, and Carbo was released after almost six months in jail. It is not hard to conceive Joe passing the clerk $100 or $500 to adjust the work ledger to his liking.

I tried again to focus on the murder scene.

"When Max was killed there were several other guys in the room, right?"

"Yeah."

"Well, Maxie Greenberg was supposed to have been reaching for his gun just as he was shot. Didn't any of the other guys go for theirs?"

Joe hesitated a minute, then:

"They just ran out the door. Nobody pulled a gun—they just got the hell out of there."

"You must have been in the room to see them."

Joe smiled: "That's what the cops told me."

I took this to mean he was informed by the police about the large number of witnesses to the murders. I didn't believe him.

I left Orlando the next day, disappointed that I hadn't received either a convincing "yes" or an absolute "no" to the all-important question.

After months of pondering the information I personally received from Joe Stassi, this is the scenario of Max Hassel's death that makes the most sense to me:

Meyer Lansky, Abe Zwillman, and Joe Adonis ordered Stassi to kill Hassel and Greenberg so they could take over the North Jersey beer business. Joe insisted that Waxey Gordon was not included in the contract. Why? Because Max Hassel was the main beerman, not Gordon, according to Stassi. He insisted that Hassel was the brains of the outfit, and Waxey took care of the rough stuff.

Gordon's claim that he was not in the room when the murders occurred was denied by Stassi. He said Gordon was among the seven or eight others in the room when the shooting started. Joe claimed he slapped Gordon but "you don't kill somebody when they tell you to kill somebody else."

That quote alone, in my mind, was evidence that Joe was one of the triggermen. I believe Joe or the big bosses also recruited Frankie Carbo, whose reputation as a hitman was well known. Investigators said they knew there were two killers. Joe also said: "I would have to say two," when I asked him, "how many?" That much about the murders was in the newspapers, but Joe's description of the murder scene seemed authentic to me.

Joe said Louis Cohn and Abe Parkowitz were among the several witnesses to the murder. Parkowitz claimed he was in another room, but the police wondered why he would have left twenty minutes before the shots were fired since he was usually guarding the door. Cohn disappeared after the murder and I never located any information that he was questioned by the police.

Stassi said he and Cohn were not on particularly good terms before the shootings, but in the months following he received several calls from Cohn who claimed he needed money. Joe said he sent him sums of "around $200 dollars" on several occasions. Was this hush money? Why would Joe send Blackie Cohn, a guy who resented Joe's close association with Hassel, money unless the mob wanted to make sure Cohn didn't talk. According to Joe, the calls from Cohn came from different parts of the country because he was a fugitive after being indicted in the Waxey Gordon tax case.

The Carbo connection adds to the theory that he was the second gunman. Why would Stassi go to the trouble of digging up information about a bellboy unless he had a very good reason to do so? If Carbo was his partner in crime that day, that certainly would have given Joe a motive to clear him of suspicion.

When I talked with Joe he willingly gave this information. After analyzing what he told me, my conclusion is that Abe Parkowitz opened the door of Room 824 for Joe Stassi. Frankie Carbo, unseen by Parkowitz through the peephole of the door, followed Stassi into the room and the shooting began. Joe then led Carbo out of the hotel using the hidden service elevator at the rear of the building. To both Stratton and me, Joe made quite an issue of knowing about the sealed staircase and service elevator because he once took a mistress out of the hotel that way.

After the murder, I believe he established an alibi by rushing to Brown's Tavern, probably slipping into the bar crowd unnoticed.

Joe Stassi offered Richard Stratton and me plenty of clues to prove he killed Max Hassel. In his search for redemption, he took us to the brink of confession, then his conscience hit the wall. Max was the "best friend" he admitted killing, so dear a friend that he couldn't say the words, "I did it."

The last I heard, Joe, fast approaching his 96th birthday, was living in a retirement home in Arizona becoming quite paranoid and troublesome. Prohibition's family tree is getting barren. Since Joe Bonanno died in the spring of 2002, possibly Joe Stassi will be the last bad apple to fall.

Bibliography

Reading Times

Reading Eagle

New York Times

Philadelphia Inquirer

Philadelphia Bulletin

Philadelphia Record

Berks County Recorder of Deeds archives

Berks County Register of Wills archives

Berks County Clerk of Criminal Courts archives

Berks County Prothonotary Archival Center

The Historical Society of Berks County

Reading City Council Archives

Reading Police Department Records

Reading Library and its Pennsylvania Room

Albright College Archives

Federal Court Archives in Philadelphia, Justice Department case 2867, June session, 1928

National Archives, Justice Department case 23-53-230, Record Group 60, FEA 2: p.p. 130-140

Immigration and Naturalization Service hearing transcript March 27, 1933

Cohen, Rich, *Tough Jews, Father, Sons, and Gangster Dreams,* Simon & Schuster, 1998

Fox, Stephen. *Blood and Power,* Morrow, 1981

Fried, Alfred. *The Rise and Fall of Jewish Gangsters in America*, Columbia University Press. 1993

Goash, Martin A. *The Last Testament of Lucky Luciano*, Little, Brown and Company, 1974

Gribben, Mark. *Bugsy Siegel,* Internet (The Crime Library) 2001

Hammer, Richard. *The Last Testament of Lucky Luciano*, Little, Brown and Company, 1974

May, Allan, *The St. Louis Family,* Internet (The Crime Library), 2002

Sann, Paul. *Kill the Dutchman,* Arlington House, 1971

Sifkakis, Carl, *The Mafia Encylopedia,* Volumes I & II, Checkmate Books, 1982, 1999

Smith, Richard Norton. *Thomas Deweyand His Times,* Simon & Schuster, 1982

Index

0-595-26013-6

Printed in the United States
64601LVS00003B/288